Thinking
Through
Craft

Glenn Adamson

⊛BERG

Oxford • New York

English edition
First published in 2007 by
Berg
Editorial offices:
First Floor, Angel Court, 81 St Clements Street, Oxford OX4 1AW, UK
175 Fifth Avenue, New York, NY 10010, USA

Berg is the imprint of Oxford International Publishers Ltd.

Library of Congress Cataloging-in-Publication Data

Adamson, Glenn.
    Thinking through craft / Glenn Adamson.
       p. cm.
    Includes bibliographical references and index.
    ISBN-13: 978-1-84520-646-8 (cloth)
    ISBN-10: 1-84520-646-0 (cloth)
    ISBN-13: 978-1-84520-647-5 (pbk.)
    ISBN-10: 1-84520-647-9 (pbk.)
    1. Art—Technique. 2. Handicraft. 3. Workmanship. I. Title.

    N8510.A33 2007
    745.5—dc22

                                                              2007027931

British Library Cataloguing-in-Publication Data

A catalogue record for this book is available from the British Library.

ISBN 978 1 84520 646 8 (Cloth)
      978 1 84520 647 5 (Paper)

Typeset by JS Typesetting Ltd, Porthcawl, Mid Glamorgan
Printed in the United Kingdom by Biddles Ltd, King's Lynn

www.bergpublishers.com

Published in association with
the Victoria & Albert Museum

CONTENTS

PLATES AND ILLUSTRATIONS

PLATES

ILLUSTRATIONS

ACKNOWLEDGEMENTS

Thinking Through Craft has been long in coming, and has incurred a number of debts along the way. The book is based in part on my dissertation, written at Yale University. Of particular importance at that stage of the manuscript's life were the encouragement of Patricia Kane and Bryan Wolf, the intellectual inspiration provided by David Byron, Johanna Drucker and Thomas Crow, and the perceptive comments made by Caroline Jones. I continued work on the project during my previous incarnation as the curator of the Chipstone Foundation in Milwaukee, where I had the support of many generous people, particularly David Gordon, Liz Flaig, Sarah Fayen, Nonie Gadsden, and Jon Prown. More recently, my colleagues at the Victoria and Albert Museum (V&A), particularly Carolyn Sargentson, Christopher Breward, Angela McShane, Ann Matchette, Marta Ajmar, and Laurie Britton-Newell, have provided both scholarly counsel and friendship. I have also been fortunate enough to have a collegial partnership with many of the staff at the Royal College of Art; I would like to especially acknowledge the help of Jeremy Aynsley.

For their sensitive readings of parts of the book I thank Andrew Perchuk, Ulrich Lehmann, Eva Diaz, Elissa Auther, Pennina Barnett, Lois Moran, Stefano Basilico, Peter Selz, Warren MacKenzie, Susanna Heron, and G. B. Carson. I have also been influenced by many other craftspeople and authors who engage with craft but do not trust the pieties often attached to it. I think of the ongoing conversations I have had with Gord Peteran, Charley Radtke, Garth Clark, Alison Britton, Linda Sandino, and Edmund de Waal as especially crucial to this book.

Like most scholars, I have inconvenienced the staff at several libraries. In my case particular gratitude is owed to the Archives of American Art, the American Craft Council library, the Yale University libraries, the University of Wisconsin-Madison libraries, and the National Art Library at the V&A.

Logistical difficulties posed by the publication were greatly mitigated by Helena Nicholls and by the team at Berg under the leadership of Kathryn Earle, who is a model of the adventurous and energetic publisher.

The Center for Craft, Creativity and Design, North Carolina, provided significant financial assistance that allowed me to conduct the final stages of research for the book.

Most of all, I would like to express my appreciation for the humane sagacity and unstinting advice of both Tanya Harrod and my mentor, Ned Cooke. I have done my best to keep their examples as pioneering craft historians uppermost in my mind.

Alicia Volk has been my intellectual partner for the past decade. Her wit, wisdom, and scholarship have made all the difference to this book, which would be much impoverished without her many contributions.

Finally, this book is dedicated to Arthur Adamson, who taught me much of what I know about both thinking and craft.

INTRODUCTION

Thinking through ... craft? Isn't craft something mastered in the hands, not in the mind? Something consisting of physical actions, rather than abstract ideas?

Well, it all depends. Writing about craft usually concerns itself with "the crafts"—specific processes carried out in specific materials. Chiefly these are ceramics, glass making, metalsmithing, woodworking, and the various combinations of process and material that fall under the heading of the textile arts. For the past century and more, a body of literature has grown around these medium-based disciplines. Most of these writings are promotional. Some are critical, and a small percentage is historical. Rare, however, is the text that deals with craft in theoretical terms: a text that treats craft as an idea. This book aims to do just that. It is a consideration of what craft has meant within the broader context of the visual arts, and what it could be made to mean, if thought through in extra-disciplinary terms.

Craft's position within the arts is a complicated affair. In some ways, it is analogous to the term "color." Just as every object must be made in some way, and hence could be considered in some sense to be crafted, every object has color. When one says that an object is colorful, this is not taken to mean that other objects lack color entirely; similarly, when we say that something is highly crafted, we are distinguishing it only in degree, and not in kind, from other things that have been made. There are artworks that are not only colorful, but are in some sense *about* color—by artists as diverse as Titian, Rubens, Monet, Kandinsky, and Richter. Equally, artworks may not only be well made, but may address the conditions of their own manufacture. And there are other parallels. Like art that seems to be about its own craftsmanship, art about color was at some points in history thought to be inferior. Finally, like color, craft is a word that most people think they understand—a commonsense term. Yet both have been subject to considerable speculation.

Of course, there are differences between craft and color too. There is no Color Council or Color Museum for the advancement of colorful art. It's not possible to make a living as a practitioner of color, unless, perhaps, you are an industry consultant. There are no academic programs teaching color as a field of artistic production, though there are many classes teaching students how to manipulate color to advantage. All of these differences point to the fact that craft has a constituency and economic basis, and hence a social presence, which color does not have. Yet, this lack of advocacy has not prevented color from being a major term of artistic experimentation and debate in the modern era. Maybe it's time for those who care about craft to allow it to flourish in a similar state of benign neglect. If craft were left to its own devices, perhaps it could happily occupy an unproblematic spot in the pantheon of art concepts. But then we would miss something else that craft has to offer, something that is most clearly (if unintentionally) proven by the marginalization of those institutions that champion it: craft, as a cultural practice, exists in opposition to the modern conception of art itself.

CRAFT AT THE LIMITS

From this perspective, craft is perhaps not so much like color after all. It is more like other terms in art theory, such as "kitsch," "dematerialization," or even "life" itself. Each of these terms has, within certain critical frameworks, been described as the opposite of modern art—a state into which an individual artwork, or even the entire category of art itself, might inadvertently collapse and thus lose its integrity and purpose. Yet, precisely for this reason, each has been crucial to the development of modern art, whether framed positively as an unattainable goal, or negatively as a means of critique. Furthermore, each of these non-art categories has been defined in a variety of ways under different historical circumstances. The art world has had within its ranks many enemies of kitsch, but also a variety of *enfants terribles* from Kurt Schwitters to Jeff Koons who have gleefully embraced it, resulting in what Thomas Crow has called "a productive confusion within the normal hierarchy of cultural prestige"[1] (Figure 0.1). Artists who have gestured towards the realm of the "dematerialized," and hence to the realm of non-art, range just as widely, from Marcel Duchamp to Yves Klein to Martin Creed. And there is also a long list of artists from Robert Rauschenberg to Yoko Ono to Tracey Emin who have claimed, quixotically, that what they really want to do is to erase the line between art and "life." Modern art might appear to be a realm of purely aestheticized and transcendental objects. But in fact, as Johanna Drucker has recently argued, it has always been an infinitely varied field defined by a series of contingent horizons.[2] This word—horizon—is apt because it conveys the idea of a border that can never be reached, but is nonetheless intrinsic to any sense of position. The condition of modern art is defined in relation to other conditions that oppose it, but always from a distance.

This book argues that craft should be thought of as one of these horizons: as a conceptual limit active throughout modern artistic practice. In order to pursue this line of thinking, one must first dispense with the simplistic formulation that the crafts can (or should) be art. Theodor Adorno has the definitive word on this matter, which has plagued and misdirected so many writers in the past: "Posed from on high, the question whether something ... is or is no longer art leads nowhere." Anything can be taken for art, craft included, and that is all there is to say on the matter. But as surely as this is a banal truism, the opposite proposition, that art is *not* craft—that it might gain something by defining itself against that category—is a rather interesting one. For, as Adorno continues: "Because art is what it has become, its concept refers to what it does not contain."[3] If craft is a frontier at which the aesthetic construct of modern art has often stopped short, then in that very stopping, art confronts its presumptions about itself. What's more, this same logic can be pursued from the other

Figure 0.1   Jeff Koons, *Diamond (Pink/Gold)*, 1994–2005. Stainless steel. Installed at the Victoria & Albert Museum, 2006. Courtesy of the Victoria & Albert Museum and the artist.

side of the horizon. It is equally possible to engage in the ongoing definition (which is to say, the history) of art by espousing a position conventionally associated with craft—but, again, only by confronting the ever-receding frontier that marks craft as extra-artistic.

CRAFT AS A PROCESS

Thus far I have been employing "craft" rather loosely, as a word, an idea, and a category. Of course, it can be all these things, but it might be more usefully conceived as a process. Rather than presenting craft as a fixed set of things—pots, rather than paintings—this book will analyze it as an approach, an attitude, or a habit of action. Craft only exists in motion. It is a way of doing things, not a classification of objects, institutions, or people. It is also multiple: an amalgamation of interrelated core principles, which are put into relation with one another through the overarching idea of "craft". Each of these principles is addressed by a chapter of this book. First, while the modern artwork has usually been held to be autonomous, the work of craft is *supplemental*. Second, where artistic practice has normally been oriented to optical effects, craft is organized around *material* experience. A third chapter, less dialectical in its arguments, presents the case of *skill*. This is the lynchpin of the book, in that skill is the most complete embodiment of craft as an active, relational concept rather than a fixed category. The final two chapters turn to craft's situation in the modern social fabric: the *pastoral* and the *amateur*, two ideological frameworks within which craft is structured. The first of these terms normally has positive overtones, and the second a pejorative quality. Yet I hope to show that both the pastoral and the amateur are conceptual structures in which craft's marginalization has been consciously put to use.

Other commentators have addressed most of these topics. But I hope to offer something new by seeing these five principles as properties of a dynamic phenomenon, open to debate and dissent as well as affirmation. Rather than attempting to define craft, I hope to show that it is a subject that gives rise to interpenetrating and sometimes conflicting historical tendencies. I also hope to redirect the debate about craft by focusing on its subordination. Understandably, partisans of the crafts are unlikely to see craft's second-class status within art theory as something to accept at face value, but this resistance has also led to a lack of serious thought about craft's inferiority relative to art. While art is a matter of nomination within an infinite field—that is, art is anything that is called art—craft involves self-imposed limits. Modern art is staked on the principle of freedom, its potential transcendence of all limits, including (even especially) those of craft. Yet in the very marginality that results from craft's bounded character, craft finds its indispensability to the project of modern art. My central argument, when all is said and done, is that craft's inferiority might be the most productive thing about it.

Before proceeding any further it might be helpful to explain, by way of examples, the various key terms that organize the book. The Piet Mondrian painting and the Anni Albers weaving seen in Plates 1 and 2 are usually seen as a work of art and a work of craft, respectively. Both are self-consciously modern, and superficially similar in style. The difference between them seems, on one level, to be rather arbitrary—one is a textile, the other a textile with paint on its surface. It is easy enough to hang an Albers weaving on the wall and call it art, and indeed museums have done so many times. It would be more difficult to upholster a chair with Mondrian's painting, but certainly not impossible. And yet there are good (if only relative) reasons to attach the term "craft" to only one of these objects. Mondrian's painting is aggressively autonomous, which is to say self-standing, not to be touched. It is intended as an object of purely visual contemplation. It was created using a technique, certainly, but without any highly developed manual skill on the part of the painter. Through the agency of specialized institutions—the Sidney Janis Gallery and the Museum of Modern Art, in particular—the painting has acquired great financial value, and Mondrian the status of a great artist. In its passage from unheralded canvas to priceless work of art, the painting has always been presented as having intrinsic, rather than purely commercial value. Its real worth as an artwork supposedly lies outside the normal flow of commercial supply and demand.

By contrast, Albers's weavings were originally meant to decorate a room, to serve a functional purpose as upholstery fabric, or even to serve as preliminary designs for mass-produced textile. Her wall hanging appeals not only optically, but also through its tactile juxtaposition of contrasting materials. To see it is not enough; one feels the need to rub it between one's fingers to fully appreciate its design. It was made by a professional employing a specialized skill, and indeed attests to Albers's mastery of loom weaving. As an object made by a woman in a sexist culture, and without any institutional authorization as an artwork, however, it carries overtones of amateurism.[4] All of these points of difference between the work of art and the work of craft can, and should, be called into question. Certainly, all have been the source of resentment over the years on the part of craftspeople. As they and their allies have perceived the state of affairs, objects that are associated with craft have been unfairly undervalued since the beginnings of the modern era.

In particular, the disregard for such objects has been convincingly critiqued as one subplot within the more general history of the devaluation of women's art. As recently as 2006 the Tate Modern in London staged an exhibition about Anni Albers's husband Josef, pairing him with fellow Bauhaus artist László Moholy-Nagy. The museum's texts made virtually no mention of the famous weaver, an art historical erasure that is unfortunately all too common. So there are good reasons to despise the lopsided scheme in which craft, often coded as feminine or even as "ethnic," is always seen as inferior to the hegemonic category of art. Yet, reclaiming objects like the Albers weaving for art history seems an insufficient goal for craft theory and history. As dismaying as the overtly sexist, classist, or racist aspects of craft's inferiority may be, that disheartening story should not blind us to the complexity and usefulness of craft's limitedness. In fact, as in most cases of asymmetrical power relations, it is precisely through an examination of the terms of its subordination that the social prejudices that attend craft can be redressed.

There is also a positive side to craft's inferiority. Conceived as a "problem," the idea of craft has fueled all manner of artistic and social changes in the past, and it will continue to do so in the future. Indeed, paintings like Mondrian's, which espouse a transcendental logic for art and radically deny their own materiality, turn out to be more the exception than the rule in modern art. The limits embodied by craft are not only psychologically comforting, but also conceptually useful. The implication of a decorative object in its surroundings; the sensual characteristics of specific materials; the regulation imposed by specialized tools when properly employed; the sociopolitical connotations of the figure of the artisan; and even the literal limits of time and space suggested by long days in a small shop all provide a kind of friction that keep pressing questions of form, category, and identity open for further investigation.

To hazard one last metaphor, "craft" might be conceived not only as a horizon but as a constellation of stars—useful for purposes of navigation, but impossible to actually inhabit. "The crafts," by contrast, are a well-defined terrain, an archipelago of discrete islands with fixed boundaries. Just as it is difficult to pin down where the pertinence of craft begins and ends, it is normally quite obvious who is a weaver and who isn't, what has been made on a potter's wheel and what hasn't. This is no reason to look down upon the crafts. Alongside others who will be discussed in this book, such as artists, architects and designers, many craftspeople will be offered as exemplary cases for study. These figures operate on craft from within, rather than without, and in so doing have caused a good deal of useful confusion.

I have found myself writing this book at an exciting and somewhat nervous time for those who are deeply interested in craft. The artist Robert Morris once defined Thomas Kuhn's notion of a paradigm as "a set of limits for response in a cultural time."[5] Modern ideas about craft constitute a classic paradigm by this definition, a structure of thinking that has performed a necessary but rather static role within modernity. These ideas only become visible when the underpinning structures of thought are reassessed. Such a paradigm shift occurred in the mid-nineteenth century, when the economic role of the artisan was partly displaced. Under these circumstances craft took on a largely symbolic and often elegiac character, most completely realized within the ideology of the Arts and Crafts movement. In the decades immediately following the Second World War, another such paradigm shift occurred, as the ground on which craft operated shifted gradually from the domain of commercial production to that of galleries, museums, and private collectors. The "designer-craftsman" of the 1930s—a figure that was itself descended from Arts and Crafts goals—was gradually though incompletely displaced by the "artist-craftsman." As this book will suggest, we are currently witnessing another such change, as post-disciplinary practice mounts a challenge to the established framework of modern craft. In the twentieth century, craft was mainly defined in terms of the crafts, but it is by no means clear that this will be the case in the future. Craft has always been an idea that transcends discipline—it pertains with equal relevance in pottery and architecture—and appreciation of that fact seems to be increasingly widely shared. Just as scholars are beginning to view craft practice from the standpoint of social history, anthropology, and economics, practitioners of various kinds are exploring the problematics of craft through increasingly diverse means.

A final, brief word on the organization and parameters of this study is in order. As will become apparent, each of the five chapters is structured in a similar fashion. Each begins with a survey of theoretical texts, moves on to historical accounts, and finally narrows down to critical analysis of individual works or texts. My goal is twofold: first, to subject the ideas in this book to the varied tools of theory, history, and criticism; and second, to show that the principles of craft have been manifested in objects and tested by artists in numerous, sometimes mutually antithetical ways. I have tried to draw my examples broadly, from craft, art, design, painting, and architectural theory, but the particular topics I have chosen are meant to be suggestive, not comprehensive. Again, craft is not a defined practice but a way of thinking through practices of all kinds, and there is no reason that any one medium or genre of production should be more conducive to this way of thinking than another.

Having said this, I want to be quite clear that this is a book about craft under the conditions of modernity, and particularly in relation to modern art. I have not tried to write a history of craft in pre-modern contexts, much less a master theory that transcends history. One failing of the book, born of my own limitations as an author, is its arbitrary geographical emphasis on the American and British contexts, with some reference to Japan and continental Europe. This is not in any way to deny the validity and significance of modern craft history in Australia, Africa, Latin America, and elsewhere. Though I regret my inability to present a broader range of examples authoritatively, I hope that this book will be taken in the spirit it is meant—as an introduction. In matters of geography, as in all other respects, I hope to open up future discussion rather than close it down.

1 SUPPLEMENTAL

The central claim made about modern art—the one on which all others depend—is that it is an autonomous field of practice. Art, the argument goes, strives to stand apart from the interests that are everywhere manifested in the rest of the world. To the degree that it succeeds, it is a zone of free practice. Both at the level of the individual artwork and that of the total field (modern art itself), it can achieve independence. This separation means that art is in a position to critique other institutions and cultural bases, whether they be commercial, political, social, economic, or religious. Art does not stand apart from history by any means, least of all its own; but intrinsic to its identity is the principle of freedom with regard to that history. Any prediction in advance of what it will (or should) do is alien to it, and equally, any attempt to fully account for it, whether through the apparatus of criticism or that of the market, is doomed to be incomplete. It is the part of our culture where we allow ourselves to think otherwise.

The writings of the Marxist social philosopher Theodor Adorno serve as a useful point of entry to this powerful, but much contested, idea about art. Though he considered his primary field of study to be music, Adorno attempted in his *Aesthetic Theory* to construct a complete analysis of the problems and potential of autonomy in art. To understand his position, it is important to recognize that he considered culture to be in a state of crisis brought on by the dehumanizing conditions of advanced capitalism. Art, if it could hold itself apart from this world of commercialization, might offer an institutional base for critique of the culture industry. Anything that intruded upon the sacrosanct domain of art would, in his view, only corrupt its potential to achieve a truly free arena of discourse. But the price that art pays for this autonomy is steep. Adorno's logic is hard to follow, but nonetheless convincing:

> Artworks detach themselves from the empirical world and bring forth another world, one opposed to the empirical world as if this other world too were an autonomous entity… By virtue of its rejection of the empirical world—a rejection that inheres in art's concept and thus is no mere *escape*, but a law immanent to it—art sanctions the primacy of reality.[1]

Adorno is saying here that, simply by separating itself from the world outside, art inadvertently ratifies that external reality. For artworks themselves are through their autonomy made into powerful commodities—fetishes, in the Marxist sense of the term.[2] No matter how avant garde an artwork may be, it cannot exist outside of the structures that enable its own creation. Yet in Adorno's view it can only exist meaningfully as art insofar as it attempts to critique those structures. Pierre Bourdieu, writing from a sociological perspective, has noted that "the virtuosi of the judgment of taste seem to reach an experience of grace so completely freed from the constraints of culture, and so little marked by the long, patient training of which it is the product, that any reminder of the conditions and the social conditioning which have rendered it possible seems to be at once obvious and scandalous."[3] It is precisely this scandal that the avant garde seeks to bring about.

On the basis of this logic, Adorno concluded: "Art must turn against itself, in opposition to its own concept, and thus become uncertain of itself right into its innermost fiber."[4] Art's continuous subject of critique must be art itself. It must constantly struggle with its own being, for it is contradictory at the core. In the final analysis Adorno's call for a "negative aesthetics" means that avant garde art must always carry within itself the implication of its own undoing. This does not, however, amount to a recipe for a single act of self-destruction, or even a static repetition of identical self-critical gestures. Anti-art will inevitably be re-absorbed by the art market (as has happened, for example, with Dada collages and assemblages, Piero Manzoni's notorious and now hugely valuable cans of *Artist's Shit*, or Sherrie Levine's appropriations of other artists' photographs). Thus art must continually re-investigate itself as a means of preserving an autonomous space of discourse. "Art and artworks are perishable," Adorno writes. "Right into the smallest detail of their autonomy, which sanctions the socially determined splitting off of spirit by the division of labor, they are not only art but something foreign and opposed to it. Admixed with art's own concept is the ferment of its own abolition."[5]

One does not need to be a committed Marxist to appreciate the force of Adorno's argument. To be sure, he wrote from a position of despair about the culture of capitalism, and his theory is premised upon the idea of radical critique. Even if one holds very different attitudes about modern political and social affairs, however, it seems intuitively persuasive that artists should be free of whatever constraints others might wish to impose upon them. Without insisting that art be "negative," in Adorno's sense, one might nonetheless want to see it as undetermined, free to pursue its own path by virtue of its autonomy. Anything less would reduce the artwork to a trivial fact, "a well-meaning cultural commodity" (in Adorno's sarcastic phrase) in an infinite world of goods.[6] From this perspective, one might accept Adorno's argument that avant garde art must always address its own freedom, and the terms on which that freedom is established. Accepting this idea means accepting the proposition that a self-imposed lack of concern for the world is intrinsic to art. If art is autonomous, then in practical terms, it will inevitably frustrate the expectations of unsympathetic audiences. To put it bluntly, avant garde art really is elitist and difficult to understand, and theorists like Adorno insisted on the necessity of that fact.

So what did Adorno have to say about the subject of craft? The answer might come as a surprise. Speaking to a meeting of the German Werkbund in 1965, he asserted: "Only unreasonable dilettantism and blatant idealism would attempt to deny that each authentic, and in the broadest sense, artistic activity requires a precise understanding of the materials and techniques at the artist's disposal, and to be sure, at the most advanced level." Rather than seeing craft as a base materialism that would drag the work into the realm of the ebb and flow of daily life, Adorno saw mastery of the technical means by which an artwork comes into being as being absolutely essential to the creation of an autonomous work. "Good handicraft means the fittingness of means to an end," he argued. "The ends are certainly not independent of the means." With these words, Adorno was participating in the modernist tradition of attitude towards form, originating in the mid-nineteenth-century writings of Gottfried Semper, which held that materials and processes should be seamlessly integrated with the final form of a work. However—and this is his central point—craft functions in this scheme as a transparent set of procedures, certainly to be deployed but not to be present in the content of the finished work: "The means have their own logic, a logic that points beyond them." Craft always subjugates itself in the interest of the overall work. Adorno is witheringly critical about those who get this wrong by making a fetish of craft itself, because of a misplaced love of its archaism or authenticity. He writes derisively of the "retrospective infatuation with the aura of the socially doomed craftsman" and characterizes the legacy of the Arts and Crafts movement as a "masquerade" carried out by "despisers of art."[7] Thus in Adorno, we find an argument that craft must be a self-abnegating path to the creation of something beyond itself—by which he meant not only paintings and sculptures, but also buildings, musical compositions, films, and so forth. His position might be summarized in the aphorism: "artworks are something made that have become more than something simply made."[8]

Thus for Adorno, craft does not function as the vehicle of self-doubt and rigorous internal analysis that art does—far from it. It is instead a *supplement* of the artwork, in the sense in which Jacques Derrida originally proposed that term in *Of Grammatology* (1977). A supplement is that which provides something necessary to another, "original" entity, but which is nonetheless considered to be extraneous to that original. Derrida describes the supplement as pointing to a "lack," which might be present in a single work or in an entire field of discourse. For example, an orchestral score might be seen as supplemental to the music that it records. Without notes on paper, the music would have no means of calling itself into existence, but the score is not in any way seen as an equivalent for the musical performance itself. Similarly, writing is for Derrida the "supplement *par excellence*," because it is supplemental to language itself. Without writing, there would be no way of fixing language, and yet we tend to view the written word as merely a transcription of our actual tongue, which is spoken. Through its own apparent transparency, writing establishes the authoritative primacy of spoken language. As Derrida puts it, "its place is assigned in the structure by the mark of an emptiness."[9]

The idea of the supplement has been applied by Derrida and others to "the decorative," a category of form that is closely related to craft. Often there is an accidental conflation of the two terms, as if craft could be reduced to its role in creating decoration. This is clearly not the case. The anthropologist Robert Plant Armstrong elegantly clarifies this point: "whereas a beautifully carved head may crown a heddle pulley, and though this head may in some spiritual sense increment the pulley, still is the object nonetheless a pulley. If an object be shorn of such additives as either power or virtuosity, it is still unambiguously object."[10] Decorated objects may or may not be crafted, and objects that are crafted may or may not be decorative. We might hazard that this is a distinction between means and ends: whereas craft is a supplemental kind of making, decoration is a supplemental kind of form. Though the decorative has no isometric relationship to craft, it is nonetheless true that the two are often found together, and have strikingly parallel positions in art theory.[11] Craft and the decorative converge in Derrida's most important example of a supplement, as explored in *The Truth in Painting* (1978): the gilt frame that surrounds a painting (Figure 1.1). Such a frame is not a part of the artwork, but it nonetheless conveys the sense of the painting's importance; it props up the work, as it were, making it seem important. It is what Immanuel Kant, in his *Critique of Judgment* (the text that Derrida aims to deconstruct) called a *parergon*, meaning that which is next to the work—"what is only an adjunct, and not an intrinsic constituent in the complete representation of the object."[12] The *parergon*, if functioning properly, seems to cut the work clean off from the world. Like a freshly cut flower, Derrida writes, when art is severed from its surroundings it does not bleed.

Figure 1.1   *Frame*, French, 1773–93. Carved and gilded wood.
Victoria & Albert Museum.

But if the frame walls out the rest of the world, serving as a guarantor (both visually and socially) of the object's autonomy, then it is in fact the frame that does the work. In Derrida's deconstructive method, the first move is to point out the disavowal entailed in a supplement—the willful overlooking of the ways in which a supplement constructs a sense of truth and immutability which is actually contingent. Thus Derrida argues that a painting needs its frame at least as much as a frame needs its painting. As he memorably puts it, the *parergon* has a "thickness," which is to say that it constitutes its own realm of form.[13] This thickness may be hard to measure. For if a frame is supplemental, then surely the rest of a picture gallery is as well—we require the full apparatus of the space to understand the work as having a certain prominence and value. And what about the parts of the gallery—the carpet, the lights playing on the painting's surface—or the building that houses the gallery, the streets and parking meters outside? (Derrida: "Where does the frame take place. Does it take place. Where does it begin. Where does it end. What is its internal limit. Its external limit. And its surface between the two limits.")[14] The zone of the supplemental starts to look alarmingly large. It is institutional, as well as formal. For Derrida this unacknowledged bleeding of the artwork out into the world is an inevitability; through his deconstruction of the frame, he hopes to show the hypocrisy of any aesthetics that lays claim to autonomy for the artwork.[15]

So where does all this leave craft? It would seem to inhabit firmly the condition of the supplemental. After all, how is the thickness of a frame made up, but through joining, carving, and gilding? The customization of the frame to the work is crucial—a great painting must not be besmirched with a cheap mass-produced frame—but the craft of the framer is not undertaken for its own sake. In a sense, it is not even meant to be noticed. The craft of the framer must not "upstage" the art of the painter. As Derrida says, the *parergon* has "as its traditional determination not that it stands out but that it disappears, buries itself, effaces itself, melts away at the moment it deploys its greatest energy."[16] To say that craft is supplemental, then, is to say that it is always essential to the end in view, but in the process of achieving that end, it disappears. And indeed this accords well with standard notions of craft. Whether it functions in relation to a modern artwork, or some other everyday need, proper craftsmanship draws no attention to itself; it lies beneath notice, allowing other qualities to assert themselves in their fullness. It is striking that even people who make their living through the crafts tend to feel entirely comfortable with this way of thinking. As the glass artist Harvey Littleton put it, "technique is cheap."[17] In an ensuing chapter, we will return again to the question of skill, and the tendency of craftspeople themselves to discount its importance. Here, though, it is important to note that even for those who are most invested in craft, it is most often construed simply as a means of getting to a finished form well. Like a hunter in snowy ground, it must obscure its own tracks.

In Britain, disciplines that are strongly associated with craft practice are often called the "applied arts," a phrase that aptly captures this sense of supplementarity. Craft is indeed always "applied," always in motion towards some objective. Yet, if we are to apply the logic that Derrida has brought to his analysis of the frame, then it is also true that in this very effacement, craft is pointing to something lacking in the artwork—something that the autonomous work of art needs, but cannot absorb into its makeup. We should, then, expect the history of modern craft to be a mirror image of the history of modern art: a supplement to its narrative of progress and conceptual discovery. The ensuing case studies attempt to bear out this supposition, offering four historical moments in which supplementary thinking was in play. First, the case of Constantin Brancusi will be taken up, partly because of his own uses and disavowals of craft, and partly because of his importance as a sort of patron saint amongst modern craftspeople. Second, the problematic field of mid-century studio jewelry will be anatomized as a struggle between its own impulses towards autonomy and supplementarity. Third is an examination of the Pattern and Decoration movement, a much more self-conscious deployment of the supplement for critical purposes. The chapter ends with two recent forays into this terrain by the artists Gijs Bakker and Gord Peteran. These two examples suggest that in the twenty-first century, supplemental craft may have finally made peace with itself—with the result being an unprecedented degree of wit and sophistication.

HOMAGE TO BRANCUSI

The Romanian sculptor Constantin Brancusi casts a long, sheltering shadow over the crafts (Figure 1.2). Often the connection is drawn through the titling of works (Figure 1.3); at other times it is done through equally explicit compositional means, in direct quotations of Brancusi's trademark stacks of contrasting masses (Figure 1.4).[18] But even beyond these overt examples of lineal inheritance, Brancusi seems to be everywhere in the crafts. He provides a stable and reassuring point of reference for functionless, formal, abstract sculpture in organic materials—a description that covers the majority of works sold in the upper stratum of the crafts marketplace. When not appealing directly to Brancusi's example, crafts practitioners often justify their practice by pointing to other sculptors who fall within a loosely Brancusian tradition, such as Henry Moore, Barbara Hepworth, David Nash, Richard Deacon, and Martin Puryear.[19] So pervasive is Brancusi's influence that John Perrault, an art critic with a longstanding interest in craft issues, sees him as a sort of aesthetic franchise: "Brandcusi."[20]

From a certain perspective, one might say that this is a perfectly acceptable state of affairs. Who doesn't love Brancusi? He invented abstract sculpture. His works have tremendous presence. He was a master craftsman, and his works show ample evidence of his skill in their carefully shaped volumes and beautifully modulated surfaces. Perhaps we should be grateful that the flame he lit is still burning in one corner of the art world. And yet, seen from another perspective, the crafts' adherence to Brancusi seems distinctly reactionary. His groundbreaking abstract works are now nearly a century old, and have not been "contemporary" since well before the Second World War. While his example was central to Minimalism and its derivatives, these developments were premised on acting out certain ideas that were only implicit in his sculptures, and rejecting other aspects of his work. So

Figure 1.2   Edward Steichen, *Brancusi in his Studio*, 1927,
with *Endless Column* at left. Gelatine silver print.
Courtesy of the Victoria & Albert Museum.

what should we make of the craft world's collective homage to Brancusi? We might simply conclude that the crafts have become a preserve for outmoded models of art. The crafts, we could argue, are an arena in which those who don't care to pay attention to contemporary art play at being involved in an art historical lineage. For them Brancusi is not only a source of aesthetic power, but also a convenient rhetorical device. His precedent authorizes craftspeople to ignore the art discourse of the present day, and permits collectors to pile up *objets d'art* without worrying about the modern and postmodern avant garde. However, though this cynical set of conclusions has more than a measure of truth to it, there is a more

Figure 1.3   Gordon Baldwin, *Vessel for Your Thoughts*
Mr. Brancusi, 2004. Ceramic. 30 cm high.
Courtesy of the artist and Barrett Marsden Gallery.

complicated lesson to draw from the strange fact of Brancusi's pervasive influence. This has less to do with the crafts themselves and more to do with the fundamental problematic of craft (construed in a broad sense) under the conditions of modernity. Broaching this subject will require a somewhat more complex understanding of Brancusi himself, and also a return to the questions of the supplement that this chapter has explored thus far.

It is helpful to turn first to Anna C. Chave's critical study *Constantin Brancusi: Shifting the Bases of Art* (1993). Brancusi is usually presented as a *naïf*, a hermit artist whose sculptures magically approached the "essence of things." Chave argues, however, that Brancusi himself carefully constructed and managed this image. His oft-repeated aphorisms ("create like a god, command like a king, work like a slave"), his studio environment, his staged photographs of his own works, and the self-fashioned legend he spun around his own life all served to create an impression of unaffected genius.[21] "For decades," Chave writes, "Brancusi shrewdly played the lone visionary peasant-sage from the far-flung reaches of the East… It is easy to get the impression [that his] art and views about art were unchanging and somehow transhistorical, the fruits of an extended quest for a perfection both spiritual and formal."[22] However, all of this was in the service of a repression. The struggle to create an abstract sculpture in the early twentieth century, Chave contends, entailed confronting

Figure 1.4   Mark Lindquist, *Silent Witness No. 1, Oppenheimer*, 1983. Walnut, pecan, elm.
Collection of Margaret A. Pennington. Courtesy of the Wood Turning Center and the artist.

a wide range of tensions, which ranged from the sexual and the ethnographic to the formal. While rifts of these sorts are routinely discussed in relation to other artists of the period—Picasso and Matisse, preeminently, who stand in relation to later painting much as Brancusi does to sculpture—the Romanian has proved to be exempt. It is Chave's project to excavate these crises in Brancusi's art, thus restoring him to the complex and contested story of modernism.

There is a striking degree of overlap between the strategies of repression that Chave identifies in Brancusi's life and work, and those of the craft movement since. First and most obviously, there is the aforementioned formal affinity to his handwrought organic abstraction. Like Brancusi's work, modern studio craft objects refer obliquely to function without being functional, and they are abstract enough to seem progressive but sufficiently "natural" so as not to be off-putting to those who are not used to radical art. In this respect they take their cue from Brancusi, who found a way to make abstraction safe for mass consumption. Skilled labor functions in both cases to disarm dubious audiences who might otherwise find modern art too similar to child's play for comfort. Quite apart from these matters of form, though, there are points of congruence that indicate a less complete concealment of the underlying problems bedeviling modern abstraction. Brancusi's affected naïveté, for example, meant that he was perceived as an outsider, but one who perceived things truly. Chave cites a New York newspaperman's 1926 description: "The look in Brancusi's eyes is the look that cannot be counterfeited; it is the look not only of an honest man, but of an artist who has been true to his ideals."[23] Like Henri "Le Douanier" Rousseau, whom he befriended and to whom he frequently compared himself, Brancusi was not much involved in the competitive discussions about art then happening in Paris, but he was invited to all the best parties. On the other hand, despite his earthy, artisanal persona, Brancusi maintained a position on the subject of craft that might have pleased Adorno. He relentlessly propounded the idea that his skill in carving was not meant to draw attention to itself—that it was entirely a necessary means of achieving form. He pointedly dismissed the early phase of his career, during and shortly after the period in which he was working as an assistant in Auguste Rodin's atelier: "My hands were so deft that I could do everything and become a commercial success, but I was not satisfied with myself."[24]

Among Brancusi's most surprising habits was his practice of making many iterations of works that differed only slightly from one another, resulting in confusion on the part of museums and collectors ever since. Are these editions, or multiples of some kind? Are they simply to be taken as autonomous works of equivalent importance, and if so, what was the point of making an "essential" form more than once? The same questions can be asked regarding many craftspeople's outputs, which have an equally uncertain and uncomfortable relationship to autonomous art on the one hand, and "production work" (that is, crafted multiples churned out to make ends meet) on the other. In both cases, making the same thing again and again assures (and perhaps reassures) a steady public, but at the sacrifice of any claim to legitimate avant garde status, for the repetition of forms over the course of years implies a quality of ahistoricism. Chave identifies this as another of Brancusi's compensatory strategies; he found it was more effective to offer essence rather than innovation.[25] A corollary to this production strategy was the necessity that Brancusi's studio not seem like a workshop—which would have been perilously close to a factory, given his repetition of object types—but a profoundly aestheticized environment. His atelier served as a means of building the mystique around his work, and hence as a highly effective sales venue. He studiously avoided of any mention of the numerous assistants whom he employed in the production of his sculptures (who, incidentally, included Julio Gonzales, the first artist to incorporate welding into modern sculpture, as well as the Japanese-American sculptor Isamu Noguchi).[26] The permanently displayed simulacrum of Brancusi's workspace at the Centre Pompidou in Paris attests to the effectiveness of this strategy. Similarly, craft artists who have achieved a certain level of success—one thinks of Sam Maloof and John Makepeace in wood, or Dale Chihuly in glass—tend to create quasi-magical working environments that serve as the backdrop for their heroic achievements. As with Brancusi, their use of teams of craftsmen is a more-or-less open secret, the discussion of which they must carefully monitor so that it does not detract from the sense that each of their works is individually handcrafted by the master.

The artist Scott Burton, who curated an exhibition of Brancusi's works at the Museum of Modern Art in New York in 1989, commented that "Brancusi's studio, like his individual pieces of furniture, was both itself and a representation of itself." This perception about the site of Brancusi's production was part of a broader investigation that Burton undertook into the sculptor's oeuvre. Of particular fascination to him were works that functioned in multiple guises. Brancusi frequently presented the same object—usually in the form of a simple table or a small bench—as a base for a sculpture at one moment, and as a free-standing autonomous work at another. For Burton, this amounted to a slippage between the conditions of a pedestal and a sculpture, so that it was "simultaneously performing a function and acting as its own sign." He saw this "doubleness" as penetrating some of Brancusi's famous works, such as *Endless Column*, which could be seen as "a mighty étagère, a quantity of little tables stacked on top of one another," or perhaps as a column that is also a depiction of a column.[27] As Chave writes, this way of seeing the *Endless Column* raises the possibility that it is radically lacking as a work—it could be seen as nothing but an enormous base whose sculpture has gone missing.[28]

Burton's postmodern analysis of Brancusi is itself descended from the critical reception of works by Jasper Johns, whose paintings *of* flags, targets and maps, because of the flatness and conventionality of those signs, literally *are* flags, targets and maps.[29] But if both Brancusi and Johns effected a collapse between things and the representation of those things, their results differ greatly in their self-consciousness. What in Johns reads as a proto-Conceptual proposition about representation comes across, in Brancusi, as an intentionally obfuscating muddle of the supplement's relation to the autonomous work. A pedestal operates in the same manner as a frame—it holds what is placed atop it apart from the world. If a pedestal is granted its own autonomy, even implicitly, its regulative function as a supplement threatens to collapse. Like a psychoanalyst, Chave interprets this confusion as the inadvertent acknowledgment of a repressed crisis. For her, Brancusi's confusion of the base with the work speaks of a deep-seated doubt about autonomous sculpture itself. Through this mechanism,

Brancusi avoided directly confronting the question that people unused to abstract sculpture might have been posed about his works—why could they not *all* be seen as furnishings rather than artworks?

With this line of thinking in mind we might return to the question of Brancusi's enormous influence on the crafts. Chave's diagnosis can be transferred without difficulty to the present day, for craftspeople still work in the same state of anxiety about the status of their creations. The most acutely self-aware of them, such as the British ceramist Carol McNicoll, make no bones about the predicament in which they find themselves, as her own hilariously self-deprecating *Homage to Brancusi* shows. A truncated version of the *Endless Column* made of stacked slip-castings of a single pressed glass pitcher (found by McNicoll in a thrift-store), the piece deflates the usual pretensions of Brancusian craft with witty concision (see Plate 3). And yet, there is another side to this story. When we are faced with the puzzle of Brancusi's "pedestal-tables" (as Burton calls them) our first instinct might be to compare the way in which they are wrought with the techniques used to create more obviously autonomous sculptures in his oeuvre.[30] If we are looking for a clue that would help us to assign priority to one object rather than another, then craft would seem to provide an indication. The objects that Burton points to—which hover uncertainly in the double position of work and supplement—tend to be roughly hewn from timber, while the more recognizably autonomous works are likely to be made in brass or marble. This is by no means to be misconstrued as an insistence on an absolute hierarchy of materials in Brancusi's mind, as if he felt that noble substances were destined to be art and others were consigned to the realm of craft. Rather, Brancusi employed craft as a nuanced means of sending (and mixing) signals about the intended status of his objects. His chosen materials may not have had absolute connotations, but they did allow him to express relative qualities of facture and refinement. This artisanal language was one that Brancusi used adeptly. His careful juxtapositions of finish and material subjugate themselves to a total compositional effect.

From this example we can draw the broader point that while craft may be supplemental, it is certainly not to be taken for granted. It is easy to fall into the trap of thinking that craft is either present or not present in a work, or that it is present in some quantifiable sense. In fact, craft is a strictly qualitative consideration, in which the goal is always effacement in the service of the total work. Such erasure is no easy thing to achieve. It is worth recalling that Adorno implied that handicraft must be *mastered* if it is to do its work in support of autonomous art. To return to Derrida's example, we might observe that a frame is not just any gilt rectangle; it must be appropriate to the work that it supplements. This is where the craft of the framer comes in. His carving skills, careful application of bole and gold leaf, and judgment in the niceties of style and form are all absolutely necessary. This issue of appropriateness—a word that is itself closely tied to the concept of the supplement, as is clear from its etymological relation to the term "prop"—brings us back to the question of the lack in the autonomous artwork. For Chave, the lack in Brancusi is historically situated. His repressions are endemic to the emergence of modern art. But we can also reiterate the broader point, tacitly suggested by Brancusi's sculpture, that under the conditions of modernity craft is a supplement to art. Modern art cannot get along in its absence but also cannot admit its indebtedness. For the artwork to emerge in its autonomous totality, craft must absent itself from the proceedings.

WEARABLE SCULPTURES: MODERN JEWELRY AND THE PROBLEM OF AUTONOMY

At the other end of the spectrum from many craftspeople's single-minded gravitation to the works of Constantin Brancusi is the wild diversity of studio jewelry production over the course of the late twentieth century. Just as potters and woodcarvers have looked to Brancusi as a beacon, jewelers have looked to precedents in modern art; but their sources of inspiration are legion. Constructivism and Surrealism (especially its offshoot, Biomorphism) were undeniably the primary influences, but beginning in the 1940s, jewelers also looked to Picasso's welded sculptures, to contemporary Expressionist painting, to what was then called "primitive art," and to artists like Salvador Dalí and Alexander Calder who included jewelry-making in their own practice.[31] Yet other styles competed and intermingled with the visual vocabularies of modern art—from medievalizing Arts and Crafts enamels to Art Deco diamonds and costume jewelry, to the smoothed forms of contemporary Scandinavian design.

In sum, modern jewelry was a magpie art form, which tolerated a high degree of promiscuity in stylistic terms but developed few if any styles of its own. Indeed, some jewelers happily shuttled back and forth between idioms that were supposed to be antithetical—austere abstraction one day and ingratiating cartoons the next. Despite its derivative character, mid-century jewelry is fascinating because it represents a conscious struggle with the question of style. It goes almost without saying that this was also a struggle with the logic of the supplement in which jewelers found themselves doubly trapped. What a frame or pedestal does for a work of art, a piece of jewelry is supposed to do for the body. It stands apart from, but also points to, the character of the wearer. The jewelry historian Toni Greenbaum describes how this dynamic played out in modern craft jewelry: "Wearable works of art proclaim allegiance to a movement; they are 'badges,' so to speak, to be worn by those advocates of a progressive aesthetic. Wearing avant-garde jewelry identifies the wearer with a particular credo."[32]

Like any good supplement, a piece of jewelry both compensates for and exposes a lack in the thing that is adorned. To wear a piece of jewelry is to tacitly admit a need for ornamentation as a means of expressing character. By wearing a bracelet or brooch, one announces oneself merely to be the sort of person that would wear such a thing—the rhetoric of jewelry is that it adds nothing new but only confirms the "real" person who wears it. So if, at mid-century, this characterization occurred primarily through the mechanism of borrowed style, what does this tell us about the jewelers themselves? Were they applying the tropes of modern art to themselves as well-dressed people would apply a pin to their lapel—as if to say, "of course I am modern"? Perhaps this is a part of the story, but in retrospect it is clear that jewelers at mid-century also felt discomfort with the supplemental condition of their art. As a reminder of why they may have felt this way, it is helpful to turn to a standard text from the period, such as *Design in Jewellery* (1957) by the British metalsmith Peter Lyon. A proud member of the Worshipful Company of Goldsmiths, Lyon was not subtle in expressing his views about the incursion of modernism into contemporary jewelry. After referring to the "modernistic school" as "probably the most uninspired and short lived of any movement in design," he claimed that it was now only to be found in "the decoration of some cinemas, the worst type of cheap furniture and, lamentably, in some of the most expensive jewellery and silver work." The problem? "The attitude is that the wearer must adapt herself to the jewellery rather than that the jeweller should design for the woman." For Lyon, this was completely backwards. It was the jewel that should set off the body, not the other way round. "In simple terms," he wrote, "a fine necklace needs a fine neck."[33]

Even if we assume that Lyon's readers would not have found his assumption of a fixed-gender economy quite as embarrassing as we do today, it is not difficult to see that his contemporaries might have wanted to draw other conclusions. Faced with the depressing prospect of their medium's complete subjugation to standards of taste, jewelers adopted two opposing approaches, which, nonetheless, shared a common goal: to avoid the implication that their creations were simply supplemental. These two strategies group themselves roughly around the poles of Constructivism on the one hand, which tended towards an unexpected assertion of autonomy from the body, and Surrealism on the other, which tended to attempt a complete integration of body and jewel. Of course both of these objectives were Quixotic. Jewelry fully free of the body, or fully melded with it, is no longer jewelry at all. Yet these two gestures propelled a great deal of activity, especially in the United States immediately after the war.

On the autonomous side of the ledger were a group of abstractionist jewelers who were highly aware of European art and design. The preeminent figure in this group was San Francisco's Margaret DePatta, who in 1941 interrupted an already successful career (she was 37 at the time) to pursue what she called "special design work" under the Bauhaus luminary László Moholy-Nagy at the School of Design in Chicago.[34] DePatta's attitudes towards jewelry making were more thoroughly conceived and articulated than those of her Constructivist-influenced peers and followers, such as Merry Renk and Peter Macchiarini. In making what she described as her "wearable miniature sculptures," she employed a range of compositional strategies that emphatically asserted the principle of autonomy.[35] First, she gravitated to forms that stood comparatively free of the body, such as brooches and pendants. When making forms that did engage with the anatomy of their wearers, she tended to de-emphasize the part of the piece that touched the body. Her rings, for example, are simple metal circles with elaborate constructions mounted atop them. Second, in an idea she adapted from the teaching of Moholy-Nagy, she established a system of dynamically counterbalancing forms within her pieces, in which cantilevered, linear elements were weighted against more compact, denser forms. The effect was to create a self-enclosed world

Figure 1.5 Margaret DePatta, *Pendant*, 1956. White gold, ebony, and cross-faceted rhomboid quartz crystal. American Craft Council Archive.

of equilibrium not unlike that of an Alexander Calder mobile, which, formally speaking, announced its independence from exterior dynamics. Third, she nearly always had her work depicted against a neutral monochromatic backdrop—the photographic equivalent of a white gallery space—rather than as worn by a human body (Figure 1.5).

Finally, and most originally, DePatta structured her compositions around cut stones with complex refractory properties, which constituted self-enclosed worlds of optical incident. She went to great lengths to achieve this effect, sourcing her signature stone, rutilated crystal, from Brazil and working closely with a local lapidary to develop new cuts that would result in dazzling optical effects.[36] When discussing Moholy-Nagy's influence upon her, she frequently quoted him as saying: "catch your stones in the air. Don't enclose them. Make them float."[37] And indeed she employed a variety of constructive means to achieve this goal. Most often she tension-mounted her stones in order to create an effect of levitation; sometimes, as in her more informal "sweater jewelry," she resorted to gluing pebbles directly onto metal struts using kiln-baked epoxy. "They should be free, as they are in nature," DePatta explained, "so I keep the metal as simple as possible and never enclose the stones."[38]

The reception of DePatta's work immediately after her death in 1965 testifies to her success in communicating the idea that jewelry could be an autonomous art form. Some writers argued that she seemed to be operating in another discipline entirely. "If Margaret DePatta could have been something other than a craftsman of jewelry, she would have been an architect," her biographer Yoshiko Ushida wrote. "Her jewelry reflects the straightforward precision and boldness of the architect, but with the freedom of the sculptor."[39] The important thing, though, is that this "freedom" was not simply asserted, as if it consisted only in a simple lack of functionality—a great mistake often made by craftspeople themselves and commentators on their work. Rather, DePatta devised positive strategies for creating an effect of autonomy. It is no coincidence that her pieces seem like hermetic worlds of form, to which a wearer's body seems largely incidental; she worked hard to achieve just that effect.

Against this clear claim to autonomy should be placed the more subtle, countervailing tendency in mid-century jewelry to achieve a compositional union between jewelry and the body. This tactic was less overtly stated but also somewhat more widespread among jewelers, perhaps because it was more particular to their medium. Other crafts might try to achieve self-standing visual languages similar in spirit to DePatta's, but jewelry had a unique opportunity to bend the body to its own logic, and vice versa. A group of jewelers who were influenced by popular Surrealism (Dalí rather than Bataille) formed the core of this tendency: among them Sam Kramer, Ed Weiner and Art Smith, all of whom had shops in the lower part of Manhattan.[40] Smith may be taken as exemplary of the general trend. Toni Greenbaum contrasts his production to the superficially similar works of Calder, who (like Smith) made much use of twisted and spiraling wire: "where Alexander Calder's jewelry could exist artistically—independent of the body—Smith's relied on the human form as armature."[41] Smith himself noted that he used negative space "very accurately, very concretely." Rather disarmingly, he claimed that he chose this approach because space was "a very cheap component," and then added more seriously, "you can find it and make it tangible."[42] His compositions must be activated through the act of wearing—they are shapeless and unwieldy affairs when experienced off the body. Smith also designed costumes for theatrical companies, and his more ambitious jewelry could be said to have achieved an effect of performance when worn. Publicity shots taken of models wearing Smith's work emphasized this through the use of dramatic poses and camera angles—a complete departure from the photographs of DePatta's studies in autonomous form (Figure 1.6). The fact that his chosen models were African-American, like the artist himself, gave this performance an implicitly political charge: in an age when the slogan "black is beautiful" was current, Smith was clearly celebrating the skin beneath the ornament.

Jewelers like DePatta and Smith were feeling their way through various styles, rather than staking out competing programmatic stances about their medium. They nonetheless set the stage for the much more self-conscious wave of jewelers who emerged in subsequent decades. The implicit dissatisfaction with the condition of jewelry that had manifested itself in earlier work now became outright antagonism. The result was the new category of "body

Figure 1.6   Art Smith, *Mobile Neckpiece*, ca. 1969. Textured bronze.
American Craft Council archive. Photograph by Lida Moser.

jewelry." Though there were American exponents of this new direction—the Californian metalsmith Arline Fisch being a particularly notable figure—there was a greater critical mass in Germany, the Netherlands, and slightly later in Britain. Again, a few examples will have to stand in for the larger picture. Otto Künzli and Gerd Rothmann, both working in Munich, created marvelously understated pieces: Kunzli's clip whose only function was to attach two people's clothing, so that each body became an ornament for the other; Rothmann's fragile brooch made by casting the palm of the wearer's hand.[43] In Britain, Caroline Broadhead created one of the iconic objects of the early 1980s, a woven nylon "neckpiece" in the shape of a cylinder that entirely shrouded the wearer's head. Wendy Ramshaw, best known for her sets of rings mounted on sculptural metal spindles, created a set of brass stamps in geometric shapes that allowed the "wearer" to ornament the skin by direct printing in ink. And Susanna Heron reshuffled the relations between performative body jewelry and autonomous abstract form in an exhibition held at the Crafts Council Gallery in London in 1980 entitled "Bodywork." The show was composed mainly of flat geometric shapes made from plastic materials—rigid acrylic, flexible polyester, and resin inlay. These works made only minimal concessions to the idea of jewelry (see Plate 4). Also exhibited were collaborative photographs of Heron taken by David Ward with patterns of light projected on to her body.[44]

At the time, the new jewelry seemed impressively conceptual within its genre. The American critic Rose Slivka wrote a rapturous review of one exhibition of the British "new jewellery": "[This] jewellery does not accommodate the body—rather it is in orbit around the body, a galaxy of planets whirling on their dervishes. Jewellery is now a body cage and a mind opener… Where before your jewellery showed your social status, now it shows where your head is at and what you are thinking about."[45] Yet for all of the seemingly open-ended and avant garde aspects of this work, in retrospect it seems entirely legible: it simply made explicit the questions of supplementarity that jewelers had been dancing around for decades. The moment was defined by the mismatch between jewelry and the normative forms of abstract art. Heron's plastic shapes, for example, might remind one of formalist paintings by the likes of Ellsworth Kelly and Kenneth Noland, but were in fact inspired by a much earlier source: a 1927 film showing a dance staged by the Dada artist Oskar Schlemmer. Inspired by the use of improbable props in this historic performance, Heron created jewelry that both altered the natural movements of the body and bestowed upon the wearer an acute sense of the spatial dynamics of those movements.[46] Like Schlemmer before her, she adapted her forms to the body—but only barely. In describing one neckpiece that she had made in 1977, which created the effect of a Saturn-like ring around the head and shoulders, she declared that she had wanted "to see how wide I could make a flat circle without it becoming unwearable."[47] The reference to early modernism in this experiment was also reflected in Ward and Heron's light projections, which seemed radical in the context of a jewelry show, but could be seen from a fine art perspective as turning the clock back some sixty years to the early "light-space" experiments of Margaret DePatta's teacher László Moholy-Nagy.

Just as Schlemmer and Moholy-Nagy had sought to escape the boundaries of autonomous form through an environmental approach to art, Heron engaged the supplementarity of her chosen medium through an act of displacement. If Margaret DePatta and Art Smith had expressed their ideas about jewelry through the medium of photography, then Heron took the next logical step, intentionally creating a situation in which photographs of her jewelry in use had as much a claim to the status of artwork as the jewelry itself.[48]

As Tanya Harrod has noted, Heron's antagonism towards the problematic position of jewelry was matched by an equally conscious attempt to achieve a break from the institutional realm of the "crafts."[49] Perhaps for this reason, her formal confrontation with supplementarity and that of her peers was almost always accompanied by a lack of conspicuous craftsmanship. Reviewing a 1982 Crafts Council exhibition of work by Peter Degen, another of the leading avant-gardistes in British jewelry at the time, critic Christopher Reed asked

> what is one to make of the flagrant lack of sophistication of these present pieces? Using the cheapest of materials and treating them in a way that emphasises spontaneity rather than technical finesse, Degen appears to suggest that the making of such artefacts need not be carried out by those who have been specially trained for the job, but that you and I, unseasoned amateurs, could do the same work if we wished to. This idea cuts so sharply against the ethos of superiority of skill and discernment that the Crafts Council is supposed to promote that people are bound to ask what sort of a reassessment (or leg-pull) is being attempted here.[50]

A few conclusions can be drawn from this narrative of ongoing discomfort. First, it is notable that the two types of supplementarity that jewelry exemplifies—its inferior relation to the body and its conventional association with craft process—are inextricably wound together in the postwar period. This suggests that while there may be no ironclad relationship between craft and decoration, there is a strong tendency for the two to be grouped together as a problematic within practice. Second, although postwar studio jewelry is routinely described as "wearable sculpture," it is clear that this formula has been a problem for jewelers rather than a solution. The fundamental impossibility of making autonomous jewelry did not discourage a figure like DePatta from setting herself exactly that ambition. Yet, as even the most prominent historian of mid-century jewelry, Toni Greenbaum, concedes, DePatta and her peers were involved in "the ornamental interpretation of modern art, using the body as a point of reference."[51] The doubly supplemental nature of their undertaking meant that the efforts that these jewelers brought to their project had little relevance to the field of sculpture *per se*. Similarly, the gamesmanship of an artist like Susanna Heron, for all its cleverness, is best seen as a reshuffling of the cards that she was dealt. It could even be said that in her attempt to wreak havoc with jewelry's supplementarity, she confirmed that aspect of the genre's identity more emphatically than any conservative goldsmith possibly could have. Ultimately, postwar studio jewelry demonstrates the somewhat counterintuitive fact that when craftspeople themselves think through craft, they often do so through a process of denial.

REFRAMING THE PATTERN AND DECORATION MOVEMENT

In mid-century jewelry and its subsequent rethinking in the late 1970s and early 1980s, we have seen artists struggling to accommodate a craft-based practice to the unaccommodating principle of artistic autonomy. But what would it look like if artists pursued the opposite course, using craft to refuse autonomy outright? This question leads us straight to the Pattern and Decoration movement, which began in 1975 when a group of artists including Joyce Kozloff, Miriam Schapiro, Robert Kushner and Robert Zakanitch, as well as the critic Amy Goldin, met in Kozloff's loft apartment in Soho to discuss their shared interest in ornament.[52] The canonical period text on Pattern and Decoration emerged two years later: John Perreault's *Artforum* article "Issues in Pattern Painting," which functioned as a kind of manifesto for the group.[53] In the essay's opening line, Perreault described Pattern and Decoration art as "non-Minimalist" (as well as "non-sexist, historically conscious, sensuous, romantic, rational, [and] decorative") but it might have been more accurate had he written that it was a conscious response against Minimalism, both stylistically and conceptually. So much is clear from a comparison of Frank Stella's early 1960s black-stripe paintings and Valerie Jaudon's 1975 *Ingomar* (named, like most of the artist's early images, for a town in her home state of Mississippi) (Figures 1.7 and 1.8).[54] As Anna Chave has argued in

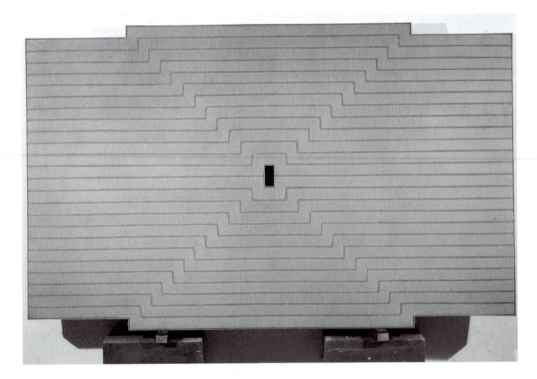

Figure 1.7   Frank Stella, *Six Mile Bottom*, 1960. Metallic paint on canvas. Tate Gallery.

a study of Jaudon's work, although these two painters clearly occupied the same aesthetic territory, their pictorial logics were diametrically opposed. The key difference is that Stella's lines are derived logically from the dimensional interaction between the overall shape of the canvas and the width of the paintbrush Stella used to paint it, while the lines on the Jaudon are composed in a seemingly arbitrary manner. Stella's "deductive structure" renders his painting self-referential, and therefore non-decorative.[55] Jaudon, by contrast, appears to abandon the rigors of self-analytic modernism in her embrace of the decorative. Her lines are in no way predicted by the overall form of the canvas, but instead are arranged in an ornamental pattern.

But are the lines of the Jaudon wholly arbitrary? Or are they arrived at through a formal logic that is simply different from Stella's—a logic that we could see as somehow craft-like? Certainly Jeff Perrone, a perceptive critic who also wrote about Pattern and Decoration for *Artforum*, thought so. He analyzed Jaudon's means of composing a picture as being fundamentally artisanal, because of its steady accumulation of organically related small-scale decisions. Jaudon's paintings, he wrote, "present a process of arriving at abstraction,

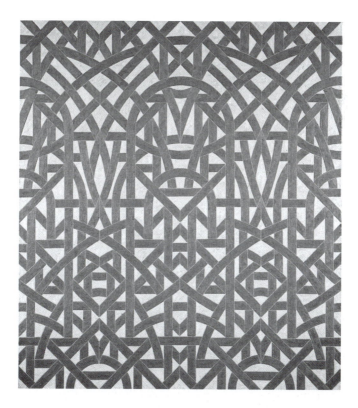

Figure 1.8 Valerie Jaudon, *Ingomar*, 1979. Oil and metallic paint on canvas. National Museum of Women in the Arts, Washington, DC. Gift of Josephine Cockerell Thornton. © Valerie Jaudon/Licensed by VAGA, New York.

as though abstraction were being reinvented ... her process unravels as we retrace the steps of her craft. Intricacies of craft are reintroduced as the primary condition of art."[56] The arcs and lines that repeat as the painting expands from its center do not cohere into a complete geometric circles and squares, but instead are interrupted in a regular rhythm. As one reviewer wrote, "[the] paintings have no beginning or ending, only centers and excrescences."[57] Instead of a painting within a frame, a painting in which craftsmanship is effaced, Jaudon has given us a painting made up of nothing but frames, each superimposed on the next, telescoping in a potentially infinite mathematical progression.

By the end of the 1970s, several writers were forwarding the notion that Pattern and Decoration works were approaching the condition of the frame. Carrie Rickey, for example, commented in a 1978 review of Joyce Kozloff's installation works that "a border signifies neither the beginning nor ending of an area but rather its interface with some beyond. In this sense borders suggest both curiosity and uncertainty about adjacency and can intimate the unknown or infinite of that outside the boundary."[58] With such arguments, we have in a sense returned to the confusion between the supplement and the autonomous artwork that we saw in Brancusi's "pedestal-tables." And again the physical process of fashioning this hybrid thing—in Kozloff's case, using ceramic tiles—is front and center.[59] But now the muddling of the two is the whole point. By inhabiting the *parergonal*, that is, by being nothing but a frame, or an unending series of frames, Pattern and Decoration constituted itself in the image of art's Achilles' heel. As Jaudon herself put it, "the decorative is both a reflection and an essential part of the world around it."[60]

Johanna Drucker has criticized the construct of modernist autonomy in the following terms: "Since it is virtually impossible to situate perception outside of the politically charged network it is equally impossible to assume some abstract and decontextualized stable condition in which to perceive the supposed autonomy on which oppositional strategies of the avant-garde are supposedly premised."[61] Drucker argues that any theory of aesthetic autonomy, even one premised on self-critique as Adorno's is, rests on an unacknowledged assumption that an artwork has "inherent and self-evident" formal properties.[62] This faith in the stable form of the work overlooks the fact that perception itself is always historically situated. Indeed, this is the full force of Derrida's deconstructivist attack—even if the artwork compensates for its lack through the prop of a supplement, this measure only defers the inevitable rush of cultural context into the work. To quote Drucker again: "For Derrida the *parergon* is not the frame that permits judgment to take place, but the understanding that erases and imposes the frame simultaneously in recognition of its effects, assumptions, and predispositions."[63] Jeff Perrone was perhaps the only theoretical supporter of Pattern and Decoration who fully grasped this point; as he wrote in 1976, "work which is called 'decorative' can cease to be only about itself and begin to explore other kinds of experience... Narrow references to art history are replaced with various cultural signs and designs of general and multivalent meaning."[64] But if the anti-formalist position outlined by Drucker was not yet established in the criticism written on the Pattern and Decoration artists, it was nonetheless very much present in their work. For these artists craft was not (as it was for Adorno) a process of self-erasure, a way of coming to terms with the materiality of the work as object; it was on the contrary a means of surfacing a cultural position.

This way of thinking through craft was exemplified by Miriam Schapiro, who, as a leader of the Feminist art program at CalArts (see Chapter 5), turned to an expressly decorative style that incorporated craft materials and processes such as fabric appliqué. A good example of what might be called her *parergonal* period is the 1976 painting *Mary Cassatt and Me* (see Plate 6), one of a series of "collaboration" works in which she constructed elaborate fabric frames around reproductions of paintings by other artists.[65] The strategy allowed her to abandon the center of the picture, shifting her own pictorial contributions to the frame. Schapiro would later describe this impulse in autobiographical terms: "Growing up, I listened to my mother and her sister talk about the world—my grandmother's world and their own. I felt the spatial limits of their lives. I saw my own future in terms of spatial expansion. I wanted to 'move out.'"[66] Of course the image's center, which Schapiro has so pointedly vacated, is not empty. It is a photographic reproduction of Mary Cassatt's *A Woman at Her Toilette* of 1909. If Schapiro formally relegates her own artistic position to the supplemental frame, and in doing so embraces her position in the margins, she does so only to allude to the cultural fact that she occupies an analogous social position to that occupied by Cassatt (as a woman artist) in her own time. Implicitly, Schapiro is arguing that the two artists face the same problem, that of gender, but that it is impossible for Schapiro to remain within the traditional boundaries of painting, as Cassatt did. Her choice of this particular painting is significant, however, as it speaks with unusual eloquence to Cassatt's interest in her own compromised position. The figure in *A Woman at Her Toilette* is caught in the act of introspection, crafting her own appearance. In fact she is already "framed" in spatial terms by the two mirrors behind her and in front of her. Cassatt depicts a woman structured entirely within her own image, in which she is evidently absorbed. Schapiro's fabric collage is a further, responsive framing, functioning in relation to Cassatt's image as an extrapolation, an expanding *parergonal* concentricity. *Me and Mary Cassatt* might then be described as achieving an effect similar to Jaudon's abstract frames-within-frames. Crucially, though, Schapiro's own frame is not abstract, but made up of the culturally freighted content of the materials and process of quilting. This is as much a double portrait as a collaboration, and Schapiro has quite literally pictured herself as occupying the space of the supplement.

As any military commander knows all too well, an act of occupation must be more than a gesture—it requires staying power. Schapiro's work, which could easily be taken as naïve, is in fact deceptively "theoretical"—an attempt to surface her own compromised subject position as a woman artist, and her relation to art history, in supplementary terms. It is on the basis of such tactics that the artist has insisted that she and her fellow Pattern and Decoration artists had "seeded" the most significant developments in the art of the succeeding decades: "the origin of pluralism was feminism."[67] Anna Chave has recently made a similar argument: "well before the term 'multi-culturalism' became a watchword in the academy, the Pattern and Decoration group had conceived a vision of multi-cultural, non-sexist, non-classist, non-racist, non-hierarchical art."[68] Yet Pattern and Decoration art was not able to sustain itself as a viable avant garde. There were various attempts to legitimize the movement in theoretical terms, notably on the part of Perrone, whose familiarity with Derrida is evident both in his arguments and in his elliptical writing style. Decoration, he wrote in 1980, "is both beside and beyond, near and amiss (*Para-* of the paradigm is neither the inside nor the outside, but the frame and the border, the *para-* of the decorative confusion of an adorned outside of cloth and an ornamented inside…)."[69] Sadly, this argument never coalesced into an accepted critical account of the movement. Commentary on Pattern and Decoration art instead revolved around ill-defined attempts to connect it to early modern instances of pictorial arbitrariness and exoticism, such as the paintings of Matisse or Chagall. These backwards-facing justifications were not calculated to bring the movement much acclaim and, after the onset of Neo-expressionism in the early 1980s, Pattern and Decoration faded from critical view. That this elision is unfortunate for the artists involved seems obvious enough, but it also represents a lost thread in the historiography of craft. In years since, craft has continued to play an important but often unacknowledged role as the basis of a pluralist, deconstructive formal language. We will see two examples of this thinking in the work of Tracey Emin and Mike Kelley in Chapter 5. For now, though, it is enough to emphasize the fact that when Pattern and Decoration artists rethought craft, they did so not by struggling to make it autonomous but, on the contrary, by inhabiting its supplementarity so completely.

PROPS: GIJS BAKKER, GORD PETERAN

In the foregoing case studies, we have seen how two very different avant gardes—one taking place within the limited scope of jewelry, and the other taking as its point of attack the more general notion of the decorative—engaged with craft as a supplemental language of form. The two examples are in some respects opposite. While jewelers attempted to elevate their brooches and neckpieces to the standard of the autonomous work, Pattern and Decoration artists dragged fine art formats such as painting into the realm of supplemental form. Both of these strategies challenged the usual hierarchical relation between the autonomous and the supplemental. Yet, before congratulating these artists for having upended the structure of modern art, it would be well to note that both gestures were dependent upon the very dialectic they sought to critique. For this reason—a crucial point for understanding the way that craft functions within the ground of art—their effect was localized. It may have disturbed a given state of affairs, but only in a limited way. Thus radical jewelers like Susanna Heron may have shifted existing paradigms with regard to bodily ornamentation and its ties to class signification, but they leave our underlying expectations about jewelry and painting, craft and art, intact. Indeed, Heron's work could never have operated without those expectations, for it is only by the gesture of temporarily subverting them that she achieves her focused critique. Similarly, Pattern and Decoration art did pave the way for a transformation of attitudes towards ornament, gender and ethnicity in the contemporary art world. This accomplishment was achieved through a manipulation of supplemental forms traditionally associated with "women's work" and "non-Western" visual culture. Even in this case, however, craft (as an abstract category and a point of reference) by no means lost its supplemental character. On the contrary, that supplementarity was the key to the entire enterprise.

To put the matter more succinctly, postwar jewelry's striving for autonomy has an interest precisely because it was so very futile. The pleasure one gets from Margaret DePatta's attempt to constitute a fundamentally contradictory genre ("wearable sculpture"), for example, is due to the combination of her work's prodigious formal verve and its conceptual paralysis. Miriam Schapiro's *Me and Mary Cassatt*, similarly, is defined entirely within the terms that it seeks to subvert. The image is rhetorically powerful and convincingly deconstructive, but like most protest art, it possesses an air of bitter finality. In both cases, then, we see craft's inferiority put to work, but in a manner that seems in retrospect to be strident and quixotic. The remainder of this chapter will consider two artists who continue to explore the logic of supplemental craft, but who depart from this impasse in significant ways: the Dutch avant garde jeweler and industrial designer Gijs Bakker, and the Toronto conceptual artist Gord Peteran, who operates in a terrain that he calls "the furnitural." Seen against the backdrop of jewelers and Pattern and Decoration artists who saw themselves as overthrowing art historical precedent, these contemporary figures will seem rather nonchalant by comparison. They pursue no grand disciplinary strategy, and they create tightly focused studies rather than open-ended manifestos. This tendency perhaps speaks to the general condition of contemporary art, which has entered an individualist phase. The avant garde no longer operates through discrete movements. But these artists' cool, clinical quality also suggests a new maturity in thinking about craft. Rather than seeing its supplementarity as a problem to be solved, or a prejudice to overcome, artists are now able to see it clearly: as an idea that can be put in the service of particular artistic operations.

GIJS BAKKER

The Dutch designer Gijs Bakker could easily have featured earlier in this chapter, given that his experiments with jewelry began in the 1960s. In fact, Bakker and his partner Emmy van Leersum were central to a Dutch and German avant garde jewelry movement that anticipated and deeply influenced Heron and other jewelers in Britain.[70] Designing and making as a team, Bakker and Van Leersum created hybrid objects in handmade brass, cast acrylic, cloth, and other materials. These were barely wearable, but spoke convincingly to contemporary progressive fashion. Bakker's instinct for mainstream resonance has paid off over the years. His design activities broadened in the 1970s, taking in furniture and other housewares, and gradually he became the Netherlands' leading figure in industrial design. Along with the design editor Renny Ramakers, he was the prime mover behind the formation of Droog, perhaps the best-known and best-publicized design collection of the

1990s. Droog is not a design group, but rather a selection of objects that are "curated" by Bakker and Ramakers and then publicized under a single brand. Bakker has also created wares for the high-profile ceramic firm Cor Unum in 's-Hertogenbosch, and helped to found Chi Ha Paura…? (literally "Who's Afraid Of…?"), a foundation based in Amsterdam for the advancement of conceptual jewelry.

Throughout his long career, Bakker has distanced himself from a professional craft identity. At the same time, Droog's initial appearance on the design scene drew notice partly for its embrace of craft imagery and processes, its implicit suggestion that, as Museum of Modern Art design curator Paola Antonelli put it, "craftsmanship is no longer reactionary." Antonelli frames the shift in terms of problem-solving, arguing that designers' interests in newly available materials on the one hand and found objects on the other motivated them to develop a craft-based practice: "Some advanced materials actually demand manual intervention, while some low-tech materials, like glass milk bottles, that respond (at least in appearance) to ecological needs, merely demand a crafts approach because of their special nature. Experimentation, be it high- or low-tech, requires a hands-on approach."[71] Droog's early output, beginning in 1993 and lasting about five years, bears out this judgment. While recent products tend to be rampantly inventive but disparate one-liners—a suburban fence with a ping-pong table set into it, a door with seventy-two key holes, only two of which operate, and so forth—early Droog design was a more unified project, based upon craft process and imagery of a conspicuously humble kind. Hobby textiles, for example, were a favored trope. Marcel Wanders cast a macramé chair in carbon fiber, Hella Jongerius cast a knitted lamp in fiberglass, and Bakker himself wrapped actual cotton knit around a porcelain teapot to form an integral tea cozy. In 1993 the designer Djoke de Jong offered a window curtain with a dressmaker's cutout pattern printed on to its surface, implying a second life for the product through the consumer's own craft work.

During this early period the group's designers also experimented with techniques of manufacture that resulted in unpredictable variations reminiscent of the handmade, as in a set of porcelain bowls by Jongerius that are fired differentially to obtain unique eccentric shapes, Dick van Hoff's plates made from randomly extruded and blended two-tone porcelain, and Tejo Remy's iconic *Rag Chair*, made from scavenged cloth scraps bound together by steel bands. More generally, a fascination with handmade "softness" in form and material typified early Droog work. From garden seating made of pressed hay to molded felt washbasins, Droog products emphasized tactility and individualization, intentionally departing from the authoritative perfection of most high design goods. Ideologically, these products signaled a return to the Scandinavian modern or the American "designer-craftsman" styles of the 1950s, which attempted to inject human warmth into the mass production process. The difference is that Droog designers delighted in the idea that craft was a source of weakness—a problem, not an answer. As Rody Graumars, one of the collection's designers explains, "I just work in lowly situations, like with an ordinary lightbulb, things that don't have much value. I love the idea of getting power out of inferiority."[72] Bakker resorts to an even more graphic image of vulnerability: "Our design is very open. Like a fish on a cutting board saying, 'cook me any way you want.'"[73]

These metaphors—a lightbulb, a fish—raise the issue of the found object, which played a leading part in early Droog work. Remy's *Rag Chair* and hanging lamp made of milk bottles, and Peter van der Jagt's *Bottoms Up* doorbell chime made from two upside-down wineglasses, were among their first successes. Craft and the found object might seem to be strange bedfellows, but they are similar in that both constitute a horizon for industrial design. Neither the handmade nor the Readymade can be said to reside comfortably within that category, and it is precisely for this reason that both are employed in Droog products. The found object and the crafted object alike are presented as fixed points of everyday life— shards of the "real"—that penetrate the frictionless, normative qualities of a serially produced commodity. This classically avant-garde attitude may have elements of the romantic at this late date, and one could well ask whether Droog's limited-run concept design has any real critical potential. There is even an unexpected return here of the problems that beset the Arts and Crafts movement, which also provided ideologically correct goods to a high-minded bourgeoisie. Ramakers and Bakker have recently spoken about their struggle to achieve wider distribution and lower pricing without becoming a sort of avant garde IKEA.[74] Yet in purely symbolic terms, Droog can be seen as an exemplification of thinking through craft, without collapsing into "the crafts" as a fixed category—a nuance that is clearly grasped by Droog's leaders. Asked in 1996 by a design journalist about their conspicuous "craft ethic," Ramakers said: "I don't think Droog Design can be described as craft. Craftsy certainly, but never craft."[75] This was not just prevarication. Ramaker's choice of words suggests that she regards craft as a crucial point of reference, but only one among others.

The found object and the handmade come together repeatedly in the Droog oeuvre, but nowhere more winningly than in Bakker's own designs. One of his most recent creations is called the *Real Series* (see Plate 5). For this return to his original *métier* of jewelry, which is produced without a direct affiliation to Droog, Bakker collected found costume jewels— made of worthless colored paste—and then hired a goldsmith to create miniature versions of those pieces using gold, silver, and precious stones. He then joined these two objects together into a single wearable brooch or ring. The results are disorienting in the extreme, traditional in appearance but strangely off-kilter in shape, and (as the title of the series wryly signals) a confusing mélange of the genuine and the fake. The "imitation" jewel functions both as an icon of the ersatz, and also (like any found object) as a bit of the real that has been imported into the design process. The handcrafted jewel that is added to it, by contrast, is authentic in its materials but "imitation" in a different sense, in its replication of the found costume jewel. The elegance of this conceptual loop is compounded by the fact that initially, one cannot tell the difference between the paste and the precious stones. They blend together into an undifferentiated, sparkling mass. When the trick of the pieces is revealed, one is forcibly reminded of the arbitrariness of the difference in real-world value between the two. Indeed, the only obvious visual difference is that the expensive part is smaller. (This is not to say that the value system of jewelry has been suspended, of course: an example from the *Real Series* will set you back many thousands of Euros.) All of this amounts to a brilliant exercise in the supplemental. The *Real Series* jewels are like miniature ecologies of lack, in which each of the two components—one mass produced, the other hand-crafted—ornaments the other, and in so doing, exposes its own vanity. Bakker's position in all of this is that of an orchestrator rather than a fabricator. Yet it is hard to believe that anyone but a former avant garde jeweler would have come up with such an idea. After his many years of struggling with supplementarity, it returns here in a state of placid resolution.

GORD PETERAN

An old wooden chair with a brass implement crawling atop it, like an alien life form, serves as our final example of supplementary thinking (Figure 1.9). This hybrid object is the work

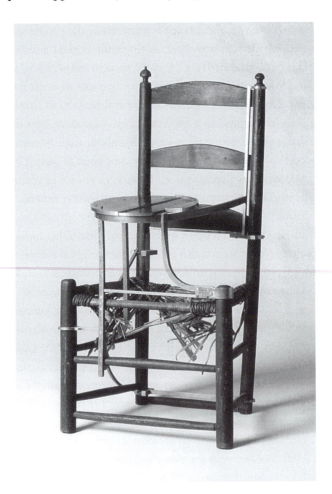

Figure 1.9   Gord Peteran, *Prosthetic*, 2001. Found wooden chair, brass. Courtesy of the artist.

of the Canadian artist Gord Peteran, who might almost be taken for one of Droog's design stable, if he were not so good at making unique art works.[76] In its conceptual structure, the work is closely comparable to the jewels in Bakker's *Real Series*. Peteran began with a found antique chair, so rickety that it had lost its usefulness. He then built a device by hand, working with whatever brass bits and pieces he had ready to hand in his studio, in an attempt to prop up the chair. The rear legs, threatening to split from rot, are bound with tight metal bands. Vertical and lateral shafts lend the chair rigidity, preventing the wounded chair from racking side to side. Flat metal plates wrap around especially weak spots in the wood. A metal disk serves as a notional seat, floating above the shredded rush upholstery. The piece is made solid and useful again, restored to its original state of functionality, but without the careful effacement that such restoration normally entails. In this case, craft conspicuously fails to cover its own tracks.

If the title of this work, *Prosthetic*, suggests a medical procedure, then this is entirely appropriate, because the work is operative in more than one sense of the term. Like a doctor, Peteran's work began with a diagnosis of the chair's symptoms. In addressing them, he followed the primary precept of medical care: "first, do no harm." If Peteran has restored the chair to life, he has done so only provisionally. At no point does the brass "enter the flesh of the patient," as he has said, and it can therefore be removed without leaving a mark on the chair's surface. Peteran recalls taking great pains to avoid moving or cutting the splayed rushes of the seat, which forced him to forge wide curves in some of the brace's struts. Such care bespeaks a degree of respect for the found object that transcends mere capitalization on its properties. As in Bakker's jewels, the handmade and the Readymade are locked in a tight embrace. They can be pulled apart, but they fascinate only when put together, each compensating for the other's weaknesses.

It is tempting to take Peteran's chair-on-life-support as a metaphor for the interpenetration of art and craft, each requiring the other to hold itself upright. But such an interpretation fails to take into account the fact that *Prosthetic* is, in its totality, an autonomous artwork. It may probe the conceptual terrain of "the furnitural," but it inhabits that terrain from a detached position. It is furniture (not only a single chair, but the entire genre) rather than art that is presented in the guise of the found object. Nor could this relation be inverted. Art's ability to absorb supplemental form is a one-way street. And yet, just as with jewelry, furniture's supplementarity can be exploited as a means to remind us what we take for granted. Like a prop on a stage, it exists to contextualize that which is beyond itself.

2 MATERIAL

As Ad Reinhardt supposedly said, "sculpture is something you bump into when you back up to look at a painting."[1] We saw in the first chapter that a modern artwork is supposed to be autonomous, and paintings perform this function admirably. They are rectangles of presence that cut themselves off from the surrounding world, either through the action of a frame or the suggestion of one (the naked edge of the canvas against the bare wall). But a sculpture is in a viewer's space. Can it be fully autonomous?

This seemingly simple question has prompted much of postwar art discourse. Attempts to establish a theoretical basis for sculptural autonomy have ranged widely, from discussions of the function of the pedestal (in which Constantin Brancusi's work has figured centrally), to Donald Judd's idea of the "specific object"—a unified form that achieves singular presence through the sheer integrity of its composition—to Rosalind Krauss's negative definition of sculpture as that which is neither architecture, nor landscape.[2] A full accounting of sculptural autonomy will not be attempted here, but it nonetheless forms a vital backdrop to a consideration of thinking about craft during the post-1945 period.[3] One strand is particularly worth picking out: the binary opposition between the material and the optical. This line of thought closely parallels that considered in the previous chapter. Just as craft's supplementarity makes it antithetical to modern art's autonomy, its grounding in *material* specificity is oppositional to the ambition of modern art to achieve a purely visual effect. This is not to say craft is somehow equivalent to materiality in itself (that is, the extension of matter in space). It would be better to say that craft always entails an encounter with the properties of a specific material. This could be wood, glass, metal, clay, paper, plastic, paint, stone—anything—or more than one material in combination. In any case, though, craft involves direct engagement with specific material properties. The normative idea of modern art, by contrast, involves the transcendence (which, as in the case of autonomy, is also a repression) of just this encounter.

Again, this is a complicated story that begins from a simple point: every artwork is made, first and foremost, to be looked at. The critic Clement Greenberg took this as the defining fact about art, and constructed his aesthetic judgments accordingly. His position has been described in the decades since using the shorthand term "opticality"—a defining idea in the history of modern painting and sculpture, not so much because of artists' assent to the theory as the energetic extension, defense, and deconstruction of Greenberg's work by his brilliant acolytes Michael Fried and Rosalind Krauss.[4] However, as Caroline Jones has recently demonstrated in her book *Eyesight Alone*, a richly detailed survey of Greenberg's career and influence, the proliferation of his ideas went far outside the inner circle of art's intelligentsia. What Jones calls "the Greenberg effect" rested on the idea that the experience of art was purely visual. The viewer was to be conceived as a disembodied entity, an "I/eye," whose disinterested vision ensured that "the encumbrances of the socialized self (family, tradition, religion, politics, ideology) appear to be stripped away."[5] Jones dissects Greenberg's position much as Chave dissects Brancusi's career, showing that the integrity of the theoretical edifice of opticality was dependent upon unacknowledged interests: bodily, commercial, and political. She depicts Greenberg as a technocratic hygienist who tried to cleanse art of its many troubling contingencies. To the extent that his way of thinking held sway in the art world, craft—conceived as the knowledge and exploitation of specific materials—could only be seen as something to be held at bay.

Though Jones's study of Greenberg is unprecedented in its comprehensiveness, it is only the most recent challenge to his understanding of modern art. As soon as Greenberg had established Jackson Pollock's primacy as the key painter of optical modernism, dissenters rushed in, insisting on the importance of the materiality in his dripped works, and of Abstract Expressionism in general. Partly because of the artist's own inability to clearly articulate his intentions, and partly due to his early death, Pollock became a Janus-faced figure. Both sides in the combat between the "Greenbergers" and their enemies, who were sometimes called "literalists," sought to claim him. As *Artforum* editor Philip Leider wrote in 1970, the latter group included artists like Allan Kaprow, Frank Stella, and Robert Morris, who "did not see, or did not see first and foremost, [Pollock's] patterns as patterns of line freed from their function of bounding shape and thereby creating a new kind of space." Rather, what seemed important to them was the way that he dripped his paint straight from the can, the way his method asserted gravity's pull, the haphazard studio detritus that found its way into the paintings—in short, "the affirmation of the *objectness* of the painting and from the directness of the artist's relations to his materials."[6]

As this insistence on "objectness" implies, it would ultimately be in the realm of sculpture, rather than painting, that the conceptual framework of opticality would be put to the test. In fact, the idea of optical sculpture seems close to an oxymoron. Yes, sculptures are made primarily to be looked at, but what would sculpture conceived exclusively as a "many sided painting" (as one aesthetic philosopher put it) look like?[7] As it happens, there is a canonical example in the form of Anthony Caro's monumental 1962 sculpture *Early One Morning* (see Plate 7). This work, composed of girders, sheet steel, and rebar, welded and bolted together and painted red, has often been taken as exemplifying the optical approach to sculpture. Thomas Crow summarizes that claim as follows: "its spare structure ensures that passage around the work will yield an unfolding sequence of surprising new visual configurations; the clean application of a single hue over the entire ensemble of the steel and aluminum sculpture effectively guides the viewer's attention towards relationships between the elements rather than towards their utilitarian origins."[8] The progression of discontinuous images that one gains by orbiting the sculpture culminates in the view along the piece's long axis. From this vantage point the work collapses visually into a "picture," centered (not coincidentally) on the easel-like form situated at the far end. It is a powerful visual experience: in that moment of coherence, the sculpture does indeed seem to transform before one's eyes, simultaneously flattening itself out and leaping out of the space of the gallery.

What makes *Early One Morning* convincing as an optical experience is its resistance to its own material condition. One feels called upon to look at it, not as an arrangement of construction materials, but as an essay in pure form. In order to achieve this effect, Caro engaged in a point-by-point denial of the sculpture's materiality. His attitude towards the physicality of the work was not just a matter of indifference, as might first appear to be the case. In fact, it was crucial that he "misused" the materials that formed *Early One Morning*'s constituent parts. Take, for example, the two sectioned girders that stand next to one another at the work's midpoint. At first they seem like a natural pair, because they have approximately the same size and visual weight. But in fact, they run in opposing directions, the heavier I-beam horizontally and the lighter-gauged piece vertically. The juxtaposition announces the fact that these are not struts that help to "construct" the work, but are rather formal elements that have been arranged for visual purposes. The same idea is conveyed by these components' means of attachment to the spine of the sculpture. Caro has employed a tangential weld, a trick borrowed from the repertoire of American sculptor David Smith (particularly that artist's *Sentinel* series of the late 1950s). The result is that the members that are supporting the load of the work seem to merely stand beside it. In a similar inversion of normal material usage, the wiry pieces of rebar, a material that would in usual circumstances be hidden inside concrete to lend it strength, are the most conspicuously gestural of the sculpture's elements. They reach out into space like stray hairs, in a playful denial of their usual constructive purpose. Or again, the horizontal bar that hovers at the opposite end of the work from the easel—a member that one would expect to be jointed at its extremities, if it were used in a building—is instead pinned at its middle, using a small bolted plate. Rather than joining and strengthening two vertical posts, it hovers in the air like a balance beam. Though Caro is using the materials of architectural craftsmanship, he consistently does so in a way that disavows any hint of thinking through craft.

A curiosity of opticality is that, while it has remained a powerful idea around which artists and critics organize their ideas about painting and sculpture, it has been observed almost entirely in the breach. As Richard Shiff has argued, "just as Greenberg was establishing such principles, many younger artists were violating the new order," so that in the mid-1950s painters from Johns and Rauschenberg to Stella were already experimenting with the relations between the visual and the tactile.[9] Meanwhile, apart from the works of Smith and Caro, very little significant sculpture in the postwar period laid claim to a purely visual effect. Perhaps this is because, once the counter-intuitive idea of opticality was articulated, it was immediately most interesting to attack it. This was certainly the intent that lay behind the reductive abstract sculptures by Judd, Carl Andre, Robert Morris, Dan Flavin and others, which have come to be classified as Minimalist. As Hal Foster has written, these works, for all their taciturn blankness, marked a crucial turning point in the progress of postwar art.[10] In testing the precept that a sculpture could in fact succeed when it was visually "contingent"—shorn of its supplemental pedestal, of optical effects, of anything, in short, that would guarantee its autonomy—Minimalism opened the door to an engagement with materiality that was not just accidental, as Pollock's arguably had been, but theoretically motivated.[11] Again, the art historical trajectories that resulted from this "crux" are too complex to summarize easily. Many artists proceeded through the movement broadly described as Conceptualism, often seen in its own day as "dematerialized" art in the service of philosophical speculation. Insofar as we still today inhabit a post-Conceptualist art world—a world in which every artwork is expected to be, in some sense, a proposition about art—craft could be seen as a persistently marginal consideration. And yet, since the days of the "Greenberg effect," material specificity, like supplementarity, has been an indispensable point of reference.

In fact, there was never a time at which craft was fully sidelined from the discourse of modern sculpture. In 1962, the year in which Caro made *Early One Morning*, Robert Morris was already beginning to work with plywood. His recollections about this moment make it clear that, just as optical sculpture was reaching its apex, craft had a profoundly liberating quality:

> At thirty I had my alienation, my Skilsaw, and my plywood. I was out to rip out the metaphors, especially those that had to do with 'up,' as well as every other whiff of transcendence... When I sliced into the plywood with my Skilsaw, I could hear, beneath the ear-damaging whine, a stark and refreshing 'no' reverberate off the four walls: no to transcendence and spiritual values, heroic scale, anguished decisions, historicizing narrative, valuable artifact, intelligent structure, interesting visual experience.[12]

It was from this attitude that Process Art, the most craft-like of the twentieth-century avant gardes, was born. Later in this chapter Morris's work in this vein, and that of his colleagues Richard Serra, Eva Hesse and others, will be discussed at some length. First, however, I will take up for consideration a range of canonical work in ceramics. If Morris was a sculptor who did not want to make a modern sculpture, then the story of postwar ceramics is primarily that of potters who did not want to make pottery. Of course, both of these efforts were doomed to failure. Ceramics, defined as such, could only continue to be ceramics, and for the most part, those who work with clay have remained identified as craftspeople rather than contemporary artists. Process Artists, meanwhile, despite their seeming attempts not to, made modern art objects that were revered as sculpture. Today the works of the most avant garde members of the studio ceramics movement are primarily to be found in the hands of specialized collectors of studio craft, or in the decorative arts collections of large museums. Similarly, the works of the most committed Process Artists reside in the permanent collections of such institutions as the Whitney Museum of American Art—heroic works to rival the Abstract Expressionist paintings against which

Process Artists sought to define themselves. These parallel failures were written into the two projects from the beginning. The two groups were traveling in opposite directions and, in some sense, each was striving for the other's condition—the one vainly trying to claw its way to the category of sculpture and the other trying to escape from it.

Somewhere in the middle, though, these two paths crossed. Both groups of artists were engaged in a struggle against the constraints of their medium—the genres of sculpture and pottery—with opposing results. For ceramic artists, materiality was initially held at a suspicious remove, while the final product of that process was triumphantly declared to be art. For Process Artists, conversely, the ends of art making were cast into doubt, but the making itself held center stage. This meant, strangely enough, that it was potters who fervently embraced the "Greenberg effect," and tried to escape the limiting constraints of craft in favor of expressive optical presence. Meanwhile artists like Morris did the reverse, renouncing the paradigm of expressive opticality and adopting the procedures of the artisan. In a few cases, interestingly enough, the results came out looking remarkably alike.

CERAMIC PRESENCE: PETER VOULKOS

In 1954, fresh from the eye-opening experimental school Black Mountain College in North Carolina (see Chapter 3) and a residency at the Archie Bray Foundation in his native Montana, Peter Voulkos began teaching at the Los Angeles County Art Institute (later to be renamed the Otis Art Institute).[13] There, he set up a now-legendary program in which he and his students, nearly all men, stayed up late, drank a great deal, and made mostly roughly painted, often huge, pots. The group's work has been summed up in the phrase "Abstract Expressionist Ceramics," the tendentious title of a 1966 exhibition at the University of California at Irvine featuring Voulkos and his students and colleagues.[14] These were potters who 'made it' as sculptors, the received wisdom has it, by dint of their savvy incorporation of the New York School painters such as Jackson Pollock and Willem DeKooning.

Much of the credit for the enduring linkage of Otis and Abstract Expressionism can be given to the art critic Rose Slivka. In 1961, Slivka published an article entitled "The New Ceramic Presence" in *Craft Horizons*, the organ of the craft movement, where she had recently taken on the job of chief editor. This essay is perhaps the most famous piece of writing on the studio craft movement in America, despite the fact that much of it is given over to rhetoric that has not aged terribly well. Beauty, Slivka wrote in a fervor of patriotic rhetoric, "is not the esthetic urgency of an artist functioning in an American climate—a climate which not only has been infused with the dynamics of a machine technology, but with the action of men—ruggedly individual and vernacular men (the pioneer, the cowboy) with a genius for improvisation."[15] "The New Ceramic Presence" is famous not for such clichés, however, but because it was so effective in providing a rationale for the work of Voulkos and his circle. Slivka analyzed the qualities of the work emanating from Otis with admirable clarity and precision:

Today the classical form has been … discarded in the interests of surface—an energetic, baroque clay surface with itself the formal 'canvas.' The paint, the 'canvas' and the structure of the 'canvas' are a unity of clay. There are three extensions of clay as paint in contemporary pottery:

1) the pot form is used as a canvas;
2) the clay form itself is used as paint three-dimensionally—with tactility, color, and actual form;
3) form and surface are used to oppose each other rather than complement each other in their traditional harmonious relationship—with color breaking into and defining, creating, destroying form.[16]

In Slivka's view, this was a style in which surface was at war with substance. She was quick to point out the inherent antipathy between a three-dimensional clay object and the depth-destroying flatness of its painted surface—a self-conscious echo of Greenberg's positive assessment of Pollock's gestural field paintings. It helped that, like Pollock, Voulkos claimed inspiration from Pablo Picasso, whose Cubist works were foundational for the modernist dialectic between real flatness and implied depth.[17]

Inspection of a typical Voulkos of the period bears out Slivka's observations (Figure 2.1). The paint that is slathered over the pot's surface is clearly meant as an act of negation, in which the substantiality of the clay is canceled by applied colors. Voulkos's process consisted of two stages. He first shaped the form through rough-and-tumble assembly, and then applied slips (clays in liquid suspension) and glazes in a manner suggested by the planes and crags that resulted from this rapid process. But the final effect belies this process: the substrate of the clay seems like an excuse for painting-in-the-round. Thus, although the technical accomplishment of his work is actually in the piling up of wet-looking slabs, the sensual underpinning thus accomplished is presented as if it were a given—an occasion for the optical push-and-pull of the surface. Sgraffito hatch-marks and scribbles emphasize this exteriority, as does the absence of an aperture. If this is a vessel, it is only minimally one and, indeed, by 1960 Voulkos was expending much of his effort on monumental accretive sculptures that either had no hint of the vessel about them, or were exaggerated to the point of absurdity by the addition of a profusion of wheel-thrown mouths.[18]

From the moment of its first appearance, Voulkos's "expressionist" work has been seen as a liberating violence done to pottery.[19] This reception was emphasized from the beginning by photographs that showed him slicing, pounding, and otherwise mauling his clay (Figure 2.2). One can well imagine why such images would raise the hackles of a traditionally trained utilitarian potter. Voulkos made no bones about it: he wanted to destroy ceramics from the inside. The entire group at Otis, in fact, rebelled against the logic, qualities, and advantages of clay as a medium, and they did so in a reflexively negative way. Their work proceeded along lines of thinking very similar to those employed by Caro in the composition of *Early One Morning*. Just as the British sculptor carefully upended the constructive properties of girders and rebar, Voulkos negated each of the significant material traits of his chosen

Figure 2.1   Peter Voulkos, *Untitled*, 1960. Stoneware.
Milwaukee Art Museum, Gift of Karen Johnson Boyd.

material. Thus, while clay is fluid and easily shaped, he fashioned huge inert slabs, and never connected these elements to each other with smooth transitions. Because of its plastic structure, clay can be fashioned into thin walls of surprising elasticity and strength. Indeed it is advisable to do so in making a pot, for the thicker a vessel's wall, the more likely it is to develop fissures or (if air bubbles are inadvertently trapped inside) even to explode during kiln firing. When working at the wheel, however, Voulkos favored rough, thickly

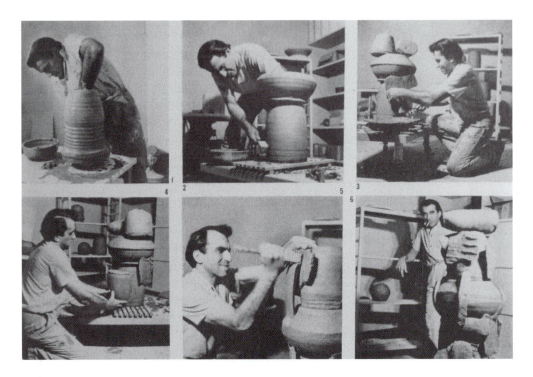

Figure 2.2   "Peter Voulkos makes a vase."
In *Craft Horizons*, 1956.

thrown cylinders without appreciable curvature. Natural clay and glazes tend to be relatively subdued in color, tending towards browns and grays. Voulkos used a vivid Technicolor palette, applying epoxy and acrylic paints after a piece had been fired. Clay is heavy when it is wet, because of its high water content, and light when it is fired, because the water evaporates in the heat of the kiln. Voulkos piled the material on top of itself, in heaps that could barely support themselves during their own construction, but which when fired were overbuilt and ponderous.

Each of the most well-known students at Otis explored a particular variant of their leader's "how not to" manner of using clay. The first thing that most of them did was to forsake the potter's main instrument, the wheel, and build by hand. One of those who did continue to throw his work, Paul Soldner, tried to deny gravity's pull—the basis for the balanced design of any pot, just as flatness serves as a point of reference for a painter—by making tall, spindly, cylindrical towers that seemed on the verge of collapse. More typical, however, were John Mason's chunky monoliths, made from cumbrous slabs that he formed on his studio floor. (A picture in the back of the Abstract Expressionist Ceramics catalogue showed him at work, in an image that seems a self-conscious aping of Hans Namuth's iconic photographs of Jackson Pollock.) Mason's signature forms were the cross and spearhead, which—as one can tell from the sloping sides supporting the wide middles of the cross pieces—were nearly impossible to execute in wet clay. Clay, unlike the metal, wood and plastic that most Minimalists used, cannot remain rigid across a horizontal unsupported span, and so this is exactly what Mason tried to do. Jim Leedy, one of Voulkos's colleagues at the Archie Bray Foundation in Montana and the member of the group most directly influenced by Abstract Expressionism, brought this tactic to extremes by building pots with dangerously over-cantilevered handles, spouts and legs. He was forced to resort to the use of ropes and armatures to assist in the drying process.[20]

John Coplans, the curator of the exhibition "Abstract Expressionist Ceramics," perfectly captured the attitudes towards clay that drove the Otis group when he wrote that they had "smashed . . . the longstanding ossified craft approach to the use of fired and glazed forms."[21] Certainly, this was not just a formalist strategy; it involved deeply personal motivations as well. Voulkos may have nursed feelings of rejection from the get-go, but in his case there was a particular, personal, watershed: his selection for a monographic "New Talent" show at the Museum of Modern Art (MoMA) in New York City in 1960. The exhibition was organized by Peter Selz, who would soon become a leading curator on the West Coast and a key supporter of artists such as Robert Arneson (see Chapter 5). The MoMA display, however, received scant critical attention. Coplans later recalled that the ceramics were "shown as a kind of a decorative adjunct" and that this was "a bitter frustration and disappointment" for Voulkos. Slivka too complained that "the show went largely ignored." Despite the fact that half of Voulkos's exhibition consisted of his paintings—which, it must be said, were second-rate and derivative Abstract Expressionist works—she attributed this to the fact that the "sculptures were in clay and New York was snobbish about the material."[22] No major East Coast museum exhibited the work of the Californian ceramists of the 1950s and 1960s in a group until the 1981 exhibition "Six Ceramic Sculptors" at the Whitney Museum of American Art. Even at this late date, several leading New York critics dismissed the historical episode as an only mildly interesting Johnny-come-lately, a regional aberration.[23] Rosalind Krauss pinpointed the reasons for this attitude in a 1978 essay on John Mason, who subsequently graduated to making Minimalist arrangements of industrially fabricated firebricks. While Krauss admired this later sculpture, she dismissed his earlier production on the ground of discursive relevance, concluding that "to be a ceramicist-sculptor in the 1950s and 1960s was in some essential way to be marginal to 'sculpture' . . . in the semantic associations to pottery, ceramics speaks for that branch of culture which is too homey, too functional, too archaic, for the name of 'sculpture' to extend to it."[24]

And indeed, the position staked out at Otis left the future of ceramics in a state of radical doubt. The concerns of technique, restraint, and nuance that had motivated studio craft potters since the early twentieth century certainly did not fade from view. But those interested in such traditional values would henceforth be obliged to constantly defend their conservatism. Voulkos had helped to initiate an endgame in which the only way to be an avant garde potter would be to deny one's status as a potter entirely.[25] Voulkos and his colleagues were the first to plant themselves at the very limits of their craft, in a gesture of dissatisfaction and ambition, but theirs was a quixotic stance from the outset. While the boundaries of workmanship could be straddled, they could not be vaulted, as there would then have been no place to gesture towards. So, as much as everyone involved would have hated to admit it, the productive friction of Voulkos's work was that it was, after all, made of clay.

In 1958, Voulkos himself moved north to teach at the University of California at Berkeley. In the early years of Voulkos's teaching at Berkeley, the strident gestural approach that had gained him such notoriety in Los Angeles was duplicated there. Voulkos's associate Harold Paris began making ceramic walls that were built up by hand from the floor, incorporating as much as three tons of clay.[26] If Voulkos's works had been implicitly savage, Paris's were literally so. He went so far as to slash the clay with a sword as he worked it. If one seeks a true ceramic version of Abstract Expressionism, this was surely it, and Paris's rhetoric bolstered the association. Invoking the well-worn Existential claims made for the gesture by such painters as Pollock, Willem DeKooning and Barnett Newman, Paris explained, "my hand and every mark in the clay is a sign that I am here now – At this instant – and this clay is what I am and will be."[27]

But Paris's violent machismo was not to prove the dominant mode in the Bay Area clay scene. After eschewing pottery in favor of bronze sculpture for several years—a transparent bid for art world acceptance—Voulkos unexpectedly returned to ceramics in 1967 following a trip to Rome. Back in California, he produced a body of work that was contained, even introverted. When Voulkos showed the new ceramics in 1968 at the David Stuart Gallery in Los Angeles, a brief notice in *Artforum* described them perfectly:

> . . . the surfaces are barely decorated by incising, and covered completely by a matte silverish black glaze. In intention they are entirely serious, rather somber, and certainly free from the bombastic Baroque rhythms of his recent [bronze] sculptures. One feels a similarity in the basic pipe-like units and in the feeling of the weightiness of the material, for the pots are as sturdy as tanks or ancient storage vessels.[28]

James Melchert, who had studied with Voulkos at Berkeley, put it more succinctly: "The group is composed of the most haptic pottery I've seen in a long time. It wouldn't surprise me if the pots had been made in the dark."[29] Voulkos had seemingly given up on the pleasures of the visual for those of touch, abandoning the combative dialectic of optical and sensual that defined his canonical work.

As it turned out, this shift was a permanent one for Voulkos. In the late 1970s, he grew increasingly interested in the exacting demands and spectacular effects of traditional Japanese wood-burning kilns.[30] The quiet, rich colors and patterns that could be achieved with these means were the result of painstaking firing—quite the opposite of the manic constructions and shiny paint of his early work. To be sure, Voulkos never became humble about his work, and he continued to cultivate the image of America's most liberated potter;

but the work itself had much more of rural Japan than 1950s Los Angeles about it. This turnabout has permitted museums and collectors to have their cake and eat it too when acquiring Voulkos's work. His reputation as a rebel is based on the powerfully incoherent anti-pots of the 1950s, but the pots that have come to seem emblematic of his work are tasteful in the extreme, sheathed in a gentle traditional ash glaze. A few summary knife slashes or embedded pieces of white kaolin clay are all that is left of the wild man of Otis.

NATURAL LIMITATIONS: STEPHEN DE STAEBLER AND KEN PRICE

In the mid-1960s, during Voulkos's stint with bronze, a host of potters had established a new set of rules for ceramics in the area. Several of these emerging figures had in fact started out as students in Voulkos's Berkeley studio, but they had rapidly turned away from the impasse represented by his early work. Of this generation, Stephen de Staebler was the ceramist who most closely anticipated Voulkos's introverted idiom of the late 1960s. De Staebler's early career should have ensured that he would be a prime exponent of "Abstract Expressionist" pottery. He had been a student at Black Mountain College (where he was friendly with Ben Shahn and Robert Motherwell) in 1951, and studied with Voulkos and John Mason at Berkeley from 1960 to 1961. He also adhered to the same Westernized, watered-down Zen philosophies that were popular with some of the New York "action school" painters.[31] Yet there is very little action, and no painterliness, in De Staebler's works of the 1960s, which explicitly reject key principles of his teacher's early style. His departure consisted of two fundamental shifts, both of which appear to date from the 1963–5 period. First, he refused to employ the bright glazes and paints that the Otis group had so thoroughly exploited, regarding them as an artificial "contrivance" that denied the integrity of the material.[32] Instead, he mixed powdered metal oxide pigments into the wet clay, or rubbed subtly hued clay slips into the surface. His colors were of a piece with the clay mass, and the exterior layer merely the exposure of an undifferentiated solid, rather than a surface in which optical effects clash with the impression of interior volume. Pure visuality disappeared, having been both literally and figuratively swallowed up by materiality.

Second, De Staebler seemed to revel in the sheer massiveness of clay. While Voulkos's work had gestured dramatically, De Staebler's forms surrendered humbly to gravity as if he was in the grip of an inability, or perhaps an unwillingness, to control the clay (Figure 2.3). Harvey Jones provided both an origin story and an intelligent explication of this passivity in a 1974 Oakland Museum catalogue of De Staebler's work:

> De Staebler can point to the sculpture he made as a student, and to the particular slab of clay that opened the door for him. What happened, he recalls, is that this slab did not do what he wanted it to do, but what it did do as he laid it on the sculpture was better. It had a life of its own and existed free from the manipulations of his hands. The power and appeal of De Staebler's sculpture derives in large part from his attitude toward the clay. He has learned by long experience to recognize the intrinsic character and beauty of the medium, and more importantly, to respect its natural limitations. De Staebler responds

Figure 2.3   Stephen De Staebler, *Seating Environment*, 1969–71.
Ceramic. Courtesy of the artist.

to the peculiar qualities which clay possesses: its plasticity when wet, its fragility when
dry, its tendency to warp, crack and slump during the drying and firing processes.[33]

De Staebler himself has repeatedly confirmed this description of his process, saying
that clay "has an inner instinct for form," and that "what I have tried to do for a long
time is find out what the clay wants to do."[34] This ambition was the opposite of the Otis
school's attempts to stretch clay beyond its physical properties, and it was haptic in the
extreme. De Staebler did not employ traditional wheel or coil building techniques, but he
also refused to use the armatures that the Otis group had used.[35] Instead, he worked huge
solid slabs into shape by pushing and pulling it with his entire body. His works were devoid
of any conspicuous marks of the hand, bearing instead the evidence of an insistent but
non-demonstrative physical interaction. Even De Staebler's working method amounted to
an analogy between the internal forces and mass of his own body, and the "natural limitations" of the clay body. Where Voulkos had approached the limits of workmanship in the
direction of action—pushing the material to the very edge of its capabilities, or denying its
mass through a covering of paint—De Staebler approached the opposite limit of inaction,

in which the material held sway over the maker. In this regard, De Staebler occupied the role of "ceramic sculptor" in a way that none of the Otis group had done. And yet De Staebler made no dramatic claims to participation in an avant garde movement. He was grounded, in every sense, in the world of clay.

Two antithetical strategies developed from the conflict that Voulkos and his circle had staged. While Voulkos himself and De Staebler opted for sensuality, others who had been directly or indirectly influenced by the Otis moment went for opticality. This could take the form of anecdotal *trompe l'oeil*, as in the work of Robert Hudson, Richard Shaw, and Marilyn Levine, or alternatively in the formalist, painterly ceramics of Ken Price and Ron Nagle. All of this work asserted the primacy of visuality over substance, to be sure, but it was essentially hedonistic, lacking the theoretical self-awareness that might have been possible through an engagement with contemporary art practice. The productive internal conflict of the Otis years was displaced by the confident deployment of technique. Hudson and Shaw pressed their mastery of porcelain into the service of visual magic tricks, while in the related but comparatively deadpan works of Marilyn Levine, preternaturally deceptive stoneware renderings of humdrum leather objects manage simultaneously to amaze and to wallow in mute pointlessness (Figure 2.4). Though Levine was arguably more a counterpart

Figure 2.4   Marilyn Levine, *Two-Tone Bag*, 1974. Stoneware with nylon fibers, engobe, luster glazes.
Los Angeles County Museum of Art, M.87.1.77. Gift of Howard and Gwen Laurie Smits. Photograph © 2006 Museum Associates/LACMA.

to the Super-Realist painters of the 1970s than a self-defined ceramist, her home and studio happened to be in the same building as Voulkos's for many years. It is therefore tempting to see her work, like De Staebler's, as a collapse brought on by the anxiety about material and image that drove Voulkos at the beginning of his career.[36]

Ironically, though, it was another potter—not Voulkos, but Ken Price—who most successfully crossed over from the Otis milieu into contemporary art acceptance. Partly, this is thanks to the support of conservative critics Dave Hickey and Peter Schjeldahl, who hail Price's work as a welcome return to sheer visual pleasure. But this is selling him far short. For decades, Price's practice has been to create simple sculptural shapes in clay, fire them, and then to cover them with dense, unvariegated, highly chromatic paint, sometimes incising or sandblasting through this sheath of color. The material underneath might as well be plastic or metal, and indeed Price was readily grouped with the "fetish finish" school of Los Angeles painters and sculptors who worked with these non-craft materials. Coplans, typically, characterized Price as "a sculptor with a full cognizance of the abstract expressionist *painter's* extreme sensitivity to color."[37] What is at stake here, though, is not simply a rejection of clay. In Price's case, the problem seems to be how to maintain Voulkos's ambivalence about the formal properties of material—surface or substance—while achieving a supremely resolved object. The effect is that of a pot that is not at war with itself, as Voulkos's were, but rather satisfied with its own contradictions.

This approach emerged in Price's project *Happy's Curios*, which began in 1972 but was not finished for exhibition at the Los Angeles Country Museum of Art until 1978 (Figure 2.5). The project was spurred by Price's own geographical removal from Los Angeles (where he had studied with Voulkos, and shown at the famous avant garde gallery Ferus) to the environs of Taos, New Mexico. Struck by the vitality of the Mexican tourist trade pottery he saw there and in the sales booths of Tijuana, Price undertook to imitate the "folk" look and large-scale replication of such wares. Maurice Tuchman, the curator of the Los Angeles County Museum of Art exhibition of *Happy's Curios*, saw Price's act of intentional impersonation as the most difficult aspect of the project:

> Price concentrated on making extensive series of basic cups and plates and vases as nearly identical as possible. This was the way a local artisan in, say, Oaxaca would inherit pottery technique from his father and then practice his commercial craft, with its severely limited vocabulary of shapes, for a lifetime. For a lengthy period, however—1972 to 1974—Price found that his very awareness of the effort to become another, imagined person directly thwarted the casual and effortless procedure of that imagined folk artist. The two processes were exactly antithetical. Hearing Price talk about these years of obsessed effort calls to mind an actor's projection into another personality throughout a long-running play.[38]

Extending Coplans's analogy, it might be said that Price's effort recalls the impossible cultural leap described in Jorge Luis Borges' essay "Pierre Menard, Author of the Quixote," in which a contemporary French writer is imagined attempting to rewrite *Don Quixote* word

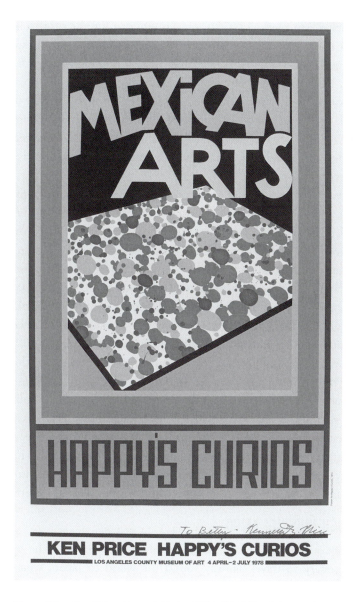

Figure 2.5   Ken Price, *Happy's Curios*, 1974–79. Offset lithograph poster.
Los Angeles County Museum of Art, Gift of the Estate of Betty Asher.
Photograph © 2006 Museum Associates/LACMA.

for word, on the basis of his own experiences rather than through reference to the original.[39] But where Borges imagines Menard succeeding in this impossibility, the subject of *Happy's Curios* became Price's inability, or unwillingness, to fully adopt the self-effacing mindset of a production potter. Price articulated his deeply felt difference from the unknown craftsman as the project developed. His discovery that his mentality was "antithetical" to that of his ostensible soul mates was marked by changing intentions for the project. In 1972, when he began *Happy's Curios*, Price intended the pieces he was making to be sold in a typical Taos shop front, expressing tacit political sympathy with ceramic workers. But when it was finally finished in 1978, the pieces were not for sale at all, but rather on display at the largest museum on the West Coast. The objects themselves went through a similar transformation. The Mexican folk pots were not replicated faithfully, but rather translated into an array of fetishized formal objects—flat ciphers of real world referents. Often the pieces are simple abstractions of the formal tropes of indigenous pottery, transformed (or perfected) into geometrically precise sculptures.

Stylistically speaking, the pots that make up *Happy's Curios* are among the earliest post-modern ceramics, and like most postmodernist art, they hover uncertainly between critique and cynicism.[40] The project had a daring whiff of hypocrisy about it, particularly because after his "projection" was over, Price was free to return to making his signature high-priced, technically polished ceramic sculptures—which, as Coplans remarked, are the very antithesis of folk ceramics.[41] Yet this was hardly an unexamined project, as Price's choice of calling one of his pots "an Inca self-portrait" implies. In repudiating the idealism of simple identification with his Taos neighbors, Price was being anything but sardonic. The schematic, cartoonish forms of his "curios" capture the flattening effects, the losses in translation, that inevitably occur when a pot is made to be looked at. This is implicit even the choice of the word "curios" itself, redolent as it is with the history of colonialist loot mounted in display cases—objects torn violently from their everyday context. In Price's rendering of the humble, earthen pot as a spectacular commodity, we see Voulkos's ambivalence about "ceramic art"—reified in a battle between substance and surface—considered at one remove. Price has managed to avoid both a resigned commitment to the tactile pleasures of the clay and a flat denial of the medium. As we will see in Chapter 5, Robert Arneson blazed a similar path out of Voulkos's impasse, using content and imagery as means to resolve a problem of material and form.

CRAWLING THROUGH MUD: YAGI KAZUO

For a provocative continuation of this narrative about the physical, the optical, and the ceramic, it is necessary to travel halfway round the world to Japan, where the terms of engagement for potters were rather different. The acknowledged inferiority of ceramics that implicitly motivated every American potter in the postwar period was not nearly so extreme in the Japanese context. The historic prestige of the medium had been compromised with the rise of westward-looking painting and sculpture during the Meiji period, but there was still a strong respect (bordering in some cases on nationalist pride) for historic and contemporary ceramics. Indeed, for progressive potters in postwar Japan, the problem was not so much to elevate ceramics as to excavate themselves from the burden of hallowed tradition. Louise Cort has shown that it was an outsider, the Japanese-American sculptor Isamu Noguchi, who provided a necessary instigation to rethink clay. Blissfully ignorant about revered materials and glazes, Noguchi freely mixed canonical references—covering

Shigaraki or Bizen clay, which was traditionally ash glazed, with shiny green Oribe glaze, for example—and rummaged about in the grab-bag of the Japanese ceramic lexicon, throwing together motifs from Jomon pottery or Momoyama tea ceramics with his own highly developed language of geometric abstraction.[42]

Of the Japanese potters influenced by Noguchi's example, the most open-minded were a group assembled in 1948 under the name of *Sodeisha*, literally the "crawling through mud association." This was an ironic reference to the patterns found on some historic Chinese ceramics, but it also was a strong presentiment of the concerns of the group's leading member, Yagi Kazuo.[43] Born into a family of ceramists in Kyoto, Yagi was responsible for coining the (again, ironic) phrase *obuje-yaki*, "kiln-fired objects," to describe the non-functional experimental wares that he and his colleagues made under Noguchi's influence. As Bert Winther-Tamaki has written, Yagi's avant garde production began around 1954 and so slightly predated the similar "breakthrough" achieved by Voulkos in California. There were certain affinities between the two. Both were influenced by fine artists such as Picasso and Miro; both gathered around them a group of like-minded followers; and both combined wheel-throwing and handbuilding in unexpected configurations. In the Japanese case, however, there was a distinctively political subtext. While Slivka celebrated "the new ceramic presence" for its full-blooded American character, Yagi's position was necessarily complicated by his adoption of a putatively Western sculptural language. After the cataclysmic defeat of Japanese imperialism, his challenge to the tradition of Japanese ceramics could not but read as a challenge to the *idée fixe* of Japaneseness itself. In Winther-Tamaki's words, "Yagi pushed the perimeter of the pottery world beyond its previous limits to the extent of internalizing something of the duality of the border itself, and to the extent of internalizing something of that imagined to lay beyond."[44]

Given this backdrop, it is perhaps no coincidence that Yagi's tactics ultimately came to resemble not Voulkos's, but rather those of artists working in war-torn continental Europe. His *shiwayose-de* ("gathered wrinkles") objects of the 1960s are the clearest example of this affinity (Figure 2.6). Made by rolling innumerable little squares of clay into short cylinders and pressing them into solid, simple masses, these wares demonstrate, in the contrast between the individual hand-formed bits and the overall shape imposed by external pressure, a sense of clay's raw physical properties.[45] They are stylistically comparable to earlier ceramics by Lucio Fontana or roughly contemporary works in plaster by Jean Fautrier, Cy Twombly and Jean Dubuffet.[46] All of these artists reveled in the physicality of *matière* and, like De Staebler, rejected the painterly qualities that could be achieved with glazes, enamels, or other colorants. Dubuffet, for example, wrote of the imperative for the painter "to plunge his hands into full buckets or bowls, and with his palms and fingers to putty over the wall surface with his clay, his pastes, to knead it body to body, to leave as imprints the most immediate traces of his thought..."[47] In the case of fired clay, there was in the wake of World War Two a suggestion that the medium should be figuratively as well as literally conceived as scorched earth.[48] Yagi also shared an interest with the European artists in

Figure 2.6   Yagi Kazuo, *Circle*, 1967. Ceramic.
Museum of Modern Art, Tokyo.

giving his ceramics a repellant surface, which in his case resembled coiled intestines, or the "gray matter" of the brain. Finally, Yagi's pressed tubes of clay have an excremental quality achieved through an uncontrived, automatic process of forming. In all these respects Yagi's wrinkled ceramics embody what Yve-Alain Bois and Rosalind Krauss have called "base materialism," a lowering and "de-class(ify)ing" of matter which opposes itself to idealistic Modernist models of artmaking.[49]

A final but especially striking similarity between Yagi and certain postwar European artists, particularly Dubuffet, was his interest in people who were euphemistically called *chieokure no kodomo* (which might be translated "young people who are slow to develop understanding"). This aspect of his activities began in the mid-1950s, when Yagi was one of several artists invited to the facilities of the Ōmi Gakuen in Otsu Prefecture. The residents there, some of whom were adults with mental disabilities and others children from "unstable environments," had a pottery facility where they made simple functional objects as part of a vocational program. Yagi visited intermittently, living and working with the residents in 1955 and again interacting with them in 1965. Nor was this the exquisitely self-conscious playacting of Price's *Happy's Curios*. According to fellow Sodeisha member

Osamu Suzuki, Yagi ran the pottery studio there enthusiastically, without any hint of ironic distance: "Rather than saying he taught people ceramics, perhaps it would be better to say that they played together with clay ... without forcing, [he] encouraged people to use their hands. And yes, there are a great many things we can do with our hands. Squeeze, slap, push, throw, bend, twist, pull, pile, cut, tear, stack, stretch, roll, pound."[50] Yagi was astounded by the products fashioned by the residents; he pronounced their roughly hand-built objects to be masterpieces, superior to the works of Picasso and Miro. The institute's director in 1965, Taichi Yoshinaga, recalled the results of Yagi's teaching: "The first time they encountered clay, everyone reacted a different way. Some bit into the clay, others spread it over their bodies, or on the table, or tore it up and threw it around the studio... The prolific students had filled the ceramics studio with their work so there was hardly room to walk." Remarkably, Yagi helped to organize an exhibition of these wares at the Hanshin Department Store, a frequent site for the display and sale of contemporary ceramics. His only regret was that he was forced to price the wares, implying that one object might have more intrinsic worth than another.[51]

Yagi's encounter with mentally disabled potters is redolent of the familiar European notion of *art brut*, Dubuffet's term for the work of children, asylum patients, and others "untouched by artistic culture."[52] Dubuffet's context and aims, however, were quite different in nature. He was involved in a rethinking of the strain of Surrealism that had been codified in Georges Bataille's journal *Documents*, and for him the work of the "mad" was at least in part a rebuke to the falsity of contemporary art.[53] For this reason, perhaps, Dubuffet's position was perilously close to the implicitly condescending stance of today's "outsider art" experts and collectors, who value objects precisely because they were created in a non-academic context and therefore have a naïve authenticity (see Chapter 5). For Yagi no such antagonism against the construct of fine art, nor any prejudice in favor of the perceptions of the untutored, seem to have been operative. It was not some eccentric authorial creativity that he found to be so moving in the ceramic work of his "students," but rather the direct experience of *tsuchi* ("clay," but also "earth" or "dirt"), just as one might have in handling a roughly fashioned traditional teabowl.[54] One might therefore speculate that Yagi found in the products of his mentally disabled colleagues the same quality he discovered in historical precedent; "old Japanese ceramics," he wrote, "belong to a mental state full of irrationality."[55] Yagi was strongly opposed to any conscious control of irregularity, as was frequent among the teaware makers of his own generation, but he also sought ways to allow the authentic irregularity of material to express itself in his work. In some respects, then, his position was surprisingly reminiscent of that occupied by Yanagi Sōetsu and the other adherents of *mingei* that we will encounter in Chapter 5, who also valued a thoughtless irregularity in the work of "folk" artisans. The crucial difference, perhaps, was that this was entirely an artistic value for Yagi—not a social or ethical one. In the end, it was the Ōmi Gakuen residents' enthusiasm for the material of clay itself that commanded his interest—an enthusiasm he shared without irony. Once, Yagi was asked to name the essence of ceramics. Was it the wheel, the traditional tool of the potter? "No, it's not the wheel," Yagi replied. "It's that feeling you get when you take soft clay and squish it between your fingers. That's the essence of clay for me."[56]

THE MATERIALIZATION OF THE ART OBJECT, 1966–72

The title of this section is a purposeful inversion of Lucy Lippard's well-known book, *Six Years: The Dematerialization of the Art Object, 1966–72*. By no means is Lippard's extraordinary documentary overview of conceptual art to be diminished. Yet it is clear in retrospect that these same six years saw contemporary sculptors engage in an outburst of experimentation with materials and processes. This was a more wide-ranging set of activities, perhaps, than the various uses of clay discussed thus far. Nonetheless, it operated within the same dialectic. The conflict between the sensual and optical that acted as the motor for Voulkos, and which De Staebler and Yagi were able to fully resolve only by committing themselves fully to the logic of material, was also central to the work of "Process Artists" of the late 1960s such as Eva Hesse, Richard Serra and Robert Morris. However, these figures offer something that Voulkos's angst, De Staebler's persistence, and Yagi's sheer joy do not: a theoretical account. One often hears claims that craft has been unfairly excluded from contemporary art discourse. In the late 1960s, though, the most interesting theory about craft was arguably that being developed by sculptors.

Clearly, Conceptual art was not the only way forward into the 1970s. Indeed, Lucy Lippard herself was the first to isolate the trend towards a new type of sculpture. For the 1966 show "Eccentric Abstraction" at the Fischbach Gallery, the critic selected a group of artists including the weaver Alice Adams, sculptors Eva Hesse, Louise Bourgeois, and Bruce Nauman, and the ceramist Ken Price, all of whom seemed to her to be reviving Surrealism in American art.[57] At first, this organizing principle seemed persuasive. The development from Minimalism to "Eccentric Abstraction" seemed like a reprise of the shift from cerebral Dada to idiosyncratic Surrealism in the 1930s. This interpretation rapidly came to seem untenable, however, as Lippard herself noted in 1971. Conceding that she had "overestimated the Surrealist connection," she wrote that the real issue that drove this group of artists was "materials and physical phenomena."[58] The exhibitions "Nine at Leo Castelli," curated by the artist Robert Morris in 1968, and "Anti-Illusion: Procedures/Materials," at the Whitney Museum in 1969, had brought the moment into clearer focus.[59] As one of the curators at the Whitney, Marcia Tucker, noted, this new sculpture derived its meaning entirely from "the activity of making a work and from the dictates of the materials used."[60]

The Process Artists had a very specific idea of what "process" meant, and it had nothing to do with the unleashing of psychological content achieved through the chance operations of Surrealism. Neither did it involve the grand gestures of Abstract Expressionism or the industrial fabrications of Minimalism. In place of these models of art making, Process Artists aimed to limit their productions to what is best called "facture." This useful term, which is associated with materialist tendencies in Russian Constructivism and German modernism, was summarized as follows by the Bauhaus instructor László Moholy-Nagy: "the way in which something has been produced shows itself in the finished product. The way it shows itself is what we call facture."[61] While artists like Moholy-Nagy devoted a great deal of attention to this principle, bringing it to the making and analysis of not only sculpture but also painting, photography, and other media, it was not until Process Art that an attempt was made to restrict the art work to facture alone. This meant conceiving of the work as a residuum of the process by which it came into being.

The key theorist of Process Art was also one of its leading artists, Robert Morris. At the beginning of this chapter, we saw how liberating craft process was for the young Morris. That was in 1962. By 1968, he was concerned with little else. He argued, for example, that Minimalist sculptures (including his own) had been motivated simply by the desire to "build well," that is, to construct in the most reasonable and consistent fashion possible. Morris explained that he had subscribed to this age-old rule of design in his own early Minimal works, such as *Column* and *Slab*, the dimensions of which were (as art historian James Meyer relates) "programmed" by store-bought plywood, either bisected or left whole.[62] Two years on, in the 1970 essay "Some Notes on the Phenomenology of Making," Morris refined his argument:

> Much attention has been focused on the analysis of the content of art making—its end images—but there has been little attention focused on the significance of the means... I believe there are 'forms' to be found within the activity of making as much as within the end products. These are forms of behavior aimed at testing the limits and possibilities involved in that particular interaction between one's actions and the materials of the environment. This amounts to the submerged side of the art iceberg.[63]

Here Morris argued not only that form should be derived from process, but also that the "limits and possibilities" of action and material should be the standard by which the success of such derivations should be judged. This seems at first to be a clear-cut endorsement of craft as the basis of sculptural practice. Yet it is not intuitively obvious how "the particular interaction between one's actions and the materials of the environment" will result, logically and necessarily, in a particular form.

To better understand this formulation we might contrast one of Morris's earliest sculptures, 1961's *Box With the Sound of Its Own Making*, with an untitled 1967 work in felt. The former is, as its title suggests, a simple cube made of walnut boards, which contains a tape recorder playing the sounds of the box's own manufacture—sawing, drilling and screwing. As Rosalind Krauss has written: "even as it performs a kind of cogito of carpentry, *Box With the Sound of Its Own Making* burlesques the idea of the closed circuit of self-reference."[64] If this complete overlap between action and result is enacted (perhaps, as Krauss says, ironically) in the *Box*, it is directly opposed by Morris's later sculpture, which is open-ended and allusive. Now, the artist's own action is not predictive of the shape of the work: Morris cut slits in a sheet of felt, hung it from the wall at two fixed points, and let it flop in a tumbled skein to

Figure 2.7   Robert Morris, *Untitled*, 1967. Felt.
Ellen Hulda Johnson papers, Archives of American Art,
Smithsonian Institution. Photograph by Rudy Burckhardt.

the floor (Figure 2.7). Interviewed in 1968, Morris noted his growing interest in "a working process which did not in any way equate with the image."[65]

His work in felt bears this out. Its form is nothing more than the direct result of the acts of slicing and hanging that initiated the sculpture, and the natural drape of the thick, soft material. Though it may not be immediately obvious, this is a sculptural reworking of Jackson Pollock, whom Morris noted had gone "beyond the hand to the more direct revelation of matter itself."[66] Pollock's drip paintings were produced, Morris wrote, by the conjunction of "the nature of materials, the restraints of gravity, the limited mobility of the body interacting with both."[67] In *Untitled*, those same factors are in play; but Morris discarded the remainder of Pollock's art, particularly its transcendental opticality. What he was left with was resolutely physical, facture in its minimum state: a kind of making that bears no evidence of intentional arrangement. Morris allowed material circumstances to overwhelm and eradicate any lasting evidence of his "design" of the object, including the imprint of his hands.

Richard Serra's short film *Catching Lead*, while very different from *Untitled*, elegantly illustrates this point. (Figure 2.8) It shows a forearm and hand (Serra's own) extending from

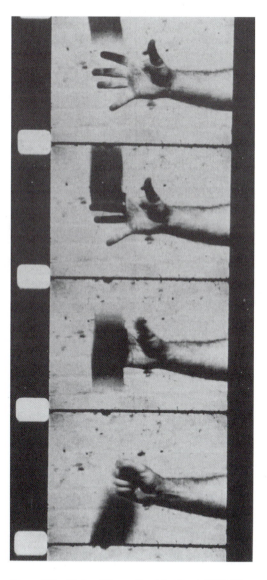

Figure 2.8   Richard Serra, *Catching Lead*, 1969. Film.
Courtesy of the artist and Gagosian Gallery.

the right margin of the screen. The hand has seen some recent use, to judge from the dark oil or soot that smears the fingers and palm. For the three-minute duration of the film, ingots of lead fall regularly from the upper edge of the screen. The hand tries to catch them— sometimes successfully, more often not. While a viewer first thinks that the moments in which an ingot is caught are the victories for the artist (or at least, the struggling hand), the message of the film could as easily be the opposite: the failures are the interesting moments, for they indicate the precise limits of the artist's intentionality.[68] It may seem counter-intuitive to suggest that Richard Serra—the artist who went on to make *Tilted Arc*, perhaps the past half-century's most famously overconfident sculpture—has an interest in the limits of artistic will. But that is exactly what *Catching Lead* illustrates. In fact, the film is one of three of the same year that revolve around Serra's unresolved or restrained gestures—the others being *Hands Scraping* and *Hands Tied*.[69]

At this time Serra also composed catalogues of verbs without objects: "to roll, to crease, to fold, to store, to bend..." As Rosalind Krauss has written, these lists "describe pure transitivity. For each is an action to be performed against the imagined resistance of an object, and yet each infinitive rolls back upon itself without naming its end."[70] This list of actions stalled recalls the purposeless actions that Yag Kazuo undertook alongside his mentally handicapped charges at roughly the same time in Japan. For Serra, too, infinitives might just as easily be described as embodying pure intransitivity *or* transitivity; they stand at the point where artistic action exists in relation to some material, but has not been directed to any specific end.[71] A similar lack of closure occurs in Serra's ingenious *Props*, which are constructed of lead slabs, cubes, and pipes. Marcia Tucker wrote of the artist's "concern with what he calls 'arrested moments,' that is, fixing a piece at its point of maximum potential change, incorporates an element of actual time into a sculptural mode."[72] The trick of the *Props* is that each part of the sculpture stays put only through the continued pressure of the other parts. The sculptures must keep on working in order to exist; final stasis is permanently held in abeyance. Despite their great weight and massive construction, the *Props* embody fragility and uncertainty as well as power and mastery. Early critics wrote of the "possibility of imminent formal disintegration" that hovered ominously about them.[73] This quality fulfilled a dictum that Morris laid down in 1970: "what art now has in its hand is mutable stuff which need not arrive at the point of being finalized with respect to either time or space."[74]

A key aspect in the works, as in Morris's felt or in the work of the ceramists discussed earlier in the chapter, is the character of material. Serra's use of lead exploited the metal's unusual properties: its delicate, easily marked surface that records what is done to it in minute detail; its high density; and its tendency to warp slightly when placed under stress. These were all advantages in constructing the *Props*, in that they dramatized the stakes of the balancing act considerably. Lead also offered Serra mutability; like clay, it can be made to fluctuate between fluid and solid states. He made use of this property in *Casting*, first executed at the Whitney Museum in 1969. To make this sculpture, Serra melted lead in a brazier and flung it at the base of a wall, gradually making a long wedge of metal. Once the lead had hardened he pried it away from the wall in order to drag it out into the room. One could see *Casting* as an attempt to create a series of perfect casts of the right-angled negative space where wall met floor. But a fragile fringe of solidified spatters betrays the means of the making. The punning title *Casting* manages to sum up both aspects of the work in one word, both in the sense of "molding" (represented by the squared rear edges of the wedges) and "throwing" (represented by the rough, splashed front edges). Just as Morris's *Untitled* marks a passage from two fixed points to the chaos of tumbled felt on the floor, Serra has found a way to invest facture with a juxtaposition of order and chaos.

Eva Hesse's work also exemplifies this craft-like approach to making art, which uses the properties of particular materials as a means for making form. Until recently Hesse received anomalous treatment from well-meaning art critics and historians, who identified her sculpture as a highly personal, even eccentric enterprise. (Indeed, she may have been foremost in Lippard's mind when she titled her 1966 exhibition "Eccentric Abstraction.") Perhaps because of the extraordinary character of her biography—particularly her struggles as a woman in a male-dominated sculpture world and her tragic early death—and the unusual availability of that biography in the form of her pseudo-confessional diaries, many writers have used Hesse's work as the basis for psychological diagnosis rather than art criticism. More recently, Anne Wagner has proposed that Hesse's variable, chaotic, and handmade works should be seen as proto-Feminist, a means of undoing the rigid, automated processes of Minimalism.[75] On this account, the artist's formal strategies are motivated by gender rather than the precepts of Modernist formalism.

Yet in terms of the way that they were crafted, Hesse's sculptures were very much in step with the trends of the moment. Certain elements of her sculptures seem almost to have been extruded, just to the point where the material begins to take on a shape of its own accord. Hesse herself noted this fact, writing of the sculpture *Addendum* (1967) that "the cord opposes the regularity. When it reaches the floor it curls and it sits irregularly."[76] As in Morris's and Serra's works, Hesse staged situations in which material is partly held in form and partly takes a form of its own volition ("it curls and it sits"). The same play between composition and non-composition appears in the *Accession* series, in which the individual pieces of plastic tubing are tied in a regular grid to a rigid metal box but are then allowed to droop willy-nilly; and again in *Right After* (1969), where cords of fiberglass are hung from hooks in an oppositional choreography of randomly intersecting curves and fixed apexes (Figure 2.9). Hesse's sculpture has often been described as more subjective than that of other (male) Process Artists because the materials in which she most frequently worked—latex, rubber and fiberglass—resemble skin, hair and flesh.[77] But she could as easily have been attracted to these artificial substances not for their metaphorical bodily qualities, but for their traits as working materials. Like Morris's felt and Serra's lead, all of these materials have a uniform texture and dull color. They engender surfaces that have obviously been worked into shape, but are almost unnerving in their lack of marks unique to the artist's own hand.

Figure 2.9   Eva Hesse, *Right After*, 1969. Fiberglass.
Milwaukee Art Museum, Gift of Friends of Art.

Hesse achieved the extraordinary break with previous sculpture that was common to all Process Art: without resorting to industrial fabrication, she was able to mimic Minimalism's lack of personalized finish.

Hesse's choice of materials was also motivated by the logic of the residuum. In her earliest sculptures she had been drawn to waste materials, beginning with textile factory refuse during a stay in Germany.[78] If the Minimalists occupied the fabrication shop and the techniques of mass production, she positioned herself on the proverbial back stoop of the factory, gleaning and picking her materials from piles of industrial leftovers. In this respect, too, Hesse was participating in a broad trend among Process Artists. Barry Le Va's first scatter pieces have been compared to "the castoffs in a textile factory at the end of an industrious day," and were literally fashioned from waste material (see Chapter 4).[79] According to his later testimony, LeVa hit upon the idea of scatter art while fashioning sculptures in his studio out of masonite, wood, canvas and newspaper:

> after I'd been constructing a piece for about three hours, I suddenly became aware of all this debris on the floor, bits of canvas and other stuff, and this residue seemed much more interesting and significant than what I was making. It had exactly what I was after.

Not so much indications of a specific process, or what had been done to the material, as of marking off stages in time.[80]

Both LeVa and Morris selected felt as a working material, perhaps because it is already a waste product composed of loose ends from other textile production. This connection was driven home by Morris's 1968 scatter piece *Threadwaste*, which consisted of copper tubing, asphalt, and felt strips mixed with powder-blue colored thread that had originally been "industrially used as lubricated packing for the bearings of freight cars."[81] Here the bright blue tangles of thread, like the felt, allude to the finished fabric that does not appear in the work; the title emphasizes the sculpture's status as (to use LeVa's term) a "marking" rather than a product—like an animal lining its territory.

The sculpture as waste product was the most suggestive means by which Process Artists investigated facture, because it brought a psychological overtone to their radically reduced processes. There is an air of scatology around these works, an air of debasement. Critic Ursula Meyer noted this quality in 1969: "these works cowered helplessly on the ground, prostrate, accessible to the next blow... To me, the new trend is indicative of the *loss of power* not only over the object but of the object itself."[82] This points to a final conclusion about Process Art. All of these sculptures—Morris's felt tangles, Serra's lead props, Hesse's fiberglass, LeVa's scatter works—are proposals about the issues proper to craftsmanship. In their evident desire to achieve a rupture with previous sculpture, they even suggest the potential for craft to upset the well-laid table of art. And yet, to perform this rupture, they found it necessary to insist on a particularly reductive idea of craft: a limiting of craft to mere facture. What Meyer calls "object mastery," the grand artistic gesture, was exactly what they sought to preclude.[83] In this sense, like Voulkos and Yagi, their project was defined negatively. Yet their conceptualization of process and material as facts to be taken account of, rather than the basis for free creativity, has been hugely influential on subsequent artists. In the next section, we will take a look at two recent artists—one working in glass, another in clay—who continue to explore the possibilities.

BREATH: DALE CHIHULY AND EMMA WOFFENDEN

Since the mid-1980s contemporary glass has captured the imagination of the public, and of a certain class of collectors and curators, like no other arena of the crafts. It has also generated a level of contempt that is equally unmatched. Much of the credit for both of these responses can be laid at the feet of the American glass artist Dale Chihuly, who is, depending on one's perspective, either a heroic sculptor whose neo-baroque creations bring delight to a mass audience, or a crass commercial operator who churns out anti-intellectual kitsch. This divergence of opinion in itself suggests the power of Chihuly's work to channel perceptions about craft as a cultural phenomenon. As has often been remarked by his critical supporters, he stands firmly within a long line of decorative artists, from the Renaissance goblet-makers of Venice to the French art nouveau artist René Lalique. And indeed, Chihuly's work shares in the raw, sensual appeal of this tradition, as well as its preening fetishization of technique for its own sake. What distinguishes his work within this tradition, arguably, is its spectacular, late-capitalist character. In this respect he might be compared to Thomas Kinkade (like Chihuly, a self-proclaimed "painter of light"), whose business model involves mass-produced color prints of saccharine landscapes, which are sometimes retouched by hand to achieve a degree of authenticity (and a higher price). As Kinkade often points out, he is the best-selling artist of recent decades, if volume of sales alone is what counts.[84] Yet it would be hard to mistake him for a "contemporary artist" in the usual sense of that term. Chihuly is, I would suggest, a roughly analogous figure, both in terms of his entrepreneurial brilliance and his cynical disregard for art's critical possibilities. Like Kinkade, he acts mainly in the capacity of an impresario, directing an elaborate production system that ensures the widespread distribution of a reliable product.

Yet, seemingly because he works in the crafts field, Chihuly's work is not confined to the mall, like Kinkade's. It proliferates in museum lobbies and galleries across the globe. Unsurprisingly, given Chihuly's huge success, many artists working in glass and other craft-identified materials have followed his lead, indulging in a free, gleefully empty-headed play of forms. Headline craft fairs, such as Sculptural Objects and Functional Art (SOFA) in Chicago and New York, or (to a lesser extent) Collect in London, are swamped with largely interchangeable glass sculptures, many of which are variations on Chihuly's historicist style. Others adhere closely to the Brancusian model described in the last chapter. The same could be said for *objets d'art* in ceramic, turned and carved wood, and other media that are clearly patterned on glass's success story. When it comes to the bottom line, the results are indeed impressive. But the price that the studio crafts pay in terms of cultural capital is equally steep. When Chihuly places one of his chandeliers in the lobby of a museum, he sends a message (on the institution's behalf, as well as his own) that craft is a matter of hedonism, not conceptualism. Whatever one may think of his work as a visual spectacle (impressive, or depressing?), there can be no doubt that when this particular banner is hung from the rafters, all notions of self-reflection are dramatically swept aside. Chihuly circumvents the theoretical struggle described in this chapter—opticality versus materiality—through the disarmingly simple method of playing up both properties to the hilt, thus draining them of any dialectical interest. If contemporary art cognoscenti still have a tendency to regard "craft" with suspicion, who can blame them? Chihuly and his followers, who are for many people the public face of contemporary craft, stand against everything that modern and postmodern art has tried to achieve.

What would it look like if a work of glass art were made with the express intent of sub-verting this state of affairs? One answer presents itself in *Breath*, a work by the English artist Emma Woffenden (see Plate 8). It is a simple object: a glass dome, more suggestive of an architectural or mathematical model than a functional vessel, with a single balloon-like void protruding into its core. The work is notable, first, for its absolute rejection of the apparatus of most contemporary glass art. There is no color, little evident technical brio, and no expressive character here. It is as cold and flaccid as Chihuly's chandeliers are superheated and triumphal. Nor is there any mystery about its means of manufacture. The cylindrical form has been pierced cleanly and then penetrated by a hollow volume, which the title implies was fashioned with a single breath of the artist into a gather of molten glass. That breath has been captured and presented like a specimen, much as a soft internal organ might float in a jar. Indeed, there is a nice correspondence between the thin-walled, blobby glass form and the artist's own inner parts, the lungs, diaphragm, and stomach that went into the making. In part, then, *Breath* is about the entrapment and preservation of the ephemeral—an updated version, say, of Marcel Duchamp's 1919 readymade *50cc of Paris Air*. But it is also, like Process Art, about facture: the residue of an encounter between the body and a particular material. The downwards, drooping curve created by Woffenden's exhalation has a pathos reminiscent of Eva Hesse's or Robert Morris's equally gravitational work, but here, the material is less incidental, the means still more direct. This is "glass blowing" in its most literal form.

In a way, Woffenden is only pointing out the obvious: a material cannot provide a full accounting of design, intention, or action, no matter how desperately the artist wills it. It will always remain partially resistant. Nor can it ever be rendered entirely "optical." Woffenden's *Breath* is the anti-Chihuly. There are no easy pleasures here, only an elegant limning of the relation between a striving body and some troublesome material. What we are left with in the end is facture as material contingency, in all its open-ended, unpredictable pathos. In *Breath*, the most demanding of craft procedures is reduced to a single, comically elementary puff of air. One might well ask: is this what advanced thinking through craft must look like? Is there no place in the climate of post-conceptual art for work grounded in extraordinary skill? The next chapter will take up this question, which, like that of craft's materiality, admits of no simple answer.

3 SKILLED

Thus far, this book has dealt with craft as a problem case within modern art history. I have presented binary situations in which art and craft have been pitched against one another, according to key terms of difference (autonomous and supplementary, optical and sensual). In such matters, craft is often seen as a sign of failure, but it can also be an escape-hatch—a means to think outside the narrow confines of the autonomous artwork. In the case of skill, matters are yet more complex. Skill, narrowly conceived as "knowing how to make something," is obviously at issue in the creation of any art, even the most "dematerialized" of conceptual works. Indeed, when an artwork is not made to the standards a viewer might expect (however those standards have been determined), skill becomes all the more present as a consideration. It is most conspicuous in its absence. And yet artists often casually denigrate skill, as if it were beside the point. Jackson Pollock voiced a typical attitude: "it doesn't make much difference how the paint is put on as long as something has been said. Technique is just a means of arriving at a statement."[1] The British sculptor Helen Chadwick, meanwhile, was even more forceful. "I feel, like a lot of contemporary artists, distrustful of the conceit of the artist's hand—this talented hand, able to tosh off these beautiful creations."[2] Skill is a precondition for all art making—one might say, its craft foundation—but at best, it seems to be taken for granted. At worst it is an outright embarrassment. Why is this? How has this apparently hypocritical position become the norm in modern art production?

This chapter will pursue the unwieldy topic of skill by focusing not on concrete cases of art history, as was the case in the previous chapters and will be again in the final two, but rather by looking at a variety of key theorists who have delivered opinions on the subject. These perspectives will be taken not just from the realm of art theory proper, but also from other fields, including art history, educational theory, and architectural criticism. The ambition is not to resolve the problem of skill but, on the contrary, to suggest that it is an inherently conflicted subject that is central to the politics of twentieth-century visual culture. Also, as a way of acknowledging the dialectical nature of skill as a subject, several of these case studies will feature a head-to-head contrast of two positions, both of which might have something valuable to contribute to an overall understanding of skill. First up is a discussion of two key British texts on craft skill, by the woodworker David Pye and the art historian Michael Baxandall. Next, stepping backwards in time to the early twentieth century, I will examine the more overtly politicized debate about skill that took place among left-wing progressive educational theorists and their opponents. In this context, skill was discussed not only as a way of making things but also as a way of making people: a means of social improvement. The focus on education then continues, via the relatively apolitical figure of Josef Albers, to two of the most hallowed sites in craft history, the Bauhaus and Black Mountain College. Finally, the chapter proceeds to the late twentieth century for an examination of the architectural writings of Charles Jencks and Kenneth Frampton. Politics returns here in a different guise, as an argument over questions of the built environment. Through all of these examples we will see that one thing remains constant: skill, the way it is learned, and the purposes to which it is put, all elicit passionate disagreement.

CIRCULAR THINKING: DAVID PYE AND MICHAEL BAXANDALL

With such a difficult topic to unravel, a good way to begin is with a couple of anecdotes. The first comes from an oral history interview of the American potter Warren MacKenzie, recorded in 2002. Although MacKenzie will be discussed later in the book (see Chapter 4), a story he tells about the famous British potter Bernard Leach seems too good to pass up here. It comes from the early 1950s, the period when he was working as an apprentice at Leach's pottery in St. Ives, in the west of England:

> Bernard worked in a part of the shop that was away from the rest of us. He had a separate studio upstairs, and so we didn't actually see him making pots so much. But when he wanted to decorate his ware, it had to come down to the glazing room, where the pigments and slips and so forth were for decorating. And one day he brought down about three boards full of pots, 20 pots, let's say, and then he got called away to the phone, and we, of course, all went into the glazing room to see what he had brought down, and we were able to pick up and handle his work. And there was a man who worked in the pottery, Bill Marshall, and Bill was technically the best thrower in the pottery. He could work with more clay; he could shape it quickly and easily and throw very well. And Bill looked at all these pots and picked them up and handled them and so on. And he finally said something which shocked us, but I guess I would have to have agreed with it. He said, "Bernard can't throw worth a damn." And we all thought, oh, well. And then Bill finished his statement. He said, "But he makes better pots than any of us."[3]

A second anecdote, of considerably more ancient vintage, communicates a very different message about the relation between art and skill. The story is that of Giotto's "O." Pope Benedict IX, having heard of Giotto's fame, sent a courtier to seek him out. When this emissary located the painter, he asked for proof of his skill. As Vasari, in his *Lives of the Artists*, relates the narrative:

> At this Giotto took a sheet of paper and a brush dipped in red, closed his arm to his side, and with a twist of his hand drew such a perfect circle that it was a marvel to see. Then, with a smile, he said to the courtier: "There's your drawing."
>
> As if he were being ridiculed, the courtier replied: "Is this the only drawing I'm to have?"
>
> "It's more than enough," answered Giotto. "Send it along and you'll see whether it's understood or not."

As a result, the pope and many of his knowledgeable courtiers realized just how far Giotto surpassed all the other painters of his time in skill.[4]

The craft world often seems like a ghetto of technique, and the art world as an arena of the free play of ideas shockingly divorced from knowledge about process and materials. Usually, this schism is described as originating in the Renaissance.[5] Yet as these two anecdotes demonstrate, this way of understanding art and craft fails to capture the complexity of the situation. When the proverbial first art historian, Vasari, was presented with the rhetorical challenge of introducing the artist who inaugurated the Renaissance, he turned to a simple story about skill as a way of proving Giotto's genius.[6] And conversely, even those who place a very high value on traditional craftsmanship (as both MacKenzie and Leach did) can have a surprisingly casual attitude towards skill. Indeed, directly after relating this event in his interview, MacKenzie underlined the moral: "it's not the technical side of it that matters; it's something beyond that."[7]

But what is that mysterious "something" of which MacKenzie spoke? Nothing could be more familiar, or less intellectually satisfying, than the idea that the truly skilled practitioner (whether artist or craftsman, musician or athlete) has an ineffable, special quality. Whether conceived as beauty, talent, magic, or genius, this is the commonplace notion of what is to be skilled. The implication is that the proper response is not theoretical discussion, but shoulder-shrugging amazement. When somebody's got "it," that certain something, we are usually content to admire, rather than analyze, that person's achievements. A few theorists have tried to come to grips with the subject, though. The most outstanding example is David Pye's *The Art of Workmanship*, perhaps the purest piece of "craft theory" written in the twentieth century. Pye offers a disarmingly straightforward consideration of the physical realities that the rather imprecise notion of skill tends to conceal. A second text, as metaphorical and elusive as Pye is precise and concrete, is Michael Baxandall's *The Limewood Sculptors of Renaissance Germany*, an art historian's attempt to ground his methodology in an understanding of craft. Through reference to Thomas Crow's recent reading of Baxandall, it is possible to argue that skill's normative quality—its seeming rightness in our eyes—makes it a profoundly cultural matter, and the heart of what it means to think through craft.

The wonderful thing about David Pye's writings about workmanship is their matter-of-factness. He once wrote, "what laymen call skill is mostly a matter of taking very great trouble."[8] This feels more like the end of a conversation than the beginning of one, and is typical of Pye—a great writer of aphorisms, but also a quintessentially scientific thinker. He wants to settle the issue, to be sure of his facts. He sometimes has a propensity to be fussy and legalistic, as when he quibbles over the question of whether anything is really made by hand: "some things actually can be made without tools it is true, but the definition is going to be rather exclusive for it will take in baskets and coiled pottery, and that is about all!"[9] But there is deep-seated commitment behind his finicky logic—a mission to recast craft in a newly relevant guise. It is no coincidence that the great line about "taking very great trouble" appears in an obituary about Ron Lenthall, the highly skilled technician

Figure 3.1   Ron Lenthall.
Pictured in *Crafts* magazine, 1982.

in charge of the woodshop at the Royal College of Art in London, where Pye also taught (Figure 3.1). Lenthall exemplified the self-effacing tendencies of craft. Indeed, he could be said to have been a living supplement himself, as he fabricated the output of many leading artists that passed through the Royal College in the 1960s and 1970s, and received no share in the authorship of those works.[10] It was men like Lenthall that Pye most respected. And yet he had little use for waxing poetic about their talents. In his defining work *The Nature and Art of Workmanship*, Pye wrote, "*skill* is not a word used in this book. It does not assist useful thought because it means something different in each different kind of work... Like 'function' you can make it mean what you please. It is a thought-preventer."[11]

That flat assertion is all the more remarkable given that Pye's book is the most compelling technical discussion of skilled work ever written. In a perceptive evaluation of his work published in 1982, Christopher Frayling and Helen Snowdon pointed out that Pye's great breakthrough was to "divorce manual skill from *mental* skill (know-how), going directly against the grain of established Arts and Crafts Movement opinion."[12] His method was to reserve the term "workmanship" for purely physical procedures, such as the actual moving of a hand plane over a board in order to smooth it, or the pressing of fingers into wet rotating clay in the attempt to make a bowl, and then to subject the mechanics of those procedures to rigorously literal analysis. In so doing, Pye was able to vacate the idea of skill of its moral overtones, and thus to depart from the established tradition of modern craft theory. Nor was this departure subtle. He heaped scorn on the writings of John Ruskin, who had previously been a virtually sacrosanct figure amongst craft commentators, particularly the moralizing aspects of his thought. (Pye pointed out that "from time to time [craft] had doubtless been practiced effectively by people of the utmost depravity.")[13] The message was clear and consistent. While Ruskin had pronounced that "art is not a study of positive reality, it is the seeking for ideal truth," Pye insisted that workmanship is a realm of discrete physical actions, each one susceptible to rational examination.

Pye's most well-known distinction is that between the workmanship of risk and the workmanship of certainty. This was a purposeful reframing of the dichotomy between craft and industry, or hand and machine. The great advantages of Pye's shift in terminology are its accuracy, mobility and flexibility. In the workmanship of risk, "the quality of the result is not predetermined, but depends on the judgment, care and dexterity which the maker exercises as he works." There is nothing here about a categorization of certain type of work or product, and Pye insisted that the workmanship of risk was just as important to the operation of certain huge factories as small artisanal shops.[14] Partly, this is because the relation between risk and certainty is relative rather than absolute. Total certainty and total risk are rarely observed, and intermediary positions between the two can be achieved through means as humble as a pair of scissors (which helps the user to cut a straight line) or as complex as an injection-molding machine. Within this elastic framework, Pye was willing to make some place for the concept of skill, but only in a very limited way. He saw it as the capacity to achieve constraint manually within the context of the workmanship of risk. In slicing bread, for example, the skill is in holding the knife continuously parallel to the plane of the cut. The force applied does not count as skilful because it does not affect the result.[15] Skill, then, is the human equivalent to a jig in woodworking or a mold in ceramics—it is control within a productive operation, the ability to reduce error. While there are certain corollary rules that attend skill, such as the fact that it tends to be compromised by increased force or speed in the operation, it is essentially a simple matter: purposefully constrained physical action. The product of such action could be a craft object like the wooden bowls that he himself made—objects that, in their obsessively regular application of free workmanship, seem like nothing so much as diagrams made for Pye's own books (see Plate 9). But it could also be a musical performance, a building, or a battleship. The crafts have no unique purchase on the matter of skill.

For all its reductive quality, this notion has a surprising appeal in today's messy, post-disciplinary environment, when artists feel ever more free to hop from one medium to another. As Tanya Harrod has recently argued, the roots of this climate may be found in the 1970s, when higher level art educators began to teach skills to their students "as and when."[16] In this system, or rather non-system, a young artist would receive exposure to a wide range of materials and techniques, read a great deal, and eventually settle on a project. The student would then learn the skills required, and then perhaps move on to something else. While few art schools have been completely unmoored from disciplinary education, the results of this general attitude are widely evident in the disappearance of medium-specific crafts courses in higher educational institutions. They are equally apparent at contemporary art fairs, promiscuous environments in which a single artist might present sculptures, paintings, and video, each with a high degree of conceptual sophistication and (unless the fabrication of the work has been hired out) amateurish production values. Pye himself might have been less than enthusiastic about this state of affairs, given his attention to detail. Yet is obvious that this postdisciplinary approach to making art is compatible with his notion of skill not as a calling in life, but as friction applied to an action in the service of any intended outcome. By these lights, our postdisciplinary world is not necessarily better or worse than the world it supplants; it has simply dedicated fewer resources to the development of particular skills.

There is one gap in this scheme, though, and it is the one that scientific approaches to artistic matters usually fail to account for: the question of intent. In one of his typically concise formulations, Pye declares, "Good workmanship is that which carries out or improves upon the intended design. Bad workmanship is what fails to do so and thwarts the design."[17] To demonstrate the point, he offered a "test-tube example," two circles representing a wooden picture frame. One circle, like Giotto's O, is unbroken. The other is interrupted by loosely fitted joints. The first circle, Pye says, will always seem like good workmanship and the second like poor workmanship. This seems clear enough. But how do we know this? How do we know that the circle is meant to be round? His answer, uncharacteristically, is a rather unsatisfying appeal to gestalt psychology. We are born, Pye says, with the knowledge that a nearly round or nearly square volume is meant to be perfectly round or square. What he does not say is that the roundness of the picture frame, whether or not it is a genetic preference, is also a cultural fact with economic consequences. Pye is of course willing to concede that making a perfectly round object is more difficult, and hence more expensive, than making an object that is only approximately round. He is not, however, interested in the question of why that expense would be worth incurring. This is a cultural question, he might say, not a question about workmanship proper. But in pulling these two things apart, he does violence to the subject.

For even if workmanship is really nothing more than an actualization of a pre-existing idea, it is still an investment. This is obviously true in the sense that craft costs money, and so wherever it manifests itself, a cultural observer should be ready to look for the interests involved. (In this sense, skill might be seen as a form of rhetoric.) Less obviously, it should be pointed out that craft skill never comes for free; it must be learned. Indeed, in a sense, skill is something that seems noteworthy only from the position of the unskilled. The skilled practitioner takes proficiency for granted. It is only during the difficult process of acquiring a particular skill that skill as such emerges. As Peter Dormer put it in his own book-length study on the subject of craft knowledge, "The constitutive rules of a craft are only learned by actually doing the activity. Indeed, they are the activity."[18] If the conscious experience of skill is intrinsically transitional, however—a matter of coming to grips with technique, rather than applying a technique that has already been mastered—then Pye's view of skill as a form of constraint must be modified. This is not to invalidate his point about the fundamentally restrictive quality of skill, but rather to insist on the incompleteness of that account. The experience of craft, precisely because it is hard won, is always a revelation. Moreover, this experience always takes place within a specific cultural context. Hitting a nail with a hammer may be an identical action no matter when and where it occurs, but both the experience and motivations involved in the hammering are always historically contingent.

Pye did not come fully to grips with this cultural dimension of craft. Indeed, his term "diversity," which he describes as the inevitable product of the workmanship of risk, masks a nearly romantic attitude to his own historical moment. Thus, Pye notes that "diversity imports into our man-made environment something which is akin to the natural environment we have abandoned," and that "there is no substitute for the aesthetic quality of [free] workmanship and the world will be poorer without it, particularly the countryside. It is impossible not to regret that it is declining but quite impossible to expect that it will survive on any scale as a means of decent livelihood."[19] The tone of these statements is elegiac, the tone adopted by a heartbroken lover rather than the coolly rational analyst we have come to expect. Indeed this passage, though it seems mischievous to say so, veers surprisingly close to the ideas of Ruskin, his *bête noire*. What led Pye to adopt such an uncharacteristic position is his inability to see craft skill as a moving target.

For clarity on this point, we turn now to the figure of Michael Baxandall. A former curator of sculpture at the Victoria & Albert Museum, Baxandall is best known for his binding together of material and cultural matters in art history. Thus, in *Painting and Experience in Fifteenth-Century Italy* (1972), he showed how the consumption of costly materials such as gold and lapis lazuli, the relative size of altarpiece paintings, and the amount of time spent by a workshop master compared to his assistants, were dictated by patrons rather than artists. (As he put it, "in the fifteenth century, art was still too important to be left to the painters." So much for the clean split between artist and artisan in the Renaissance.)[20] Here, though, I want to focus on Baxandall's equally famous study of Northern Renaissance wood sculpture, *The Limewood Sculptors of Renaissance Germany* (1980). Thomas Crow has written an elegant, short study of this work, which gives us a model in which social art history is draped on the framework of a history of attitudes towards production.[21] For Baxandall, Crow demonstrates, the ties between physical process and the expression of shared culture are multiple, occurring at the level of metaphor as well as praxis. The central point in this process of interpretation is material itself. "In what terms," Baxandall asked, "are we to think of a piece of wood as having a character to be respected?"[22] It was a double-sided question, for the respect in question was not only historical—that felt by an artist like Veit Stoss or Tilman Riemenschneider—but present-day, that felt by the historian. Indeed, for Crow, the stakes are those of art history itself. Through an in-depth study of material properties, the scholar can recreate some aspect of his quarry's mentality, for one thing is sure: the artist dealt with material. Like a manuscript in an archive, the wood of a carved Madonna preserves the thought process of its maker, if one can only extract the data. Even the title of the book demonstrates the primacy that Baxandall accorded to the material as a matrix of interpretation.

In the case of German Renaissance sculpture, the material was limewood, a large-growing and evenly porous hardwood taken from the lime or linden tree. Unlike oak, which was imported in significant amounts into Germany, limewood was a local material. But it had a key weakness, which Baxandall introduces with deceptive nonchalance: "The typical cracking in a log of light hardwood like limewood is a radial pattern of splits running from its ends, for which the term is 'starshake.' The cause is uneven shrinkage in drying, and it is these lines one must read."[23] The effect of radial cracking described by Baxandall here—not too different, really, from the interrupted circle that seemed to Pye to be a guaranteed sign of poor craftsmanship—turns out to be the determining factor in the period's sculptural compositions. What Baxandall calls "sublimated starshake" can be detected in the lines of Renaissance sculptures, which feature radially extended, vertical forms that are unlikely to suffer tangential shrinkage, and hence disastrous cracking (Figure 3.2). Baxandall pushes this logic as far as it can reasonably go, using it as a metric to judge individual carvers' styles. Thus, while certain sculptors opted for a relaxed, stable approach to carved form, he argues that others flaunted the properties of the material by creating "knowingly hazardous" shapes that curved across invisible lines of potential fracture.[24] The terms employed by Pye—certainty and risk—return here, as does his deep respect for the complexities of particular materials.[25]

For Baxandall, skill as a management of risk is not just a technical matter. It is fixed firmly within the decision-making process and the stylistic sensibility of the sculptor. For Crow, there is yet another level of meaning to this engagement with material. He interprets the craftsman's concern with starshake—the tendency of limewood sculptures to blow apart of their own accord—as a deep-seated cultural metaphor. For the limewood sculptors, starshake was a figure for iconoclasm, a terrible storm that was about to visit itself upon them, destroying their livelihoods as image makers and even endangering their lives. As Crow reports, Riemenschneider himself, one of the greatest of the limewood sculptors, "was imprisoned during a peasant's revolt and, as one story has it, suffered his hands being broken." For Crow, the historical reality of religious warfare, and the extraordinary pressures it placed upon art, open up the possibility of reading sculpture in the way that it was meant to be read in the first place: "One lesson of Baxandall's *Limewood Sculptors* is that in special circumstances history itself has enacted the violence necessary to understanding, so the

Figure 3.2 Tilman Riemenschneider, *Angel*, c. 1505.
Germany (Würzburg). Limewood, formerly painted.
Victoria & Albert Museum.

willful interpreter can withdraw from center stage, let his or her material do the work, and thus restore some validity to the ideal of objectivity."[26]

We might now take a step down from the lofty perch of Crow's analysis, and consider what Baxandall's method might suggest for a larger understanding of craft. Whether or not the specter of iconoclasm was at the forefront of German sculptors' consciousness as they worked is impossible to know. But that they formed their representations, their culture, through a process of coming to know the lineaments of wood is certain. Their cultural ideas—conceptions of its proper use—were written into that experience of skilled craft. The example of Baxandall suggests that skill is not just knowing how to make something, but rather knowing how to make something seem "just right." Pye's argument that skill is essentially a matter of restriction, rather than potential, seems initially to be at odds with this line of thought. But in fact, Pye's insight might help us to understand the political valence of Baxandall's argument in greater depth. For skill is, in the end, much like Giotto's circle. It has an inside and an outside; it both includes and excludes. The manner in which it performs this action—through absolute roundness, for example—is only effective within a certain cultural perspective, such as that quintessentially Renaissance mentality that recognized circularity as a sign of perfection. What Pye helps us to see is that skill's traditional claims to authority, to "just rightness," reside primarily in the craftsman's refusal to do it any other way.

LEARNING BY DOING

If this is the case—if skill is, at base, a way of achieving cultural authority—then we might well expect skill to be challenged by those who position themselves as progressive. This seems a truism of avant-garde art in general (hence the contemporary art viewer's commonplace "my child could do that"), and probably has much to do with the disparagement of technique by artists such as Jackson Pollock and Helen Chadwick mentioned at the beginning of the chapter. Yet there have been many more subtle forms of challenge to the authority of skill. One particularly rich vein of this discourse can be found in modern educational theory, which was perhaps little read by non-specialists, but was nonetheless tremendously influential in that its ideas transformed the schoolroom experiences of countless children.[27] The discussion of vocational education is of particular interest in that it is one of the few arenas in which craft has been extensively examined as a political subject. This was especially true in the 1930s, when debate was defined largely in terms of Progressivism—broadly speaking, a politically left-leaning movement in which educators tried to make schools into mechanisms of social reform. The emergence of Progressivism took place against the backdrop of an expansion of schooling to the working class, and a corresponding curricular change. Craft-based teaching had been common in European and American schools for younger children in the late nineteenth century but it was not until the interwar years that such courses were considered to be appropriate to a general liberal arts education for older students. Eventually, in the late 1940s, when the teaching of craft came to be firmly entrenched in British and American universities (partly as a way of coping with a sudden influx of war veterans), arguments for and against Progressive education structured the gradual expansion of vocational education.

During the three decades of its greatest influence, Progressivism generated an enormous and varied literature on the ends and means of teaching. Although it is difficult to generalize about Progressive theorists as a group, all were to one degree or another social reformers. Much of their work dealt with the issue of broadening curriculum to include craft courses, an idea which went through changing fortunes over the course of the early twentieth century. In the earliest days of the Progressive movement, vocational educators already connected manual training to the goal of abstract learning rather than the acquisition of marketable skills. They looked back to such examples as Felix Adler's Workingman's School, founded in New York City in 1880, which in turn had been inspired by the *slöjd* (or *sloyd*, meaning "craft") elementary schools of woodworking in Sweden.[28] Adler's school included programs in simple engineering, woodwork and clay workshops as "an organic part of regular instruction," and not in order to inculcate "an aptitude for any particular trade."[29] Similarly, John Dewey's early "experimental school" in Chicago incorporated the teaching of carpentry as early as 1897, as well as assorted craft activities, which he called "social occupations."[30] Dewey's books *Democracy and Education* (1916) and *Art as Experience* (1934) proved to be hugely influential on the Progressive education movement. His central idea was "experience," defined as a moment of interaction with objects and processes.[31] The goal of all education, Dewey argued, should be to shape experience so that it encourages moral and aesthetic learning. Vocational teaching should adhere to this principle: the idea was that the experience of materials that could be gained via the acquisition of craft skill would produce in the student a general physical and mental "readiness."[32] Dewey thus saw craft as entirely compatible with a liberal arts education.

Dewey's influence on the Progressives began to take shape at the end of the First World War. In 1918 the US Congress, spurred by the need for skilled workmen that had been demonstrated during the conflict, passed the Smith-Hughes Act, appropriating federal funds for vocational schools.[33] Though these new resources immediately resulted in an expansion of crafts courses across the country, Dewey attacked the bill vigorously, arguing that it "symbolizes the inauguration of a conflict between irreconcilably opposed educational and industrial ideals."[34] This was because the new funds were primarily used to set up trade schools as alternatives to academic high schools. By 1925, the enrollment in vocational and technical schools had already risen to about 50,000 students nationwide.[35] As this system was constructed, it inevitably raised the question of class prejudice. By attending such schools, some argued, the working classes were encouraged to engage only in manual work, while the children of wealthier and more educated families at non-vocational schools were encouraged in intellectual pursuits. "To my mind," one educator wrote, "we may as well give up the boast of democracy if we are to have industrial education for the masses and a liberal education for the favored few."[36]

This problem was only exacerbated when vocational education for youths was introduced into the relatively new junior high schools. Increasingly, these schools acted as two-way turnstiles through which students were directed either to work or to further education in an academic high school.[37] In one of the more candid descriptions of vocational education's role in this process, the junior high school was described as a "transition stage" in which the child "is groping to find his place in society," so that its proper role was "determining the field of endeavor to which the child is best adapted," thus maximizing " economic efficiency."[38]

The system was one of social instrumentality. In many cases, craft-based occupational programs such as woodworking, which had been introduced in earlier trade schools and elementary schools, were supplanted by mechanics and machine shop courses that provided a more direct preparation for working in industry. Supporters of this shift argued that it was only due to the misapplication of European educational techniques that Americans had introduced craft-based programs into schools in the first place: "we did not realize, apparently, that there was no peasantry here as in Danish countries; that the continental 'whittling knife' and all that it illustrated in economic life would soon be succeeded by the automatic machine."[39]

By the onset of the Depression, then, the high-minded vision of the teaching of manual craft skills espoused by Dewey (who had written in *Democracy and Education* that "the only adequate training *for* occupations is *through* occupations ... to predetermine some future occupation for which education is to be a strict preparation is to injure the possibilities of present development") had already been replaced by a much more practical brand of directive, industrial vocational education.[40] For Progressive educators, who grew to the height of their influence in the 1930s, this situation seemed one of the most pressing problems in American education. Faculty at the Teachers College at Columbia University, a center of Progressivism that included in its numbers such prominent figures as George Counts and Harold Rugg, launched attacks on the industrial orientation that vocational instruction had taken. Their arguments were based directly on the themes Dewey had established in the 1910s (indeed, the Teachers College group formed the core of the John Dewey Society, an influential leftist educational organization).[41] Employing Dewey's vocabulary, the Columbia theorists insisted that the "experience" of craftsmanship should be provided for the sake of general "readiness," rather than as job-specific training.[42] George Counts's essay "Dare the School Build a New Social Order?" warned darkly of the anti-democratic implications of an "industrial feudalism" in which the means of technical production are concentrated "in the hands of a small class."[43] He argued for an alternative model of teaching which would eschew the traditional "three Rs" for a politically oriented curriculum, and which would place emphasis on the experience of skill in a general sense, rather than the acquisition of particular economically useful skills: "the important consideration is not the content of the course pursued but rather the method by which the pupil works."[44]

With the onset of the Depression came a more overt politicization of the Progressive educators' message. Counts and the other Teachers College theorists put forward their ideas in the *Social Frontier*, a leftist journal that also printed articles by communist luminaries such as Leon Trotsky. The Progressives' association with such figures led to the condemnation of their ideas as subversive; in one chilling anticipation of the red-baiting of the 1950s, their writings were attacked as "a mere protective smokescreen for a communistic offensive."[45] While the *Social Frontier* did not necessarily embody an orthodox Marxist position, contributors such as Earl Browder, who was indeed affiliated with the Communist Party, were not afraid to demand that educators "open wide the door of the school for the examination of all social and economic problems" and to insist that education, "an ally in the worker's struggle," should be *related directly to the material interests of the masses, political and economic.*"[46] By the end of the decade, even Dewey, who had been a relatively apolitical figure throughout his career, was arguing that "intellectual organization is not an end in itself but is the means by which social relations ... may be understood and more intelligently ordered."[47] With this increasingly socialist orientation came a broader agenda for Progressive vocational education. Less emphasis was placed upon the experience of the individual, and more on the importance of manual craft as a kind of training in leftist civics. In a 1935 *Social Frontier* article, one professor of industrial relations at Columbia wrote that craft courses should be used as a means to teach students of all classes the value of manual work: "from now on the effort has to be to train in the practice of industrial citizenship, no less than for vocational skills."[48] At the same time, he affirmed the importance of the aesthetic and cultural experience to be had in vocational courses: "all the cultural values which can be related to instruction for each vocation must be injected... Every technique has its history no less than its artistry."[49]

It is important to note that the Progressives were not by any means anti-modernists. They had no objection to modern technology, and assumed that craft and industry were natural partners in social change, rather than adversaries.[50] Harold Rugg, the wartime editor of *Social Frontier* (in its last years of publication from 1939–43) and a member of the Greenwich Village avant-garde (alongside figures like John Marin, Marsden Hartley, Alfred Stieglitz and Georgia O'Keeffe), can be taken as an exemplar of this point of view. Like Dewey, he brought an idealistic moralizing tone to his writing on art, characterizing creative thought as an inherently redemptive and enlightening activity.[51] And like Counts, Rugg held that social power lies in "the interplay of many small interest groups," and that through education, designs for a more equitable society could be effected.[52] In the 1930s he had had the unique opportunity to expound on these ideas through a successful series of elementary and junior high school textbooks. In one of these, entitled *Man At Work: His Arts and Crafts*, Rugg wrote to his readership of schoolchildren that the social function of art holds "as true for you as curtain makers or as garden-makers or as playwriters or craftsmen of any kind, just as they have held true for the great builders, painters and sculptors throughout history"[53] (Figure 3.3). For Rugg, any craft had inherent moral integrity as a creative experience, so it followed that every child should be educated to become "self-expressive craftsmen with words or tone, with clay, wood, or stone, with light or shade."[54] The inclusion of artistic and vocational courses in a school's curriculum was not a way to make education a more efficient way of building the economy, but rather a means of working towards "a sound society."[55]

THINKING IN SITUATIONS: JOSEF ALBERS—FROM THE BAUHAUS TO BLACK MOUNTAIN

If it is intriguing to see craft through the lens of left-wing educational theory, it is positively fascinating to observe those same principles in action at Black Mountain College, founded

Figure 3.3 "The New and the Old in Education."
From Harold Rugg and Ann Shumaker, *The Child-Centered
School: An Appraisal of the New Education*, 1928. British Library.

in 1933 in North Carolina. The school is widely celebrated for its history as a cauldron of the postwar avant-garde but it was also a notable milestone in educational practice. The organizers of the college had come from Rollins University, which was itself a bastion of Progressivism; but what really made Black Mountain unique from the point of view of educational theory was the presence of Anni and Josef Albers on the faculty.[56]

As a student at the Bauhaus in Weimar beginning in 1920, and then as the master of the preliminary materials course there (after 1923), Josef Albers had direct experience of an alternative model of craft pedagogy that corresponded to some degree with the American model of Progressivism. Here the strands of influence are difficult to disentangle. Some of the initial precepts about the teaching of craft at the Bauhaus, notably the guild organization of the school, the focus on hand-work as a guarantor of good design, and the importance of master-apprentice relationships, were descended from the same turn-of-the-century Arts and Crafts movement ideas that had influenced Dewey. And Dewey's early writings, in turn, had achieved a certain currency in Germany through the Work School movement led by Georg Kerschensteiner prior to World War I, which focused particularly on teaching manual crafts to young children.[57] But the Bauhaus leadership, particularly architect Walter Gropius, also had the benefit of hindsight in constructing their own version of the utopian production community. To an extent unrealized even by those Arts and Crafts organizations that had been sympathetic to machine production, the Bauhaus actively pursued relationships with industry. The teaching of craft served as the instrumental basis for this ambition. "True creative work," Gropius wrote, "can be done only by the man whose knowledge and mastery of the physical laws of statics, dynamics, optics, acoustics equip him to give life and shape to his inner vision. In a work of art the laws of the physical world, the intellectual world and the world of spirit function and are expressed simultaneously."[58] The physical qualities of material and the constraints of use, both held to be objectively verifiable, were used as parameters (or in Gropius's words, "pre-ordained limits") within which artistic practice could flourish.[59] The workshop was a "laboratory" for the creation of "type-forms" according to "theoretical and formal laws."[60]

Gropius's ideas about craft skill had much in common with Dewey's. Both resisted the hierarchical division of fine and useful arts, and saw artistic potential in all modes of technological production. Like Gropius, Dewey had specifically attacked the artist who "attempts to engage in self-expression that is isolated and without reference to the context out of which inquiry into materials arises."[61] He argued that technique applied through materials gives access to a universal whole.[62] However, there were important differences as well. Though both men were politically to the left, Dewey gradually came to side with those who hoped to erect a barrier between vocational education and industrial training, out of a fear that children would be taught craft skills only to serve more effectively as factory workers. Gropius's objectives were no less politically motivated—he hoped that craft would serve as the basis for a democratic, mass-produced modernism—but he remained steadfastly instrumentalist.[63]

Josef Albers's departure from the Bauhaus to Black Mountain was therefore a transition between two models of progressive education that were similar, but in some ways antithetical. His unexpected removal to North Carolina forced him to confront this difference. The teaching strategies that he developed there were strikingly non-instrumental, an approach to thinking through craft that might have been borrowed directly from Dewey's *Art as Experience*. The roots of this attitude can be detected in Albers's time in Germany as the leader of the Bauhaus foundation course, which lacked the direct application to industrial design that was favored by Gropius, and taught in the more advanced craft-based courses at the school. "The best education is one's own experience. Experimenting surpasses studying," Albers said in 1928. "Invention, and re-invention too, is the essence of all creative work (proficiency is a tool and hence is secondary)."[64] His pedagogy put this principle into practice. It was premised upon continual "unprofessional" experimentation with materials such as newspaper, often without using tools of any kind. As Frank Whitford notes, the idea was that "the simplest and least likely materials could be used to teach important lessons about the nature of construction that were of relevance to engineering as well as art" (Figure 3.4).[65]

It is unclear the extent to which Albers may have read Dewey's books or have been influenced by them. When asked about this in an interview, he remarked only that his tenure at Black Mountain "was already the time when self-expression came up, very much lubricated by John Dewey. Well, I do not believe in him so much."[66] This lack of enthusiasm may reflect a difference on the issue of self-expression, which was central to Dewey's theory, but which (as we will see) Albers found to be completely counterproductive. In most other respects, however, Albers promoted ideas that were consonant with Dewey's writings. In the approved Progressive manner, his teaching eschewed the transmission of pre-established technique, and (unlike other pedagogical models propagated at the Bauhaus) also avoided setting out fixed abstract principles. Instead Albers exposed his students to a continuous experience of process, by which they would acquire skill in the most generic sense. This philosophy had practical consequences. As at the Bauhaus, Black Mountain students engaged in craft production partly with a view to becoming economically self-sufficient; but they did so mainly by producing necessities for themselves (including the building of the school itself) and goods for informal craft sales in nearby Asheville. There was also nothing in his teaching that implied that the Black Mountain students should develop models for industry—somewhat surprisingly, in light of Anni Albers's continued commitment to this goal. While the preliminary course at the Bauhaus had as one of its expressed aims "the choice of a vocation: recognition of the area of work and the kind of materials that suit the individual," no such decision awaited a student at Black Mountain.[67]

In a 1965 interview, Albers recalled:

> at Black Mountain we did quite some drawing and there I found out it is not just a matter of aiming with the eye. It's also drawing with our motor sense... It's a matter of feeling, not seeing. You don't watch what the arm does, no. You go by the feeling within the arm, you see. And this motor sense business I have developed, still more, and that indicates already that I was not just repeating Bauhaus stuff.[68]

This emphasis on physical action, obviously, has little to do with craft's position as a preparatory stage of industry.[69] The laws of design that Gropius and other Bauhaus instructors had emphasized no longer take center stage. Instead, the experience of the physical object is stressed. Learning is done not through the mastery of theory or knowledge, but the

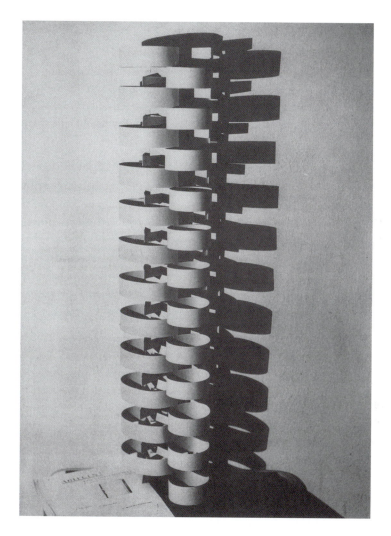

Figure 3.4   Gustav Hassenpflug, form study in paper, 1928.
Made in Josef Albers's foundation course at the Bauhaus.
Bauhaus-Archiv Berlin.

inductive experience of doing. As Albers said when a local carpenter came to demonstrate at the Black Mountain woodshop:

> I said to the master: you saw a board, and don't make any comment upon the doing. You do as you always saw, as all carpenters do... If you have experienced and have done wrongly and know why it is wrong, and have done rightly—that sticks with you. And not by reading printed matter. You have to watch ... all this practical work is thinking in situations.[70]

This encounter can be contrasted to the similar experiences that Albers had arranged for his students at the Bauhaus. As he recalled:

> we visited the workshops of box, chair, and cabinetmakers, of coopers and cartwrights, in order to learn the different possibilities of using, treating, and joining wood. Then, we tried to apply our knowledge to the making of useful objects… Soon, however, we expanded our practical work to allow more inventiveness and imagination, as a fundamental training for later specialized design.[71]

While the distinction between these two narratives may seem slight, it suggests the distance that Albers had traveled in his thinking about the objectives of craft education. At the Bauhaus, the encounter with real live woodworking was one step on the road to "specialized" design. At Black Mountain, however, it was simply an experience, which might be applied by students in any manner.

Another way to express this difference might be say that, for Gropius, craft was a matter of technique, a body of knowledge particular to an externally defined matrix of materials and processes. This model was influential on Albers early in his career as an educator, and the direct experience of material would always remain at the core of his pedagogy. Increasingly, though, Albers approached teaching not as the transmission of a discrete set of skills, but rather as an opportunity to give students the sense of what it was like to be skilled at all. This educational approach also reflected Albers's own seeming indifference to the products of creative activity, even his own. "What was art to me or was not some time ago," he said in 1944, "might have lost that value, or gained it … Thus art is not an object, but experience."[72] The exercises Albers set for his students were therefore not intended to produce a concrete outcome, or to convey a self-standing and finite body of abstract principles, but rather to encourage the active exploration of material contingencies. His notion of skill had to do not with results, but with potentiality per se. It could not exist outside of the context of learning—the processes of acquisition and application—nor could it be taught effectively through language. (As Dewey had argued in 1937, the teaching of craft knowledge "cannot be put into words because it is the work of the artist-designer himself and no one can tell him just how to do it. If they could tell him, his work would be mechanical, not creative and original.")[73] Albers's teaching of skill was adaptive, rather than final, and evolutionary, not perfectible. The artistic object was but a stage within an ongoing process, rather than an end in itself, even the end of "self-expression"—thus, perhaps, his refusal to allow his students to sign their pieces. As a former Black Mountain student recalled, Albers "wasn't terribly concerned with what we felt. He was concerned with what we saw and that we learned to see. And he would say, 'If you want to express yourself do that on your own time. Don't do it in my class.'"[74]

Rainer Wick, the leading authority on Bauhaus pedagogy and its influence, has been extremely critical of the reception of Albers's ideas, particularly his material exercises, which he argues "were robbed of their genuine intentions" by later educators and "locked into formalism."[75] Certainly, the establishment of certain teaching strategies—paper cutting exercises, comparative color theory, the collaging of found materials, and the like—as a rote part of European and American art school curriculum in the postwar period reflects the difficulty of maintaining a truly open-ended pedagogy at mass scale. What was experimental at the Bauhaus and Black Mountain College gradually became a new orthodoxy. On the other hand, the effect of Albers's own pedagogy has been impressively multivalent. While many of his students at Black Mountain (and, after 1949, at Yale University) emerged as leading Conceptualists with a positive antipathy to any notion of craftsmanship, others involved themselves deeply in craft theory and practice. This multiplicity is itself the best testimony to the efficacy of Albers's conception of skill.

CHARLES JENCKS AND KENNETH FRAMPTON: THE AD HOC AND THE TECTONIC

One would think that architecture would be the last discipline in which one might look for a continuation of the foregoing discussion. In Dewey's and Albers's theories of education, we find a celebration of the open-ended exploration, an engagement with materials that may result in "readiness" in the mind, but nothing in the way of product. Architects, meanwhile, care most about getting their work built. They may engage in speculation of both theoretical and visual varieties, and certainly the archives of architectural libraries worldwide are stuffed with images of unrealized projects. But in the end architecture must contend with the challenge of shaping the world in the most concrete, political sense. Yet, of course, every pedagogical theory takes for granted the fact that education itself is a preliminary stage in the construction of culture. Even if the results of teaching are not prejudged, the impact of education on society in the broadest terms must be a cardinal concern. It will be recalled that the lack of goal orientation in Dewey's writings was itself a moral position, in which the values of critical awareness and adaptability are preferred to the inculcation of standard civics lessons. Albers too saw in his seemingly formalist teaching distinctly political implications.[76]

In architectural theory of the 1970s and 1980s, one can observe a hotly disputed return to these questions of process, product and politics, as a part of a broader theoretical confrontation with a perceived crisis in the built environment. Educational theory and craft both figured centrally in this discussion, but this fact has been little remarked upon— perhaps because it has been somewhat obscured by the formulation of "postmodernism" as a concept, style, and condition of culture in these same texts. With the invention of the idea of postmodernism, architecture (not unlike photography during the same period) emerged from decades of marginality within the visual arts. Not since the interwar period and the figures of Gropius, Le Corbusier, Mies, and other modernists had architecture seemed to be the medium that dictated the tenor of the times. And indeed, as broadly applicable as the debates that swirled around postmodernism proved to be, they were also very much the internal discussions of a field that was revisiting its own recent past. As the very term "postmodernism" implies, the crucial question for writers on architecture in the

1980s was the proper interpretation of the 1920s and 1930s. So much is clear from the writings of Charles Jencks and Kenneth Frampton, nearly exact contemporaries who were adversaries in every respect but one: both operated from the now familiar precept that open-ended skill (rather than fixed technique) was the only way to build successfully for the present. Yet in following this principle the two drew very different conclusions, so much so that they became antagonistic, postmodernist spokesmen for two conflicting strains within Modernist architectural discourse, which Folke Nyberg summarizes as a debate between "those architects who consider building an ontological activity and those who maintain that architecture is codified practice used as an academic and autonomous language of style."[77] That Frampton and Jencks drew almost diametrically opposed conclusions from this same starting point demonstrates the complexity of modernist attitudes towards skill, and the unexpected continuations of those conflicting attitudes in the era of postmodernism.

Our two protagonists could be said to have defined their academic personae, as well as their relationship to one another, as early as 1969, when Jencks included an essay by Frampton in a volume he co-edited entitled *Meaning in Architecture*. This publication would be a sign of things to come in several respects. Jencks eagerly adopted a principle of multiplicity, going so far as to print critical comments in the margins of each essay by the volume's other contributors. Frampton, by contrast, delivered an impassioned application of Hannah Arendt's book *The Human Condition* to architecture, using her political philosophy to deliver a moral indictment of the built environment.[78] This divergence—the arranger and the activist—would go on to define their approaches to their own careers and writings, but also the actual substance of their architectural theories. From the beginning Jencks was determined to embrace pluralism, a "relative relativism" which was centrally committed to the peaceable maintenance of difference within a heterogeneous society, while Frampton has championed a craft-based architecture that would dramatize the physical connections between a society and its locality.[79]

CHARLES JENCKS: LABELISM

The great weapons in Jencks's rhetorical arsenal are the label and the diagram, and he has been an inveterate compiler of both. Though the word "postmodernism" itself has been his greatest success in the labeling department (he did not coin the term but was responsible for its popularization), it is only one of a thicket of categories and trends for which he has coined a neologism: Adhocism, Late Modernism, en-formation, New Tuscanism, slick-tech, neo-vernacular, Radical Eclecticism, and so forth. This welter of terms amounts to an identification (or perhaps an invention) of the lineaments of contemporary architecture, and conveys the strong sense that Jencks views the contemporary architectural landscape as defined not by fixed principles but infinite variety. To reinforce the point, Jencks has repeatedly constructed elaborate visual diagrams that map the field of architectural practice, much in the manner of Alfred Barr's notorious 1936 flow chart of modern art.[80] But while Barr's explanatory diagram is a mapping of forward progress, Jencks's are more like notes from an archaeological dig. Chronology plays a part in his system of historical organization, but everything is retrospective, and there is no narrative of advancement. In this respect he too he was responding to the 1960s, a time that (in cultural geographer J. B. Jackson's memorable phrase) said "goodbye to evolution."[81] The judgments that Jencks makes are consistent with this, in that they tend not to be sweeping statements of philosophy but analyses of individual buildings or architects. The model for his position is that of an art critic, who may have a declared position on the state of things, but is most interested in making incisive aesthetic determinations. To the extent that Jencks speaks of architecture as a whole—as an ethical and social discipline—he limits his moral claims to the principle of pluralism.

Multiplicity lay at the heart of Jencks's first major statement on contemporary architecture, *Adhocism* (1972), written with Nathan Silver. Dedicating itself to the ideal of "a purpose immediately fulfilled," the book examined the phenomenon of self-built housing that was strongly associated with the counterculture of the time.[82] In this period, as historian Terry Anderson has noted, "living cheap became an art, and being poor was hip in America's throwaway society."[83] The attitude was imperfected, as it were, by so-called "woodbutchers," DIY builders whose ramshackle constructions attracted enough attention that a small publishing craze appeared to document them.[84] A few of these self-built houses were in fact well-crafted, but most relied on forms that required little or no skill to construct, such as geodesic domes and adobe huts.[85] The lack of craftsmanship in such buildings became a point of pride in itself, and propagated a down-at-heel aesthetic that was imitated by sculptors as well as professional architects. Jencks approved of this development, later writing that the "approximate craftsmanship" of Californian woodbutchers, the example of their "improvisation, creativity, incongruity and iconic imagery," was crucial in the formation of leading architects such as Frank Gehry and Eric Owen Moss.[86] He adopted the phrase "ad hoc" ("for this" in Latin) to convey the motivations that lay behind such anti-craftsmanship—an ingenious inversion of the thinking about open-ended skill that Dewey and Albers had espoused.

While *Adhocism* is not a text about education per se, Jencks provided his own distinctively polyvalent account of the process of acquiring skills:

> If we are to believe that the experience of art and the learning of skills have any effect on us, then it must be for the most part indirect. That is, our mind is developed and changed mostly unconsciously in multiple ways... If we learned only one skill at a time, or if we were always affected directly by a work of art, it would be a very inefficient way to progress and we should always be victims of our environment. Luckily, learning is much more total and flexible than the Platonic theory of direct influence would have it.[87]

For Jencks, this meant that the kind of controlled experiments with material that Albers had conducted in his classroom (and which had become common in architectural education due to the influence of the Bauhaus) were due for revision: "adhocism consists of a general and loose approach to a problem rather than a tight and specific one."[88] Jencks appealed to Claude Levi-Strauss' anthropological theory of the *bricoleur*, "someone who works with his hands and uses devious means compared with those of a craftsman," and whose "universe of instruments is closed and the rules of his game are always to make do with 'whatever is at hand.'"[89] By taking up this figure as his emblem, Jencks argued that present-day architects should not conceive of their work as heroic or progressive, as Modernists had done, but rather as hostages to fortune—"responsive, individualized, [and] differentiated."[90]

At this early phase in his writing, then, Jencks placed great store by the concept of reactive skill, but distinguished it from the values of exacting craftsmanship. In this respect he was entirely in concert with Robert Venturi, the American architect. Venturi's use of the vernacular, both in his writings and works, is too well known to reprise here; suffice to say that Jencks hewed closely to the precept set out in the architect's groundbreaking 1966 text *Complexity and Contradiction in Architecture*: "it is from the everyday landscape, vulgar and disdained, that we can draw the complex and contradictory order that is valid and vital for our architecture as an urbanistic whole."[91] Of course, Venturi did not consider himself, in terms of architectural method, to be an actual vernacular "builder." (Jencks concurred: "An architecture cannot afford to name everything, spell out all its messages in a clear, denotative language. To insist that it do so would be to reduce it to a revivalist genre: building rather than architecture.")[92] His fascination with the Las Vegas strip, the billboard, and the "almost all right" qualities of Main Street storefronts had nothing to do with the subtleties of their construction and everything to do with their clearly legible symbolism. Indeed, as Jencks pointed out, Venturi specifically premised his work on the realities of "economy and industrial standardization on the one hand and lack of craftsmanship on the other," which left only imagery as a means of creating distinctive buildings.[93]

This focus on symbolism became increasingly central to Jencks's writings. In his most influential book, *The Language of Post-Modern Architecture* (1977), Jencks described the effect that could be realized through what he called "double coding." This was in some ways an extension of the principles of the multiple and the ad hoc that he had previously espoused, but now Jencks's emphasis was on the professional architect rather than the individual consumer. Indeed, while he continued to uphold the principle of a pluralist public for architecture, that public was becoming increasingly abstract, and increasingly defined by their consumption of the built environment rather than their shaping of it. Jencks explained that "Post-modern architecture is doubly-coded, half-Modern and half-conventional, in its attempt to communicate with both the public and a concerned minority, usually architects," noting that unlike a traditional society, in which "the architect, craftsman, and public implicitly understand the same meanings in buildings," there is in contemporary culture an "inevitable disjunction between the elites who create the environment and the various publics that inhabit and use it."[94] He saw postmodern architects like Venturi as populists; the true elitists in his view were "Late Modernists" who insist on the "restricted and hermeneutic language" of their built forms.[95] For Jencks, this was unpardonable egotism. In view of the pluralism of contemporary society, he argued, all authentic responses to a building must be considered equally valid—whether they were incompatible interpretations by specialists, or intuitive misuse or even simple inattention on the part of the public.[96]

If the idea of "double coding" marks a broader transit in Jencks's thought from the ad hoc to the postmodern, then this same transformation could be observed in the broader world of design culture at the time. In a textbook case of sublation (the process by which disruptive cultural elements are absorbed by a hegemonic culture), the ad hoc had become an up-market style.[97] Tanya Harrod has tracked the commodification of the "salvage baroque" look in craft and design, noting that the glass furniture of Danny Lane, for example, "looked subversive while functioning as a good investment."[98] This is another kind of double coding, of course, and while it is not exactly what Jencks had in mind, it could be seen as consistent with his own top-down pluralism. Indeed, in his attempt to avoid centralized elitism, he could be said to have inadvertently exemplified it. It is no coincidence that the grand finale of Jencks's period of centrality to architectural discourse was the design and ensuing publicity campaign of his own home in London. Called "the Thematic House," the space was (as Harrod notes) "hardly ad hoc or alternative."[99] A pretentious arrangement of classical, mythological, and literary motifs, the house was a temple to "symbolic architecture," a theatrical spectacle in which every scene was premised on its own postmodern cipher.[100]

As we will see, it was just such "scenography" that Kenneth Frampton objected to so strenuously. But while the oppositions between Jencks and Frampton are real (and acknowledged in mutual *ad hominem* attacks) it is worth repeating that in the early stage of their careers, both were deeply interested in the notion of open-ended skill, comparable to Dewey's notion of "readiness" or Albers's principle of "thinking in situations." As we have seen, Jencks valued this type of skill because it was necessary to expedient bricolage, something completely separate from the deep commitment of craft. Indeed, he was quite happy to concede that postmodern landmarks such as Michael Graves's 1982 Portland Building were successful partly because they could be built on the cheap: "People sometimes think that Post-Modern buildings are more expensive than Late-Modern ones, because of the ornament, polychromy, and sculpture. But often it's the reverse case because these very same elements can 'hide faults in construction'"[101] (Figure 3.5). Nothing could be further from the lessons that Frampton drew from a similar set of ideas about skill. The possibility that Jencks rejected out of hand—that architecture is best conceived as a craft—would gradually become the central message of Frampton's writing.

KENNETH FRAMPTON: CRAFTING ARCHITECTURE

The genesis of Kenneth Frampton's conceptualization of craft skill can be detected in an early essay on architectural education, focusing on the history of curriculum development at the Hochschule für Gestaltung (HfG) at Ulm. Because the HfG was the direct descendant

Figure 3.5   Michael Graves, Portland Building, 1980. Portland, OR.
Image Courtesy of Michael Graves Associates.

of the Bauhaus, debates about design education there were effectively debates over the legacy of modernism itself. As we have seen, the Bauhaus idea was already multivalent, encompassing Gropius's regulatory notion of technique as well as Albers's nascent conception of skill. Frampton staged his own narrative around the notion of "scientific operationalism," a model that was propounded by the HfG's foundation course leader Tomás Maldonado, which attempted to resolve this underlying conflict between instrumental rationalism and undirected preparedness. There was no chance that the HfG would pursue a course akin to Albers's at Black Mountain; the school was a training ground for architects and industrial designers, pure and simple, and as such it was unapologetically oriented towards producing "specialists" and opposed to generalized "artistic" training.[102] It maintained little investment in craft training. Workshop teaching of any kind was minimal and mostly limited to the fabrication of prototypes. Maldonado was quite conscious of the craft-based teaching of the pre-war modernists, but he wanted to update their precepts so that they would function within the post-war industrial economy. Frampton explained it this way:

> Maldonado praised the progressive aspects of the Bauhaus for its commitment to the 'learning through doing' approach of Hildebrandt, Kerschensteiner, Montessori and Dewey, and for its pragmatic opposition to the verbal emphasis of the humanist tradition. Nevertheless, it was clear that this particular pedagogical approach had now outlived its usefulness and that a new philosophy of praxis was needed. To this end, Maldonado proposed scientific operationalism, of which he remarked, '... it is no longer a question ... of knowledge, but of operational, manipulable knowledge.'[103]

What Maldonado was looking for was a way to rationalize the style of learning championed by Albers—to teach through practice but to do so in a rigorously evaluative manner. His course at the HfG therefore placed great emphasis on mathematics, logic, and information theory. Rather than throwing pots and cutting paper, students now mapped topologies and learned to draw projections of a single form from all sides, as if it were rotating in space. Predictably, this turn in teaching methods did not entirely end the tension between means and ends, but rather displaced it from the ground of craft practice into that of scientific method itself. As Frampton wrote, "the rigour rapidly developed into a form of heuristic determinism and into a logical positivism of design that would often tend to forgo a solution rather than arrive at a synthesis that could not be entirely determined algorithmically."[104] Faculty at the school who were most committed to "practical design," such as Otl Aicher and Hans Gugelot, found this fascination with theory for its own sake to be intolerable, while Maldonado himself was troubled by what he called "method-idolatry."[105] The tension was never fully resolved prior to the school's closing in 1968.

For Frampton, the failure to arrive at a unified curriculum at the HfG was emblematic of a continuing tension between modernist design and modern culture. It was the same old dilemma that had existed in different forms at the Bauhaus, and arguably even in the Arts and Crafts Movement: the fundamental incompatibility of autonomous design values and the realities of economic exigency. Frampton ended his article on the impasse at Ulm with a surprising departure into the broadest of cultural terms:

> Having started its existence as a school of design, in lieu of a school of politics, it was paradoxically returned to its political destiny by men whose lives were dedicated to design. The vicissitudes that their respective theories passed through, over a decade, tend to confirm that this development arose naturally out of adopting a certain attitude towards design. For design as the self-determination of man on earth, through the exercise of his collective *consciousness*, still remains with us as a positive legacy of the Enlightenment.[106]

This seems a non sequitur, perhaps. Yet with these words, Frampton made the leap that would become most characteristic in his work: from questions of design directly to questions of cultural value. He was attracted to the conflicts in curriculum at the HfG because they showed that instrumentality, in contemporary culture, would always remain at war with principles that were authentically based upon material and form.

Though it would be difficult to glean from his seemingly neutral historical account, Frampton was looking to Ulm for confirmation of his core convictions about architecture. These were drawn primarily from his reading of Martin Heidegger and Hannah Arendt. The influence of these two controversial titans of twentieth-century philosophy was decisive for Frampton; in particular, Heidegger's essays "Building, Dwelling, Thinking" and "The Question Concerning Technology" were foundation stones for him. Without attempting to completely review this case of intellectual lineage, it is still possible to discuss Frampton's work of the 1980s in light of the principles that he drew from both essays. Frampton's choice of Heidegger as an intellectual forebear must be counted as something of a surprise. His own politics were Marxist (unlike Jencks's, which might best be described as casually liberal), while Heidegger has been seen as a problematic figure throughout the postwar period because of his association with Nazism.[107] Even more surprising, perhaps, is Frampton's adoption of some of the mystical and essentialist aspects of Heidegger's philosophy at the very moment that deconstruction and postmodernist theory were reaching the height of intellectual currency.[108] None of this prevented him from placing two of Heidegger's ideas at the very center of his writing: first, an opposition to instrumental technology; and second, a conviction that to build is a spiritual activity, in which one's very way of "being in the world" is at stake. These two principles are not only interrelated, but might even be seen as variant expressions of a single, more fundamental idea about "authentic" being and creation.

Heidegger's thinking about architecture rests on the observation that building is only possible from the standpoint of a particular ground. Any construction within space is also the founding of a place, and conversely, as Mark Wigley puts it, "the figure of a building as a grounded structure cannot be discarded to reveal any fundamental ground, as the sense of the 'fundamental' is produced by that very figure."[109] In a lovely evocation of this idea of mutuality, Heidegger writes that a bridge "does not just connect banks that are already there. The banks emerge as banks only as the bridge crosses the stream . . . The bridge *gathers* the earth as landscape around the stream."[110] From this point, Heidegger derives the less self-evident argument that building must acknowledge and address its groundedness in the earth, as the essential character of dwelling. In making this move, he is mounting an objection to the very divide between means and ends with which we have been concerned throughout this chapter:

> Dwelling and building are related as end and means. However, as long as this is all we have in mind, we take dwelling and building as two separate activities, an idea that has something correct in it. Yet at the same time by the means-end schema we block our view of the essential relations. For building is not merely a means and a way toward dwelling—to build is itself already to dwell.[111]

Heidegger applied the same reasoning to craft (which he conceived in the broad sense of *technê*, a Greek word that could mean craftsmanship, art, or simply making) as he did to building.[112] Indeed, as mentioned already, it would be a signature feature of Frampton's writing to presume that building was itself a type of craft, and this too was a premise he borrowed from Heidegger. Just as the creation of a structure results in a dwelling that reveals both the character of the place and that of the people who inhabit it, in craft, the making of a thing "reveals" both the material and the maker simultaneously (in Heidegger's difficult language, "what is brought forth by the artisan or the artist, e.g., the silver chalice, has the bursting open belonging to bringing forth not in itself, but in another, in the craftsman or artist").[113] Modern technology, by contrast, lacks this mutuality and wholeness in the relations between means and ends. Heidegger sees the technology of his own time as purely instrumental, and as "challenging" nature, rather than revealing its authentic being. This was not the case in premodern times, according to Heidegger; in "The Question Concerning Technology," he wrote memorably that "the peasant does not challenge the soil of the field."[114] This particular feature of Heidegger's thought encapsulates the mix of regressive and progressive thought that fascinated Frampton. For if Heidegger here expresses a type of cultural conservatism all too close to that of the Nazi party, he also seems to be ecological theorist *avant la lettre*—he is both a conservative and a conservationist.[115]

Frampton freely acknowledged all of this, and in fact framed his own polemic "Towards A Critical Regionalism" (1983) as an explicitly Heideggerian manifesto for "rear guard" resistance to the prevailing technological culture. "Today civilization tends to be increasingly embroiled in a never-ending chain of 'means and ends,'" Frampton argued, and therefore "the mediation of universal technique involves imposing limits on the optimization of industrial and postindustrial technology."[116] He enlarged on Heidegger's somewhat mystical discussions of actual building with a list of concrete proposals, all of which were directly opposed to the postmodernist, symbolic architecture for which Jencks was the spokesman. Against postmodernism's "gratuitous, quietistic images" Frampton called for an engagement with tactility. Against "pure scenography" (a phrase that irresistibly suggested the highway strip architecture advocated by Venturi and his collaborators Stephen Izenour and Denise Scott Brown) Frampton appealed to the "tectonic . . . a potential means for distilling play between material, craftwork and gravity," an idea to which he would return in greater depth, as we shall see. And against the mobility and "time-space compression" that had been identified as one of the key features of the postmodern condition, Frampton invoked the Italian architect Mario Botta's motto of "building the site."[117] This last point, while seemingly of the least concern to our inquiry into the question of skill, was the most widely discussed feature of "Critical Regionalism," perhaps because the distinction between Venturi's own vernacular imagery and Frampton's emphasis on local conditions was a subtle one—the difference, in effect, between space and place. In a related essay, Frampton distinguished between his critical regionalism and "populism" (the school of Jencks and Venturi, though he did not name them in this context), which he described as a non-critical dispensation of signs.[118] Thus the literal act of building—"the craft enrichment of both form and space" that Frampton found in the work of architects like Botta—was unexpectedly cast in the role of criticality's guarantor.

Like Jencks, Frampton articulated his position through the consideration of specific architects. In light of his early conclusions about the HfG, it is perhaps unsurprising that none of his chosen subjects inhabited a clear modernist or postmodernist position. Rather, he was attracted to architects who turned back the clock to an imaginary moment before that impasse, who exemplified regional modes of building—not only in terms of imagery but also in terms of materials and construction techniques. In addition to Mario Botta, whose works were clearly meant as a return to classical Mediterranean architecture, Frampton's pantheon included historical figures such as Frank Lloyd Wright, Mies van der Rohe, Alvar Aalto, Carlo Scarpa, and Louis Kahn, and contemporaries Alvaro Siza, Arata Isozaki, Tadao Ando, David Chipperfield, and Richard Meier. This was a fairly selective list—as is suggested by the fact that all of these architects were also discussed at greater or lesser length by Jencks, who damned most of them to his purgatories of modernism and "Late-Modernism" (the latter being the brush that he used to tar Frampton himself).[119] Jencks was not above caricaturing Frampton's position, only to damn it with faint praise: "For many ex-Modernists the only way forward is via constructional logic," he wrote:

> and the corollary of this: for strong defenders of Modernism, such as Kenneth Frampton, any use of symbolic or decorative detail is kitsch! This is, of course, an absurd position, but it does help explain the passion with which Neo-Rationalism, or the New Tuscanism, is promoted. Its defenders believe it will further an authentic architecture in an era of commerce. In fact, the approach is also a style like any other and quite defensible as a genre. It has all the beauties of simple prose.[120]

This was a reductive and perhaps even an intellectually dishonest response to Frampton's ideas—it made him out to be a latter-day Adolf Loos, an anti-ornamentalist, which was an unfashionable position indeed in the early 1980s. It would have been more accurate by far to see Frampton as an intellectual descendant of Gottfried Semper, the nineteenth-century proto-modern design theorist. For Semper, all elements of building had an intrinsic logic based on their primordial associations with certain materials and constructive techniques. It is only natural, he argued, that walls should bear ornament, because this is an expression of their ultimate historical root in textiles hung to divide space.[121] Similarly, the articulation of structural members naturally corresponds to basic means of jointing timber uprights and beams—hence the classical column with its capital and entablature. As these ideas suggest, Semper thought that constructional logic could have a life of its own. It could migrate from one medium or situation to another, so that a way of thinking about craftsmanship might develop in the literal hanging of textile and continue to find new applications in the construction of patterned brick walls. These ideas are familiar enough; what is novel in

Frampton's work is the attempt to extend them to create a moral basis for contemporary architecture. The capstone to this line of thinking was the 1995 magnum opus *Studies in Tectonic Culture*. Beginning from the observation that "architecture" derives from the Greek for "master carpenter" (*archi tekton*), Frampton returns us to Semper's discussion of process and material, and tries to set out an idea of architecture as "tectonic," that is, completely bound to thinking through craft. Frampton borrowed this term from the 1963 essay "Structure, Construction, and Tectonics" by the eminent Harvard architectural historian Eduard Sekler, which proposed that tectonics was a way of creating an intensified experience of the abstract principles, the "play of forces," by which a modernist building comes together: "structure, an intangible concept, is realized through construction and given visual expression through tectonics."[122] Citing the Enlightenment philosopher Giambattista Vico's principle *verum ipsum factum* (roughly, "the true is that which is made"), Frampton elaborated this idea into a Heideggerian account of craft, writing that tectonic architecture inhabits "that state of affairs in which knowing and making are inextricably linked; [the] condition in which *technê* reveals the ontological status of a thing through the disclosure of its epistemic value."[123]

One point of particular interest arises from this reframing of craft skill as the paradigm for architectural design. Semper had argued that the joint (*verbindung*) was the crucial detail in architecture, the basic unit of any building's lexicon. Frampton extended this insight, arguing that the devising of a system and a detailed articulation of joinery expressed an architect's complete philosophy of building (and hence, following Heidegger, dwelling). The joint, then, might be described as a central motif within Frampton's broader theory. He does not wish to argue that it is different in kind from any other aspect of a building's creation, but it is nonetheless a juncture at which a building's "tectonic syntax" must be clarified, because it occupies the position where the pressures and tensions of the structure meet. Frampton pointed to the poetry of joining in the work of "seemingly retrograde" architects like Alvar Aalto, who exhibited "deep concern for an appropriately organic aggregation of parts and for the integration of the resultant assembly of parts into the site," or Carlo Scarpa, who "evolved his joints not only as functional connections but as fetishized celebrations of craft as an end in itself."[124] Both of these figures were notable for their drawings as well as their buildings, and Frampton was fascinated by their ability to pursue a unified aesthetic from the moment of setting pencil to paper to the final exquisite detailing of the tectonic structure—he describes Scarpa as possessing a "gesturing impulse passing almost without a break from the act of drafting to the act of making."[125] The Japanese architect Tadao Ando, who was untrained in the discipline apart from a brief apprenticeship with a traditional Japanese carpenter, is perhaps the best contemporary exemplar of this theory of "tectonic syntax." Frampton has approvingly quoted Ando as writing: "Detail exists as the most important element in expressing identity... Thus to me the detail is an element which achieves the physical composition of architecture, but at the same time, it is a generator of an image of architecture."[126] Ando is in Frampton's view "a builder rather than an architect" (note the inversion of Jencks's description of his own emblematic architect, Venturi), whose work achieves through exacting craftsmanship "the palpability of things in all their characteristic purity."[127]

But this is not to imply that Frampton espoused a simple celebratory materialism. Frederic Jameson, in a précis of Frampton's thought, has noted that his emphasis on detail and tactility, which initially seems to be a conservative call for exquisitely built form, is in fact a call for architects to "reopen and transfigure the burden of the modern" through a fundamental and structural engagement with "forces in opposition."[128] This point can be clarified by comparing Jencks and Frampton's readings of particular architects. The figure of Mies van der Rohe, for example, functions for Jencks as a cartoon villain, or perhaps a father-figure to be slain through Oedipal critique. For Frampton, by contrast, he is a model of productive engagement with the tectonic. This difference results in completely opposing readings of Mies's buildings. For Jencks, formal languages of architecture must read didactically and clearly; architecture is a means of communication. For Frampton architectural form is at its most interesting when it is caught in an internal dialectic—crafting space in a way that shows the intrinsic tensions of the medium. Thus Jencks sees Mies's modernism as a "univalent" system of reductive form, "fetishized to the point where it overwhelms all other concerns (in a similar way the leather boot dominates the show fetishist and distracts him from larger concerns)."[129] Frampton, on the other hand, is fascinated by Mies's struggle between building and architecture, objective craftsmanship and abstract space, and sees this opposition as the key to an understanding of his career. In Mies's greatest buildings, such as the Barcelona Pavilion, "the suppression of the tectonic in the planar space-endlessness of the interior finds its countervailing reification through the careful placement of material and the precision of small-scale detail."[130]

A similar divergence between Jencks and Frampton manifests itself with regard to the Japanese architect Arata Isozaki. Both critics perceive Isozaki as working in a language of disjunction. For Jencks, this is a matter of mannerist "Late-Modernism." Isozaki's vivid juxtapositions of unrelated masses (which Jencks calls "smash joints") express structure "vehemently" rather than "honestly."[131] Frampton, however, sees exactly the same qualities in Isozaki's buildings as an expression of the conflict between architecture's tectonic ontology (the simple being of the building) and its social aspect (the communication of institutional identity through symbolism). For Frampton this dialectic has guided Isozaki's entire career, beginning with a modernist "dematerialized neutrality" in the 1960s, in which an abstract space is established through rectilinear concrete frames, and moving to an emphatically regionalist, fragmentary tectonic style in the 1970s and 1980s.[132] Frampton describes Isozaki's buildings of this mature period as resolving the conflict between the ontological and the semiotic. Thus he praises the 1975 Yano House, with its massive vaulted concrete roof placed disjunctively atop a thin, planar box of concrete and glass, for its "inscription into the site," its reference to ancient Japanese burial mounds, and its economical manner of construction, poured into molds on the site in order to perfectly

Figure 3.6   Arata Isozaki, *Yano House*, 1975. Kawasaki, Japan.
Image Courtesy of Arata Isozaki and Associates. Photograph by Yasuhiro Ishimoto.

match the meandering topology of the ground (Figure 3.6). For Frampton, Isozaki is an architect redeemed by the symbolic use of craft.[133]

Though Frampton has written little about the notion of skill, his theoretical edifice is in some sense built upon it. In Frampton's view, one learns architecture by doing. Despite the fact that he is a faculty member at a graduate school of architecture, he insists that "architecture is a craft-based practice closely tied to the lifeworld and, for this reason, it sits uncomfortably within the university."[134] Learning and making are, for Frampton, different aspects of the same activity of architectural becoming. The process never stops—not when the architect leaves school, not when the first sketches of a building are finished, not when the construction is in place, not when the final details are complete, not even when the public experiences the "presencing" of the resulting structure by inhabiting it. To draw a building is already to implicate oneself in the world that it will constitute, and to dwell in a building is to grasp it as a site of continual revelation, attained through direct engagement with the resistances and possibilities of site and material. Every stage of building must also be a moment in which one learns how to build, for it is only in this way that the tectonic can come into being.

CONCLUSION: SKILL AND THE HUMAN CONDITION

Today, the disagreements between Jencks and Frampton—an overlooked debate about craft within the very heart of postmodern theory—may seem remote, and our two protagonists somewhat unfashionable. Jencks's breezy classification schemes doubtless paved the way to today's architecture culture, with its orientation toward celebrity architects and its prioritization of the visual over the tactile—though the scenographic has now arguably been largely replaced by the photogenic. Yet no one seems to need Jencks to explain the map to them anymore. He is so closely identified with the emergence of postmodernism that he has become something of a museum piece. Frampton's reputation, meanwhile, suffers from his deep affinity (never fashionable in the first place) with essentialist mystical philosophy. More importantly, perhaps, Frampton's key ideas of critical regionalism and the tectonic seem ill-suited to the present moment of breathtaking global fluidity and computer-aided design. Rem Koolhaas, architecture's currently reigning theoretical high priest, regards Frampton's essentialism of place to be deeply suspect, if not naïve. "Critical regionalism has turned into hyper-regionalism," he argues, "a fabrication of regional difference after its erasure and disappearance."[135] What Frampton might call the "technique" of mass culture has radically improved, so that its ability to simulate individuated needs and even histories (or, from a marketing point of view, demographics) has become nearly total.

Equally, Frampton's rear-guard move into craft has led to the traditional criticism leveled against the modernist avant garde—that resistant formalism, even if nobly conceived, can never be effective in changing the wider state of affairs. Margali Sarfatti Larson, for example, wrote in 1993 that "Frampton's idea of critical architecture returns to an ideological concentration on the aesthetic and semiotic properties immanent in single architectural objects, as if they were by themselves capable of reversing the effects of modernization. The effect is to render the real social implications of building even more opaque."[136] In this respect, perhaps Jencks was on to something when he dismissed critical regionalism on the grounds that it was "not very radical (it was after all an in-house revolution)."[137] Yet Frampton's theorization of craft still has the clarifying effect of redirecting attention to the underlying realities of the built environment. His writings on the tectonic, and his championing of "architecture as a unique form of craft-based knowledge," have the real potential to serve as a corrective to the post-postmodern architectural environment in which we find ourselves, with its "Bilbao effects" on the one hand and complete mall-like standardization on the other.[138]

Most importantly for my purposes, Frampton shows how profitable it can be to think about craft skill in the most general of terms, as Dewey and Albers conceived it: not as a discrete set of techniques, but as a way of being within society. His mobilization of materialist analysis in the service of cultural critique is strongly reminiscent of the perceptions that Michael

Baxandall found in the lineaments of limewood. Frampton reminds us that through the mechanism of skill, the builder (like the carver) engages with the internal forces of material; these, in turn, provide a set of constraints that test and shape the building. In the process, the material becomes the cultural. He also encourages us to think about craft broadly, in a way that both respects the qualities of particular disciplines (like architecture) and transcends their self-assigned limits. It is a set of ideas that seem overdue. What Baxandall was able to do for sixteenth-century woodcarvers, after all, we ought to be able to do for ourselves.

4 PASTORAL

Even if you've never done it yourself, you can probably imagine what it's like to depart from a summer craft program after a few days, weeks, or months (Figure 4.1). Ideally, you are refreshed and ready to rejoin the regular flow of life, but you also look back on your time with a twinge of longing. You might even be nostalgic—though your longing will be for something that has only just ended. This sentiment might be fleeting, or it may stay with you for a time, but eventually it will fade from memory. After all, the whole point of summertime idyll is that it doesn't last forever. Yet, despite its seeming transience, it might be said that this backwards-looking moment, and its distinctive tenor of pleasant regret, is in fact the big payoff for spending a summer in the woods. It is a feeling of having

Figure 4.1   The Pines dining hall at the Penland School of Crafts, Penland, North Carolina, c. 1977. William J. and Jane Brown papers, Archives of American Art. Photograph: Bill Brown.

participated in something pure and fragile, which is distant from the "real world" but also yields deeper understanding of that world—a bit of perspective, perhaps. It is, in short, the pastoral feeling.

Pastoral. The word, and the sense of removal from worldly affairs that it connotes, has been a fixture in literature since classical times. In ancient pastoral poems the main figures are shepherds (*pastores* in Latin), whose freedom from labor permits them to spend their time indulging in philosophical rumination. The shepherds' meditations are invariably set in idealized natural surroundings, a fictional "no-place" (*Utopia*). The Roman poet Virgil set his pastoral works in Arcadia, named after a region of Greece renowned for its scenic rusticity. The first known pastoral poems, the *Bucolics* of Theocritus, amount to a loosely organized evocation of the pleasures of tranquility. The shepherds in the narrative discuss matters of philosophy and love; as far as subject matter goes, their conversation might be occurring at any place and in any time. Their removal from the world of affairs is not only spatial but also temporal: the shepherds played the starring role in ancient pastoral literature not only because they stayed in the fields all day, but because their profession predated the dawn of civilization and law.[1] The shepherd is, then, an allegorical figure, who stands for removal not only from the city but also from history itself. The countryside that the shepherd inhabits is an asylum that, even in the earliest pastoral poems, seems to be in the process of slipping away.[2]

The crucial feature of pastoral, then—and the aspect of it that makes it so useful as a stance in everything from art to literature to the crafts—is that it occupies two levels of meaning simultaneously. While reading a pastoral text, we are aware that the action is intended as a symbolic ideal, rather than as narrative for its own sake; furthermore, we are aware of our own awareness of that fact, and it is this higher order pleasure that constitutes the interest when reading the text. In his 1935 study *Some Versions of the Pastoral*, the literary theorist William Empson broadly reinterpreted the mode as the general practice of "putting the complex into the simple."[3] With this formula Empson claimed for pastoral a whole range of literary phenomena that had nothing to do with retreat into nature *per se*. As Thomas Crow has written, Empson saw the pastoral as "any work in which a distinctive voice is constructed from the implied comparison between an author's suitably large artistic ambitions and his or her inevitably limited horizons and modest strengths."[4] This strategy would include such conventions as placing great poetry into a shepherd's mouth, or setting out the hard truth about King Lear through the words of a fool.

Despite Empson's attempts to rehabilitate it, however, pastoral has always occupied the lowest rung on the ladder of literary modes. It has often been said that the pastoral mode wins its reflective qualities only at the price of an inability to deal concretely with cultural reality, as the author takes refuge from complex cultural problems in evocations of an imagined, simpler realm.[5] And it is striking how completely craft exemplifies both the positive and negative aspects of pastoral: its double structure—in which making a chair or pot is valued not only in itself but also as a symbolic gesture about the value of lifestyle, integrity, and so forth—but also its tendency towards sentimental escapism. Both aspects of the pastoral lie at the heart of the history and the mythology of the craft movement. The summer schools just mentioned, places like Haystack in Maine or West Dean in Sussex, are obvious examples. Sited at a conspicuous remove from cities, they are places where one encounters vernacular architecture, natural food, and fund-raising events that recall a livestock auction at a country fair. Yet despite their seeming purity and innocence, summer crafts schools are highly self-conscious and purposefully constructed places. They are the direct descendants of such reformist enterprises as the Byrdcliffe colony in Woodstock and Dartington Hall in Devon, sites that were organized by wealthy benefactors for the purpose of idealistic social experimentation. From William Morris's rural retreat Kelmscott Manor to Sam Maloof's woodworking studio in an Alta Loma lemon grove, the pastoral stance has animated many of the sacred sites of the craft movement.[6] It would not be too much to say that the ambitions and limitations of craft as a cultural force cannot be sufficiently described *without* using the self-reflective language of pastoral. In schools, communities, and individual workshops, the dream of wise shepherds is re-enacted annually, as craftspeople eagerly suspend their worldly entanglements and join in the collective pursuit of "true" experience.

Of course, it would be wrong to say that the pastoral inclination is particular to crafts-people. Empson found it throughout modern literature, and as we will see, it is a theme that runs strongly through postwar art as well. Nor would it be correct to say that craftspeople are universally in thrall to the pastoral ideal. The "designer-craftsman" impulse of the 1950s, in which traditional hand skills were placed at the service of mass production, is an obvious exception. So too are the ambitious artistic careers of such figures as Peter Voulkos and Dale Chihuly—or, at the other end of the status spectrum, the small-batch commercial producers who ring the cash registers at innumerable high-end craft fairs. Yet even such attempts to insert craft into the center have won much of their success from an underlying pastoral myth. Designer-craftsmen, for example, often appealed to the argument that a craftsperson offered a pre-industrial legitimacy that would indirectly ennoble the eventual mass-produced object. It is crucial to the lasting reputations of craft heroes like Voulkos and Chihuly that they are seen as outsiders who triumphed over the supposed prejudice of an unsympathetic art world. And similarly, the main thing that distinguishes the craft fair from the suburban mall that is supposedly its antithesis is the resonance of the "old days" when vendors pitched their booths in the fields. From such examples it is clear that in the crafts, authenticity always seems to be just out of view, around the historical bend. This way of thinking can be seductive, but it can also be misleading. As the literary critic Raymond Williams has observed, the pastoral often hides the hard truths of commerce behind a veil of decorous sentiment.[7] Yet when the pastoral is not simply a pair of rose-colored glasses—when it is occupied self-consciously, rather than in a celebratory or promotional manner—it can be a powerful way of envisioning social and artistic change.

The question of pastoral cuts to the core of craft's potential as a cultural instrument. To what extent does craft constitute an opportunity for real creative freedom, in which critique, perspective and individualism can flourish? And, conversely, to what extent is it simply a Utopian prop, a story we tell ourselves to assuage our anxieties in an increasingly fluid, technological society? This dilemma cuts across all cultural contexts for craft. A commune emphasizes process and experience over product and aesthetics; a museum, the reverse. But how should craft be grounded at these two sites economically, geographically, and spiritually? On what grounds should it be encouraged, by what standards judged? Many of the claims made for craft have been structured around varied and competing responses to this dilemma.

One can imagine these claims along a continuum. At the "right" end, to use an overly simplistic political metaphor, one finds artists and events that focus on elevating the mainstream status of the movement. The main venues for advancement at this pole are private galleries and museum exhibitions, particularly large-scale undertakings such as *Objects: USA* (which toured thirty museums in America and Europe between 1969 and 1972); *The Craftsman's Art* (held at the Victoria & Albert Museum in 1973); and *Craft Today: Poetry of the Physical* (organized by the American Craft Museum, 1986). The effect of such projects, whatever their internal variations and inconsistencies, has been to consolidate the idea of craft as an institution, a community, or a field. As weaver and basket-maker Ed Rossbach put it in 1972, *Objects: USA* "seemed to formalize the past, chronicle it into a permanent bound volume, the authorized version. Modifications and corrections would be accomplished only with great difficulty."[8] Against this centralizing tendency there has been a "left"-leaning, pastoral desire to see craft as something loose in the landscape, unfettered by any particular institutional configuration. While less coherent by definition, this perspective has certainly had moments of dominance—the peak of craft's popularity as a cultural phenomenon, after all, coincided with the rise of the counterculture and quintessentially pastoral ethos of "dropping out."

As in electoral politics, however, it is not at the poles that craft's identity is decided, but in the broad middle. As palpable as the success of a big city museum exhibition or the purity of a backwoods pottery may seem, such extremes are in fact the exception rather than the rule. For most people involved with craft, advance and retreat are inseparable from one another, and blend in contradictory (or at least confusing) ways. Pastoral craft is at its most interesting when it collides head on with reality, and shapes itself to fit. For, as Fiona MacCarthy has written, "the simple life was never for the simple minded."[9]

REGIONS APART

Raymond Williams's *The Country and the City* of 1973 was conceived as a critique of the tendency in traditional pastoral "to promote superficial comparisons and to prevent real ones."[10] Whereas Empson, in *Some Versions of Pastoral*, had been content with the symbolic literary strategy of containing "the complex within the simple"—thus implying that the simple itself was unexpectedly complex—Williams wanted literature to speak of the class inequities of the real world.[11] He was deeply suspicious of the backwards-looking character of pastoral writing, and its tendency to view rural culture as static and harmonious, rather than dynamic and conflicted. He therefore insisted upon careful attention to "the roots that are being defended" in a pastoral text, "the natural economy, the moral economy, the organic society, from which the critical values are drawn."[12] He argued that pastoral was a weapon, which could be used on both sides of class conflict. The projections of a rural "golden age" in the writings of country-house poets, a pastoral literature which tacitly claimed the inherent superiority of the gentry, was answered by the (equally pastoral) folk idea of an ideal time of equality, prior to gentry ownership of the land.[13]

There is an important sense in which Williams's book is itself a pastoral text: a tribute paid by a sophisticated writer to the independent rural yeomanry. But there is nothing of condescension in *The Country and the City*. Nor does Williams ever abstract the pastoral to the point at which it is completely disconnected from the actual field of cultural production. Nowhere is this clearer than in the autobiographical portions of the book, in which he vividly describes his own experience of Welsh farming community as anything but a fixed abstraction.[14] When Leo Marx reviewed *The Country and the City* soon after its publication, he expressed sympathy both with Williams's dissatisfaction with the classical pastoral, and with the argument that "rural life is no less a part of the cultural environment than urban life... To equate the country with man in nature and the city with man in society is simply wrong, a false dichotomy that has contributed to a lot of muddled thinking."[15]

To what extent has craft, in the twentieth century, been a means for achieving the self-conscious, realist model of the pastoral that Williams advocated? And to what extent, conversely, has it been a means of effacing the realities of rural life through a combination of idealism and abstraction? There is no easy answer to this question, because craft has been implicated in every variation along this spectrum. In many cases, pastoral craft has been part of a purposeful invention of an "authentic" past—as in the romantic nationalist movements of the turn of the century. We might think very differently about particular cases of such constructions of imaginary craft history, depending on the politics of the revival in question. Thus, while we are charmed by the fanciful medieval design of Scottish Arts and Crafts jewelry, textiles and furniture, we are repulsed by the rather similar gestures to lost cultural purity that were associated with Italian fascism.[16] Faced with such complexity and difference, I have chosen four examples to indicate a range of possibilities —rural Gloucestershire in England, the Southern Highlands of Appalachia, Korea, and the American Midwest—that are as disparate ideologically as they are geographically. Scholars have discussed all of these examples previously, and they could easily be exchanged for other, similar stories. But it is my hope that juxtaposing them will show the remarkable prevalence of that characteristically pastoral combination, laudable idealism and tragic self-deception. Taken together, these examples provide ample validation of Terence Conran's epigrammatic observation: "the crafts revival is a very tangible metaphor of a culture at odds with the very industrial principles that made it possible."[17]

THE COTSWOLDS

The dichotomous nature of pastoral craft was already present in the British Arts and Crafts Movement, with its conflicting roots in romantic anti-modernism and revolutionary social-ism.[18] Nowhere was this split personality more evident than in the Cotswolds, an area of Gloucestershire, England. Much has been written about the occupation of this economically backward region by Arts and Crafts figures. The chief protagonists were C. R. Ashbee, the idealistic leader of the Guild of Handicraft, which moved from the East End of London to the town of Chipping Campden in 1902; and a group of three architects—the brothers Ernest and Sidney Barnsley, and their friend Ernest Gimson—who established a workshop near Sapperton in 1894 and continued working in the area. The difference between these two cases bears out what seems to be an unwritten law of pastoral: the more purposefully a practice is distinguished from the normative state of affairs, the less likely it is to sustain itself.

The Barnsleys and Gimson were certainly no commercial pragmatists, but their ambi-tions were modest in scale. When they moved to the countryside, they had little desire to either engage with or disturb the realities of their new environment. They lived the pastoral dream with gusto, inhabiting scenic surroundings while making crafts in a small shop. All were well-to-do, and did not need to rely on their crafts as a way of making a living. Initially they lived in a dilapidated manor house at Pinbury Park, on the estate of their patron Lord Bathurst, moving subsequently to homes of their own design in the nearby village of Sapperton. As Tanya Harrod has written, their work "reflected the social extremes of this semi-feudal ambience," vacillating between self-conscious "grandeur" and unaffected simplicity.[19] Though their absorption of a regional vernacular is celebrated— chamfering drawn from the vocabulary of the wheelwright, joints taken from the bracing on field-clearing rakes, the subtle curves of axe hafts, and heavy lattices imitating the side of local haycarts—these borrowings were purely symbolic details grafted on to the trappings of pretentious middle-class living, such as sideboards, writing desks, china cabinets, and elaborate metal firedogs (Figure 4.2). Sidney Barnsley, a good candidate for history's first "studio furniture maker," was the most avid of the trio, working by himself in his own shop and executing only his own designs. Gimson, who did little furniture-making himself, made the somewhat eccentric choice of concentrating his efforts on plasterwork in direct imitation of Elizabethan court interiors.

The three men were literate in the history of furniture, having become well acquainted in London with the rich holdings of the South Kensington (later the Victoria & Albert) Museum through their design work. As a result, the basic forms of their work were drawn from an array of sources that were anything but local. German baroque cabinets, the Spanish *vargueño*, and the fielded panels and applied moldings of seventeenth-century *ébenistes* all exerted an influence. When a trained Dutch cabinetmaker named Peter van der Waals came to work in Gimson's shop, the local oak that previously previously been the mainstay of production was abandoned in favor of figured exotic veneers. Yet the same men, particularly

Figure 4.2   Ernest Barnsley, *Wardrobe*, 1902. Manufactured at the Daneway House Workshops, Gloucestershire, England. Oak. Victoria & Albert Museum.

Sidney Barnsley, produced "country" furniture of an obviously pastoral kind—trestle dining tables, humble rush-seated chairs in imitation of regional ladderbacks, and massive lidded chests.

The equanimity with which Gimson and the Barnsleys shuttled between these two opposing tendencies attests to their relaxed, non-ideological approach to the Arts and Crafts experiment. In nearby Chipping Campden, however, a very different kind of pastoral was unfolding. C. R. Ashbee, a follower of William Morris and a remarkably pure exponent of Arts and Crafts movement philosophy, determined to move his Guild of Handicraft (previously located in London's East End) out to the country. Ashbee too was willing to be flexible—"directing the life and work of artisans on one day, hobnobbing with the aristocracy the next," as Stefan Muthesius has noted—but only in the service of his own wide-eyed idealism, which was non-negotiable.[20] Indeed, if one had to identify a single impractical pastoralist standing at the heart of the Arts and Crafts Movement, then Ashbee would be an outstanding candidate. He was marvelously idealistic in ways both good and bad, doing his best to eliminate class distinction within the Guild's shops, creating an environ-ment of genuine equality between the sexes, and dedicating himself to the improvement of education in the village. At the same time, he inadvertently allowed "real" cottagers to be turned out of their homes to make way for the Guildsmen, who were willing to pay higher rents, and was initially blind to the inequities in pay between his own craftsmen and local workers.[21] He underestimated the suspicion and outright hostility that his group of socialists would encounter in Campden, as well as the privations the Guildsmen themselves would experience in what seemed to them to be "primitive" surroundings. Ashbee was also a poor businessman (and in some respects rejected even the principle that one should have to manage a group enterprise), and completely unequal to the task of handling competition with the Guild's products when it arrived in the form of jewelry by the London firm Liberty. In the end his rural experiment lasted just five years, from 1902 to 1907. As Alan Crawford, Ashbee's biographer, puts it: "It was naïve of Ashbee to think that a workshop employing as many as seventy men could be set down in the country all at once and survive; its skills belonged to the city, and so did its patterns of employment."[22]

The story of Ashbee is poignant, and would be faintly comic were it not also disturbing. Even those without a trace of nostalgia for the "simple life" must feel a twinge when re-flecting on the Guild of Handicraft's conclusive demonstration that craft for its own sake was untenable. But Ashbee's complete failure to comprehend his own situation—the real nature of either his own goals or the community around him—is precisely the fault that Raymond Williams identifies as typical of pastoral thinking. As Annette Carruthers has succinctly written, no sooner had Ashbee arrived in Arcadia than he "was impatient to change the place to suit his vision of how it should be."[23] Yet, as Tanya Harrod has shown, the Cotswolds lived on in the British pastoral imagination well into the 1930s. Writers continued to extol its "Arcadian" qualities while worrying over its poverty, just as Ashbee had done, while Peter van der Waals and Edward Barnsley (Sidney's son) carried on producing furniture in the "Cotswolds" style.[24] In more recent years, somewhat counter-intuitively, Ashbee's failed experiment has been used as a stick with which to beat the present. In 1984, for example, the British woodworker Richard LaTrobe-Bateman contrasted the "Englishness untouched by the cosmopolitan pursuit of style" personified by Gimson and the Barnsleys with the "Art Camp" of his own day. "We can guess what the Sapperton group would have thought of jewellery that is intended to be unusable and grab attention by this unusability, pots that hold nothing, don't even stand up, and chairs that are a menace in use, however metaphorically elevating they may be."[25] LaTrobe-Bateman himself took the pastoral challenge quite literally, involving himself in such site-specific tasks as building ecologically sound bridges in natural settings (Figure 4.3). In such works it is clear that the underlying conflicts of the Cotswolds continue to linger in the minds of British craftspeople—a

Figure 4.3 Richard LaTrobe-Bateman, *Diamond Truss Bridge*, 1995.
English oak and galvanized steel. Engineered by Mark Lovell.
National Pinetum, Bedgebury, Kent. Courtesy of the artist.

testament to the peculiar nature of pastoral, which seems most convincing when it is most disconnected from reality.

APPALACHIA

There is of course another common meaning of the term "pastoral," which refers to a clergyman's shepherding of his flock. In the early part of the twentieth century, the Appalachian region of the American South witnessed this overtly religious meaning intermixed with the socially committed impulse common to pastoral, with impressive results. The protagonists of this moment were well-to-do women, self-styled missionaries who saw themselves as bringing propriety, prosperity, and Christianity to the backward population of the Southern Highlands.[26] Charlotte Yale and Eleanor Park Vance, for example, founded Biltmore Estate Industries in 1905, in order to put their own Arts and Crafts training (in ceramics and woodcarving, respectively) to use. With the backing of George and Edith Vanderbilt, they organized local men, women and children in the production of carved boxes and furnishings, baskets, embroidery, and woven "homespun" coverlets.[27] Frances Louisa Goodrich, who came from wealthy Presbyterian stock, had studied art at Yale prior to her own move to Appalachia. Her career in the mountains also began with missionary work, but grew steadily in ambition. By the 1920s she was running a sort of craft empire called Allanstand Cottage Industries, based in Ashville, North Carolina. Though Goodrich was just as much a pastoralist as C. R. Ashbee, her strategy could not have been more different. Assigning herself the responsibility "to save from extinction and to develop the old-time crafts of the mountains," she worked tirelessly to make Highlands craft activity commercially viable.[28] Her efforts culminated in 1930 with the chartering of the Southern Highland Handicrafts Guild, an umbrella organization that set policy for the region's craft production, helped to organize archives and educational initiatives, tried to "raise and maintain standards in design," and most importantly, promoted Appalachian crafts nationally.[29]

To put it mildly, the ambitions and perspectives of women like Yale, Vance and Goodrich were not necessarily reflective of those held by the workers under their administrative guidance. Nor was there any dissimulation on this point. While Ashbee had tried his best to break down class divisions between himself, the Guildsmen, and the Cotswolds locals, and even the comparatively wealthy Gimson was quite pleased when on a trip to London he was mistaken for a farmer, the Appalachian missionaries had no intention of merging with the population they sought to help. Theirs was a paternalistic pastoral, which envisioned the Highlanders as something like a different race magically preserved from times long gone by—"our contemporary ancestors" in William Goodell Frost's phrase.[30] The region's crushing poverty was central to this attitude, because it simultaneously justified intervention into a situation that was perceived to be pristine, and seemed to somehow prove the Highlanders' authenticity. This hypocritical attitude towards local hardship was a real-world version of one of William Empson's perceptions about the devices of pastoral literature: "The simple man ... can speak the truth because he has nothing to lose."[31]

A telltale sign of the fundamental difference between the Appalachian craft "revival" and its superficially similar precedents in the Arts and Crafts movement is its extensive use of two means of promoting mountain crafts: the photograph and the demonstration. These two techniques framed craft activity for middle-class consumption, and permitted Highlands crafts promoters like Goodrich to do their benevolent work while remaining at one remove from actual production. Photography's role in presenting Appalachia to the outside world has been much commented upon because of the prominence of Walker Evans and James Agee's *Let Us Now Praise Famous Men* (1941), a piece of artful agitprop that found pastoral poetry in the grinding destitution of three mountain families. Less well known, but similar in tactics and intent, was the 1937 publication *Handicrafts of the Southern Highlands* by Allen H. Eaton, with images by Doris Ullman. Evans's colleague in the Works Progress Administration corps of photographers, Ullman (who died in 1934, before the book was published) contributed images that were carefully staged, sometimes using costumes and props for effect (Figure 4.4).[32] Eaton, for his part, may not have been the writer that Agee was, but he conveys the attitudes of craft missionary work with great effectiveness:

Figure 4.4   Doris Ullman, "Corn Husk Seats."
In Allen H. Eaton, *Handicrafts of the Southern Highlands*, 1937. The
caption for the image reads: "Mrs. Lucy Lakes of Berea, Kentucky,
is an expert weaver of corn husks. Her hands are shown here
splicing, twisting, and braiding the corn husks for a stool seat."

That great penalties have been paid by many mountain families for the privations they
have endured and that a heavy toll has been taken in both physical and mental debilities,
are grim facts which those who know the situation admit. Nevertheless these secluded
people have won the devotion of persons who in one capacity or another are lending
aid to the various enterprises in the region, primarily because Highlanders crave above
everything the opportunity to develop their own potentialities.[33]

In the postwar period, photography has continued to be a mainstay of the rhetoric surrounding Appalachian "folk art." The fetishization possible through a camera's lens even extends to the fragmentation and isolation of the functional parts of a craftsman's body. As Julia Ardery has argued, if it is vital that a mountain carver be described as working with his "old pocketknife" (even if he actually needs to replace his knives frequently because the blades become dull), then it is equally important that his gnarled hands be shown in closeup.[34] A photograph of a Highlands artisan is always more still life than portrait.

Live craft demonstrations have been no less effective in conveying the romantic ideal of Appalachian crafts to the broader public. It may be difficult to imagine a time when such entertainments were not commonplace but in fact it was only in the context of international expositions, beginning (tellingly) with ethnographic displays in the late nineteenth century, and continuing in the Century of Progress exposition (Chicago, 1933) and the National Folk Festival (St. Louis, 1934), that the craft demonstration was developed in its modern form.[35] The demonstration, like a photograph, is a second-order phenomenon, a representation.[36] In staging craft as a performance—play-acting, often in costume, in a manner that was analogous to singing, fiddling, or story-telling happening at the same events—a demonstration powerfully condenses the unreal construction of Appalachia in general. Nor has its popularity subsided in decades since. The craft demonstration is now a sacred tradition in its own right, kept alive by such organizations as the Ozark Folk Center in Arkansas, the Kentucky Guild of Artists and Craftsmen, and the Southern Highland Handicrafts Guild itself. It remains one of the main tourist draws of Appalachia to this day.

KOREA

Another broad and rich vein of pastoral craft in the twentieth century was the Japanese *mingei* movement. The term (a contraction of *minshuteki kogei*, or "folk craft") was coined by the theorist Yanagi Sōetsu and embraced by a nexus of Japanese artists and intellectuals including the potters Kawai Kanjirō, Kaneshige Toyo, Kitaoji Rosanjin, and Hamada Shōji, the printmaker Munakata Shikō, and the English émigré Bernard Leach. It has been used mostly to refer to peasant crafts—baskets, ceramics, woodcraft, ironwork, fabric dyeing, and other media.[37] These seemed to Yanagi and those who subscribed to his ideas to possess an unblemished, pre-modern, natural, and hence universal integrity. Comparable folk craft traditions in disparate areas of the world were identified and heralded for a similar preservation of cultural home truths. Leach, for example, found *mingei* characteristics in the slip-decorated ceramics of seventeenth-century England, and duly imitated them in his own work (see Plate 10). Hamada's Mingei Reference Collection Museum in Mashiko, a pottery town situated a respectable distance from Tokyo, included material from Okinawa, Spain, the Americas, and the Middle East. But Korean ceramics, particularly white wares from the Yi dynasty, were the objects that the *mingei* group most admired. What distinguished these pots, in the minds of their modern admirers, was their concentration of skill and subtlety into deceptively unpretentious forms—the ceramic equivalent of "putting the complex into the simple."

What has disturbed some recent historians of *mingei* is that this attitude implied that Koreans themselves were "simple." Yanagi, for one, left no doubt as to his commitment to this principle. In perhaps his most famous essay, extolling the virtues of "Kizaemon," a Korean stoneware rice bowl that had been elevated to the position of a treasure by tea connoisseurs, he wrote:

> In Korea such work was left to the lowest. What they made was broken in kitchens, almost an expendable item. The people who did this were clumsy yokels, the rice they ate was not white, their dishes were not washed... But that was as it should be. The plain and unagitated, the uncalculated, the harmless, the straightforward, the natural, the innocent, the humble, the modest: where does beauty lie if not in these qualities?[38]

The problem for those who believed in such rhetoric was twofold. First, Korea was not a fictional Arcadia. Beginning in the 1870s, Japan had gradually involved itself in a struggle with China and Russia over the question of influence on the Korean peninsula and Manchuria. In two wars, first with China in 1894–5 and more conclusively in 1904–5 with Russia, Japan had asserted its interests militarily. It formally annexed Korea in 1910. Though these developments were cloaked in a language of "protection" of the Korean people against foreign aggression, in fact they were a key turning point in Japan's long climb to imperialism, which would have such disturbing political consequences in ensuing decades. As the historian Yuko Kikuchi has forcefully argued, Yanagi found himself in a conflicted position with regard to the Korean question.[39] On the one hand, he frequently condemned Japanese expansionism, particularly after atrocities were committed in 1919 and 1923 in an attempt to suppress Korean uprisings against colonial authority.[40] On the other hand, Yanagi could be seen as complicit with Japanese policy. His regular trips to the peninsula (on some occasions in the company of Leach, Hamada, and Kawai), his collecting of Korean ceramics and other artifacts, and especially his official activities organizing exhibitions in Seoul, would have been impossible without the enabling mechanisms of the imperial occupation government.[41] More disturbingly, Yanagi also used formulations in his writings that were common amongst imperial apologists. The description of Koreans as "childlike," for example, was a staple of writings in *mingei* commentary and in imperialist rhetoric alike.[42] For Yanagi, the political plight of the Koreans even seems to have become a subject of aesthetic appreciation in its own right. As Kikuchi has shown, central to his writings on Korean art was the "sentimental and dogmatic" idea of *hiai no bi* ("beauty of sadness"), which could be found in formal features as diverse as a milky white glaze or the meandering line of a jar's profile.[43] Leach had made similar claims in 1920: "The unique and excellent Corean line runs through it all, sharp, sweet, sad, and twines itself round one's heart. I saw it in the hills, in the hats of the men, the hair of the women, and the shoes of both."[44] It is difficult not to see in such mysterious characterizations the pastoral erasure of real history that Raymond Williams warns against.

A second problem in *mingei* theory was less specific to the context of early twentieth-century politics, but just as thorny: how could the artistic attitudes of a medieval peasant be recreated in twentieth-century Japan? *Mingei*'s combination of veneration and condescension towards the country potter was difficult to resolve into an image of the modern craftsman. Edmund de Waal has argued of Yanagi's essay on the Kizaemon teabowl that it exposes the "self-abnegating" aspects of this ideal. The modern craftsman, in De Waal's analysis, is cursed by "the Edenic fall into self-consciousness, the fall into language that comes in childhood."[45] In the face of this loss of innocence, the modern craftsman's grasping towards authenticity entails a discipline of self-denial.

Hamada Shōji is the best example of this idea put into practice (Figure 4.5). From his Korean tortoiseshell glasses to his attitudes towards pot-making, his persona was composed

Figure 4.5   Hamada Shōji, *Bottle*, c. 1935. Stoneware.
Victoria & Albert Museum.

of contradictory pastoral signs—what might be called imitations of genuineness. As his dedicated biographer Susan Peterson writes, Hamada felt that

> the only way to make a tea bowl is to make it the way Koreans made bowls before they knew about tea ceremony, or the way a potter in a foreign country who knows nothing about tea makes a bowl. Hamada tries not to think as a Japanese making a bowl for tea when he is making a tea ceremony bowl. He tries to think like those other potters.[46]

The acid test for such an attitude, for Hamada, was not the quality of a particular pot but a potter's total production, which was not the result of individual artistic judgments. "Anyone can choose one-tenth of his work and put on a good show. That's easy. But if you can exhibit your own work, almost all of it, and still have a good show, that's better," Hamada told Peterson. "Yi dynasty craftsmen in Korea were very good, they were like this."[47]

Leach held similar views. One of the most cherished experiences from his time in Japan was his visit to a pottery village in Kyushu, whose inhabitants he interpreted as direct descendents of the Korean potters who supposedly immigrated to this region following Toyotomi Hideyoshi's invasion of Korea in the 1590s. (This legend has been much debated by historians of Japanese ceramics, but Leach took it as fact.) He recalled that "pots filled an open field, some over-fired, some under-fired—all varieties of plain black but nothing personal or decorated and not a bad one amongst them." Yet this ideal eluded the *mingei* potters. Hamada sadly concluded that he would be lucky to achieve high quality in even a third of his pots, while Leach maintained a distinction at his St. Ives pottery between utilitarian "standard ware" made by a team under his direction, and individual "art pieces" that he himself made for exhibition.[48] Leach's vast influence in Britain during the postwar period meant that potters there inherited the insoluble problem of *mingei*. This dilemma was entrancing in itself. Michael Casson, a follower of Leach's and a staunch promoter of his ideas, wrote in 1967 about the "very different state of mind at the moment of creation" which ensured that "all pots made on the wheel are individual." Production pottery, he argued, rather than the creation of unique masterworks, "is the field where individual talent shows most clearly if the skill is there as a vehicle for expression."[49] Yet, within *mingei* theory, the notions of true creativity and individual talent were meant to be antithetical. A craftsman who was aware of the true spirit of folk craft was, by virtue of that very awareness, unable to achieve the thoughtless state necessary to the creation of true beauty.

THE MIDWEST

The message of *mingei* was the right one at the right time for America in the 1950s, precisely because of this aestheticized ideal of culture without conscious content. Given that the United States was peaceably occupying its former enemy, it was far easier to recast the image of Japan in purist "folk" terms than to confront the realities of the recent past.[50] The transplantation of the *mingei* movement to America is not usually seen in relation to this broader political context, though. Rather, it is presented as the result of a single stroke of inspired promotion, when the trio of Yanagi, Hamada, and Leach toured America in 1952 and 1953 at the invitation of Warren and Alix MacKenzie.[51] In fact, the influence of Asian ceramics in the United States much predated this event, but these three men captured the American imagination because they were exotic, cultivated, and committed to proselytizing the message of *mingei*, and their visit has often been seen as the cause of America's postwar craft-oriented *japonisme*. In actuality, the relationship between the American and Japanese craft movements was not so one-dimensional. Over the years it would evolve under the influence of such diverse figures as the potter Daniel Rhodes, the furniture maker George Nakashima, the wood and stone carver J. B. Blunk, and the curator Martha Longenecker.[52] The idea of Japanese crafts as an undisturbed repository of timeless beauty was also presented to American audiences in innumerable books and exhibitions.[53]

By the 1960s, the *mingei* ideology had spread far and wide in America, but it settled with particular firmness in the Upper Midwest. The credit for this goes mainly to the Minnesota potters Warren and Alix MacKenzie, who had been apprentices of Leach's at his workshop in St. Ives, England.[54] Partly through their teaching and partly through leading by example—Warren MacKenzie recalls lectures "to the flower clubs, art students, and the girl scouts"—the couple helped to instigate an explosion of pastoral pottery in the area.[55] Among the key exponents of the group are Jeff Oestreich, Wayne Branum, and Linda Sikora in Minnesota, Randy Johnston and Mark Pharis in Wisconsin, John Glick in Michigan, and Clary Ilian in Iowa, to name only a few.[56] "Hiding out" (as Glick once put it) in their shops, such potters made ceramics that seemed to them symbolic of the private rewards of craftsmanship, some of them modeling their work directly on Asian *mingei* prototypes.[57] Potters sympathetic with this position, whether in the Midwest or elsewhere, even had their own journal. This was *Studio Potter*, founded by New Hampshire ceramist Gerry Williams in 1972 as an "irreverent, opinionated, occasionally misspelled, and earthy" periodical.[58] It was intended as a "service to the field … rather than a display vehicle for individuals' work," an antidote to the mainstream presentation of *Craft Horizons* and its successor *American Craft*, and it wore its reverence for pastoral retreat like a badge of honor. "Friends, some words of advice from Chairman Mao," Williams wrote in 1974. "Dig tunnels deep, and store grain."[59]

One might expect the actual ceramics made by American adherents of *mingei* to be exclusively backward-looking, given the fount of nostalgia upon which they were built. As the potter Harriet Cohen wrote in 1977, these earnest, brown pots "are the deliberately primitive output of a sophisticated culture driven to nostalgia for the primitive."[60] And certainly, a great deal of negligible work came out of this wave of popular *japonisme*. Garth Clark and Margie Hughto quipped in 1979 that "an archaeologist of the future, digging through the shard piles of the mid-1950s, can be excused if he deduces that during this time the United States was overrun by an army of fourth-rate potters from China, Korea, and Japan."[61] And yet, the American pastoral potter was perhaps a more self-examined figure than might first appear to be the case. It is no coincidence that the Midwest proved to be

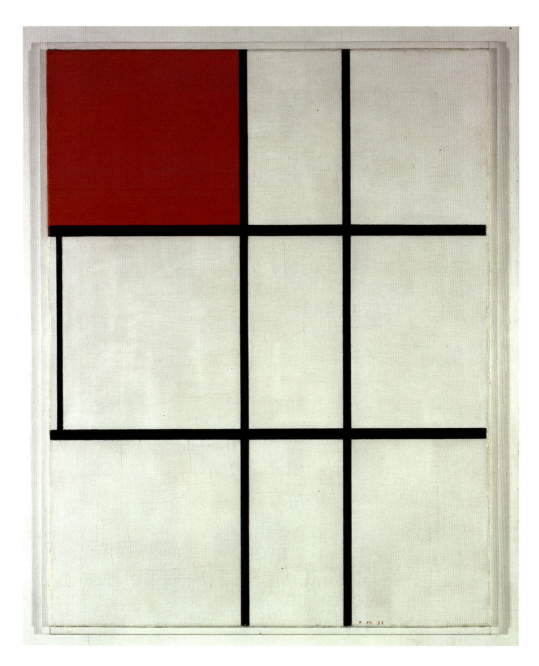

Plate 1   Piet Mondrian, *Composition B (No. II) with Red*, 1935.
Oil on canvas.
Tate Gallery.

Plate 2 Anni Albers, *Hanging*, designed 1926, woven by
Gunta Stötzl in 1967. Woven silk.
Victoria & Albert Museum. Courtesy of the Josef and Anni
Albers Foundation.

Plate 3   Carol McNicoll, *Homage to Brancusi*, 2001. Slip-cast porcelain,
aluminum base.
Courtesy of the artist. Photograph by David Cripps.

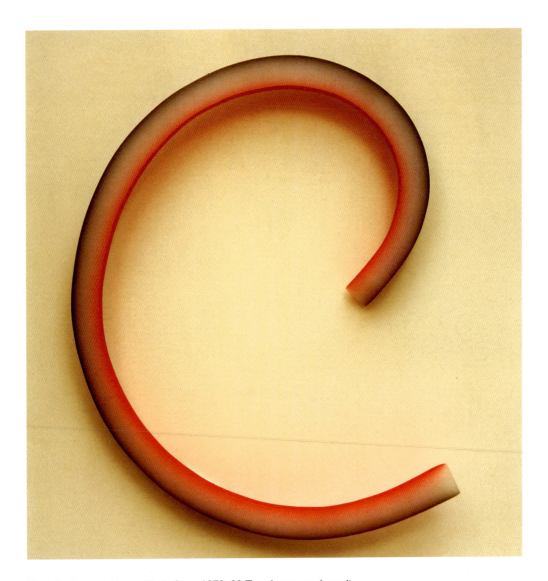

Plate 4   Susanna Heron, *Neck Curve*, 1979–80. Translucent opal acrylic,
paint on sides.
Collection Stedelijk Museum, Amsterdam. Photograph by David Ward.

Plate 5   Gijs Bakker, *Brooch: Blue Oil*, 2006. Sapphire, diamond, 14K white gold, metal, glass, color folio.
Executed by Pauline Barendse. Courtesy of the artist. Photograph by Rien Bazen.

Plate 6   Miriam Schapiro, *Mary Cassatt and Me*, 1976. Collage.
Private collection. Courtesy of the artist.

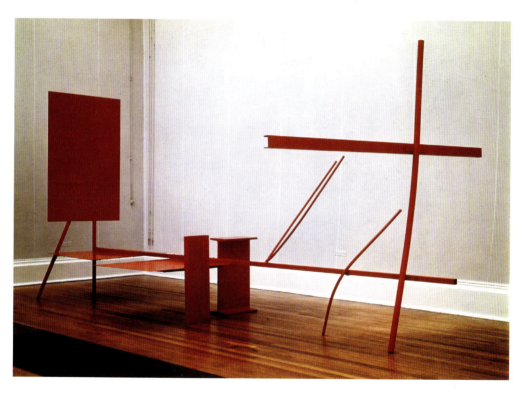

Plate 7   Anthony Caro, *Early One Morning*, 1962. Steel and aluminum,
red paint.
Tate Gallery. Photograph © Barford Sculptures Ltd.

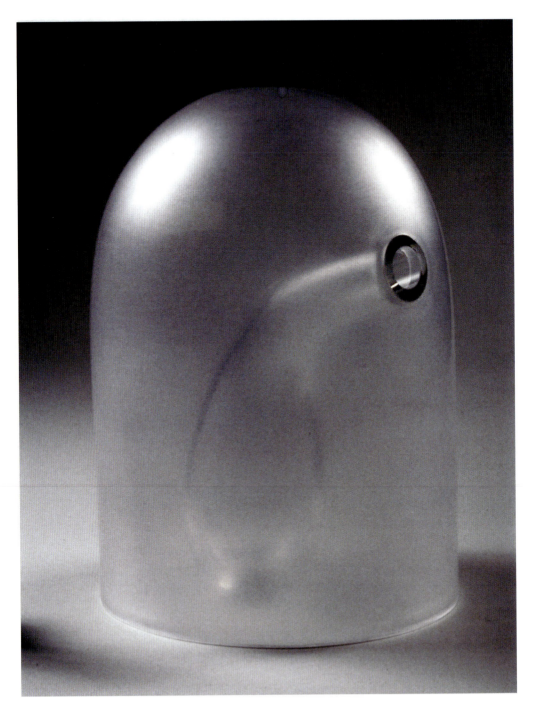

Plate 8   Emma Woffenden, *Breath*, 1992. Glass.
Victoria & Albert Museum.

Plate 9   David Pye, *Carved Dish*, c. 1980. Wood.
Wood Turning Center Collection. Photograph by John Carlano.

Plate 10   Bernard Leach, *Dish*, 1953. Slip-decorated ceramic.
Chipstone Foundation.

Plate 11   Tom Loeser, *Folding Chair*, 1982.
Courtesy of the artist.

Plate 12   Richard Slee, *Landscape with Horses*, 1997. Handbuilt glazed
earthenware with found glass figures.
Courtesy of the artist and Barrett Marsden Gallery.

Plate 13 Thalia Campbell, *Greenham Common Banner*, c. 1985.
Courtesy of Women's Art Library/MAKE.

Plate 14   Mike Kelley, *More Love Hours Than Can Ever Be Repaid*, 1987.
Stuffed fabric toys and afghans on canvas with dried corn; wax candles
on wood and metal base.
Whitney Museum of American Art, New York; Purchase, with funds from
the Painting and Sculpture Committee.

Plate 15   Tracey Emin, *Hate and Power Can Be A Terrible Thing*, 2004.
Appliqué blanket.
Tate Gallery.

Plate 16   Simon Starling, *Shedboatshed (Mobile Architecture No. 2)*, 2005.
Wood.
As installed at the Kunstmuseum Basel, 2005. Courtesy of the artist and
the Modern Institute.

the best home for pastoral practice. This was not a magical Arcadia at all, as the Cotswolds, the Southern Highlands, and Korea had seemed to be, but rather the relatively characterless backdrop of a post-agrarian, incipiently suburban landscape. Nor was it a land remote from the pastoral potter's own cultural milieu. Indeed, the principal attraction of the region was that it offered enough in the way of support, such as teaching opportunities and a ready clientele in the form of nearby urban centers, that pottery was a reasonable professional choice. If the Midwest was hospitable to the pastoral ethos, ironically, it was because it provided a site in which there was actually very little romance.

Warren MacKenzie exemplifies the articulate and self-examined position of Midwestern pastoralists (Figure 4.6). He is known for his rural shop, below-market pricing, and home-spun public persona. As mentioned above, along with his wife Alix, who passed away in 1962, he played a key role in promoting *mingei* ideals in America. But he also has departed in certain respects from Yanagi and Leach's thought, for example in his rejection of the idealization of the country potter: "I don't mean to subscribe to the myth of the idiot thrower who without thinking makes thousands of pots and hopes that out of the lot some might be good."[62] He points out that his move to the countryside in the first place was

Figure 4.6   Warren MacKenzie, *Bowl*, 1986. Stoneware.
Victoria & Albert Museum.

motivated less by romance than reality—the cheap real estate, the room to build a kiln, and the opportunity to live in a place "where our mess and pollution would be forgiven."[63] It might also be said that one never sees a classic MacKenzie pot, not only because he has avoided settling into a repetitive style, but also because the ongoing experience of making is for him the real interest of craft. As he has written, "the potter does not preplan a major piece ... each work is approached as part of a continuum of ideas and concerns that make up the potter's life."[64] MacKenzie even seems quite unconcerned about his results at times, and tells his sympathetic audience that his pots are "extraordinary objects only and precisely because they are ordinary objects."[65] As a demonstration of this ethos, he had a show in 1976 at the Rochester Art Center in which every ceramic object from a single kiln firing was exhibited in one group, implying that the notion of relative quality was a distraction from the unity of process. In the catalogue, MacKenzie stated, "I don't believe in striving to make every pot a super pot. First of all, because I don't know what that is, and secondly because I think that the best pots come almost without your expecting them."[66]

MacKenzie and other potters have found, in the modest Midwest, a place where the committed pastoral of *mingei* can be practiced in a low-key and independent manner. Their lifestyle there affords insulation from contradiction—the vexed relation between integrity and individuality that plagued more public figures like Yanagi and Leach. MacKenzie has said that his pots are "much better understood in the Midwest than they are on the East Coast or the West Coast. I can sell them on the East or West Coast, but not because people understand them, but probably because they're buying a Warren MacKenzie."[67] Yet if *mingei* ideology has existed quite happily in such a forgiving climate, it has nonetheless come under withering attack from other quarters. Partly this is simply a matter of fatigue with the "Anglo-Oriental" style of the pots themselves, but it is also an objection to the underlying hypocrisy of pastoral. (As Rose Slivka wondered in 1976, "Is getting out of the system creating its own system?")[68] The ceramic historian, critic and gallerist Garth Clark has directly criticized MacKenzie for his idealism: "to refuse to acknowledge that the economic structure of the crafts has radically changed is irresponsible ... I suspect that Doulton's has a far more rational idea of what it costs to make a teapot today than MacKenzie does."[69] Artists associated with the Funk movement in ceramics also repudiated the pastoral potter's ethos of retreat. With their professional and fine art ambitions, artists like Robert Arneson (see Chapter 5) and Erik Gronborg explicitly rejected nostalgic retreat into the rural. Gronborg argued the point by insisting that the Funk potter "has learned to live with his city, and his ceramics are as natural a part of his environment as the water jar and tea bowl were to the peasant. His ceramics are not a rebellion or a romantic wish for a past and simpler life; they are part of his own time."[70] Yet for all the apparent realism of the critical, commercial, and urban voices that have been raised in opposition, there remains something attractive about MacKenzie's practical pastoral. His example suggests that, despite the uglier aspects of the romantic idealism chronicled here, regions apart may still be places to bear in mind.

TWO VERSIONS OF PASTORAL: PHIL LEIDER AND ART ESPENET CARPENTER

The greatest single piece of writing on pastoral craft is without doubt Philip Leider's "How I Spent My Summer Vacation... Or, Art and Politics in Nevada, Berkeley, San Francisco and Utah." Published in *Artforum* at the end of the summer of 1970, just prior to the Leider's resignation as editor of the journal, the article is a document of disillusionment with the political potential of art, and his corresponding flirtation with a pastoral craft ethos as a possible solution.[71] The piece takes the form of a bittersweet travelogue, describing a pilgrimage undertaken by the author across the West Coast. Leider presents each station on his trip as one possible solution to the problem of art's social relevance: Michael Heizer's earthwork *Double Negative* in the middle of Nevada; a "movement" (that is, leftist) art gallery in Berkeley; a separatist commune near Berkeley named Canyon; and finally, Robert Smithson's famous earthwork *Spiral Jetty* on the Great Salt Lake in Utah. What do all of these sites have in common? First and foremost, all lie off the beaten path. None is more far-gone than the town of Canyon: "[a] peculiar community, almost all of it being illegal."[72] All of the inhabitants there are refugees from what they see as capitalist state control, and are constantly hounded by the authorities because of the supposed inadequacies of their hand-made homes (such as their lack of plumbing). Leider makes his sympathies clear by juxtaposing Canyon with the nearby town of Moraga, where the commune kids go to school. While Canyon is unique in its inviolate preservation of humane social values, Moraga is Everytown, USA—where "the paved highway is laid down even before the houses are built."[73]

The leading player in Canyon is Leider's friend David Lynn, a Berkeley sculptor who has given up on the avant garde and turned himself into a house builder. He is clearly meant as a symbolic representative of pastoral craft. For Lynn, art has become synonymous with community building, and with knowledge that is tied intimately to the land:

> We didn't talk about sculpture at all; it seemed pretty clear that as far as Lynn was concerned, every sculptural idea he ever had was in his building. The revolution in Lynn's art, if there was one, was dictated by the terrain: with Moraga just three miles down the road, and coming closer all the time, what serious artist could do otherwise?[74]

Lynn is not alone, of course. Canyon is replete with self-sufficient craftspeople, all of them fighting governmental assaults on their community.[75] For Leider, the most astounding thing about the people of the commune is their unbridled optimism. Every time they lose a case in front of the conservative zoning board, a scene of pastoral idealism gone mad ensues: "as soon as court lets out the Canyon people rush home and start building, not as if there was *no* tomorrow, but as if there were an infinite number of tomorrows."[76]

Throughout his article, Leider emphasizes humble deference to the landscape. Heizer's sculpture *Double Negative*, despite its huge scale, "took its place in nature in the most modest and unassuming manner, the quiet participation of a man-made shape in a particular configuration of valley, ravine, mesa and sky."[77] In Canyon, "it is worth your life to cut down a tree," as the inhabitants are determined to "effect no change in the natural ecology of the region."[78] The suggestion is that the future of not only political radicalism, but art-making itself, lies in an intimate connection to the land instead of New York art galleries. As a creature of this internecine urban society, Leider himself is an outsider in places like Nevada and Utah, Radical Berkeley and Canyon. He presents himself as a modern Dante, fascinated by each of the stations on his pilgrimage, but nonetheless foreign to them. Richard Serra, who (taking the part of Virgil) accompanies Leider at the beginning of the trip, is similarly engaged with the possibilities of an artistic retreat into the wilderness, but he too is an alien in these parts. "Every time you thought you found your place in a site," he mused, "the site kicked you out of it. Makes you feel like a fool."[79] Leider thought that the future might be "out there," in the landscape; but it could not be captured or tamed. The landscape is uninviting and resistant, and the action of the city, the feeling that it is the site of real change, exerts an inexorable pull. Leider's essay reflects these conflicting impulses. It is the self-portrait of an insider who yearns for the critical powers of the outsider, yet wishes to stay in the game. He clearly idolizes David Lynn, but all he can do is sing the pastoral house builder's praises—not actually join him in Canyon, the town of endless summer.

If Lieder's article in *Artforum* tells of escape from the hothouse of art into the wilds of the progressive pastoral, then furniture maker Art Carpenter's 1982 article "The Rise of Artiture" enacts a movement in the opposite direction.[80] The sage of the Bay Area pastoral craft community, Carpenter was throughout his career a somewhat reluctant mentor to generations of countercultural apprentices. (Though he lived in Bolinas, a center of left-wing culture, he moved there before the people he called "hippie-dippy types" arrived.)[81] He built his own shop and house by hand following his move to the countryside in 1959, including a number of dome-shaped structures that replicate in hand-crafted form the general outlines of Fuller's geodesic structures.[82] This site became the epicenter of the main counter-cultural craft organization of the era: the Baulines Craftsman's Guild. Founded in the northern Bay Area in 1972 by furniture maker Tom D'Onofrio, the Guild was not a commune by any means, but a dispersed apprenticeship system based on eighteenth-century models of workshop training.[83] A dropout from the political protest environment in Berkeley, D'Onofrio found Carpenter's detachment from society to be every bit as inspiring as the quality of his furniture.[84]

It is not difficult to see why Carpenter's furniture was so exciting for the young radicals of the late 1960s. His work combines formal sophistication derived from Scandinavian design with a rough-and-ready lack of pretense regarding technique. This internal dichotomy offered younger makers a style that breathed the honesty of exposed, simple joints, with the added advantage of a manageable set of challenges in the shop. The organic feel of Carpenter's furniture also played perfectly in northern California, where wood's natural beauty was valued by craftspeople and customers alike. A few years later, Californian woodworker Alan Marks began an overview of the region's furniture with an energetic attempt to connect this devotion to wood with the ideology of the counter-culture:

A plank of wood comes to us cut from a tree which weathered years of drought and storm, seasons of heat and cold, sheltering man and beast with its branches, and which died with a personal history recorded in its grain structure. Whatever we do with that plank should be done with respect... Today we can manufacture plastic that looks like wood and wooden furniture which could as well be plastic. We are impressed by the sheer amount of mechanical energy expended in transforming wood into a predetermined shape, but should we really be? Some feel a new era is dawning, an era in which man lives in harmonious interaction with the resources and materials of his world. Perhaps this attitude will make itself felt in design as well.[85]

Even if the plainspoken Carpenter might have distanced himself from such grand ideals, his furniture fit in with them perfectly. The hallmark of his style, an all-over softness of edges and corners, was made efficiently using a motor-driven router with minimal hand finishing, but it seemed to be the product of patient rasping and sanding. This particular feature was imitated widely in the Bay Area, especially by Carpenter's apprentices in the Baulines Guild, and came to be called the "California Roundover."[86]

Interestingly, Carpenter gave increasing prominence to these rustic affectations in his furniture as his career progressed. His earliest pieces tended to be indebted to the curvilinear designs, hidden joinery, and clean webbed upholstery of Scandinavian designers, such as Bruno Mathesson. The rougher side of Carpenter's aesthetic did not find its expression until the development of his Wishbone chair, a form produced as early as 1960 but not perfected until the end of the decade (Figure 4.7). A comparison of this chair with a rocker by Sam Maloof, the most prominent Californian woodworker and perhaps the archetypal American studio furniture maker, shows the individuality of Carpenter's approach (Figure 4.8). The two chairs share the use of wood with subdued color and figure (indigenous walnut in both cases), and curves that sensitively echo of the sitter's body. Both are clearly indebted to the precedent of the plywood furniture that had become commonplace in the 1950s, as is evident from the ingenious laminated construction of the legs in Carpenter's chairs and the rockers in Maloof's. However, the Wishbone chair is well supplied with unpretentious details such as leather strap upholstery, projecting wooden screw caps, and (in many examples) obvious flaws in the wood.

Against this biographical background, it is unsurprising that most readers think of Carpenter's article "The Rise of Artiture" (if they think of it at all) as a statement of conservatism, and in particular an objection to the new avant-garde trends in furniture. Though it was written some time after Carpenter's peak moment of influence had passed, the essay is well-known in furniture circles, and the term "artiture" still has some currency as a critical putdown today. In actuality, though, Carpenter's essay is a much more complicated document than that: an instance of the pastoral attitude of the 1960s colliding with the newly commercialized, gallery-driven craft world of 1980s. It both embodies the pastoral strategy and sheds light on its continuing pertinence for the craft movement.

Figure 4.7   Art Carpenter, *Wishbone chair*, 1969. Walnut, leather.

Published in the magazine *Fine Woodworking* in 1983, the article starts with a brief statement of Carpenter's perspective on things. His voice is that of a modest west coast boy gone
to New York City to see what the kids are doing nowadays:

> Last summer I was invited east to view a number of woodworking shows, so that I might
> offer in this magazine some reflections on the state of the craft. After a full week devoted
> to touring various galleries, museum exhibits, and the perennial great fair at Rhinebeck,
> I have concluded that woodworking has come of age. Thirty years ago wood was not part
> of the sophisticated craft scene. It was rarely included even in craft fairs, much less in
> museum and gallery exhibits, and even then only in the form of small objects… I recall
> the hesitant acceptance that was given me in the in the mid-1950s, particularly when I

Figure 4.8   Sam Maloof, *Rocking Chair*, 1975.
Museum of Fine Arts, Boston.

became a member of a Bay Area cross-media craft group. It was only ten years ago that furniture and treen began to bloom and that wood came to take its place unabashed in the craft world. Now wood in furniture form is even being made into sometimes metaphoric objects of non-utility, metaphor being the usual sphere of the painter and the sculptor.[87]

Carpenter here occupies the now-familiar pastoral stance, asserting his own relative innocence, his long experience, and his reliance on good old common sense, all of which establishes him as outside the new trends but also as an effective commentator on them. He tacitly claims a type of authority that a sophisticated city critic could never have.

After establishing his pastoral credentials, Carpenter launches immediately into a withering dismissal of "artiture," an apparent contraction of "art furniture," or perhaps "arty furniture," and everything it stands for. "Some woodworkers seem to be going … toward fame by investigating material and form to the exclusion of function," he writes. "My daughter Victoria calls this work 'artiture,' artifacts that have the traditional form of furniture, but are not of any practical use." It is worth noting that Carpenter attributes the neologism to his daughter, dodging authorship of the most contentious, critical, and thus altogether un-pastoral term in the essay. Otherwise, his opinion of artiture seems identical with the conservative stance that we have already encountered in the figure of Richard LaTrobe-Bateman. "I am not sure what the impulse is for making much of the artiture I saw, whether it is for play, pun, farce, or a quick ego fix," Carpenter writes. "But to cut a chair in half, paint it striped, and hang it on a wall draws much more attention, brings ten times the money, and is much easier than making a chair that works, and that sings with the care of its maker." So much for artiture, the reader thinks.

Reading on, however, one becomes increasingly aware that it's not as cut-and-dried as Carpenter has indicated it might be. Certainly, he goes on to forward a good many cantankerous jabs at specific pieces of "artiture," which he finds to be wanting in functionality. But it gradually emerges that function is less important than one would have thought. When Carpenter encounters Tom Loeser's *Folding Chair* (see Plate 11), "an ingenious mechanism [that is] uncompromisingly artiture," he responds in curiously conflicted terms: "I think [Loeser] should fabricate a whole series labeled 'people-traps,' for I saw no other work more siren like." Despite the fact that he had railed against striped chairs cut in half and hanging on walls only a few paragraphs earlier, when brought face to face with the object, Carpenter admits to both an irrational fear (recalling Latrobe-Bateman's attack on furniture that is a "menace in use") and an experience of seduction, an enjoyment of the use of space and color. Similarly, when Carpenter encounters Wendy Maruyama's tall-backed chair *Mickey Mackintosh*, he at first professes disappointment in its obvious suggestion of Mickey Mouse's ears. But when Carpenter later discovers that the chair was intended by the artist as a perverse combination of Walt Disney and Charles Rennie Mackintosh, he finds himself delighted: "I don't know whether Maruyama sees it this way, but artiture when it teases the seriousness of furniture, even gratuitously, does service." In saying so, even in his self-consciously abashed way (of course Maruyama sees it that way, the reader thinks) Carpenter was among the earliest writers looking at studio craft to pick up on this cleansing effect of the satirical aspects of postmodernism. Carpenter's essay today seems somewhat behind the times—particularly in its narrow focus on questions of functionality—and its context in a how-to woodworking magazine is humble indeed. Yet it is nonetheless a model of the productive ambiguity of craft as pastoral. Just as Leider is ultimately left in agonized conflict by his attraction to Canyon, Carpenter leaves the reader without a clear sense of his opinion of artiture—except that perhaps he himself is unsure of its relevance.

NORTH, SOUTH, EAST, WEST: CARL ANDRE AND ROBERT SMITHSON

In Leider and Carpenter, we have two examples of figures moving within the landscape: a city critic heading out to the country, and a rural furniture maker hazarding the urban setting. The ambivalence that beset both writers as they did so was partly a result of their individual biographies. But it also reflects the underlying pastoral structure of their thought, which rested on a notion of the landscape itself as dialectical. This idea was also important to two figures mentioned in Leider's essay, Carl Andre and Robert Smithson. Both were colleagues of the artist Robert Morris, who, looking back from 1981, encapsulated the art history of the late 1960s this way: "As the dialectical edge of Minimalism grew dull, as it had to in time, and as the radicality of its imagery, contexts, or processes became routine, its options dwindled to a formula: use more space."[88] This centrifugal tendency manifested itself in so-called "scatter" work, which Morris himself, Carl Andre, and Barry LeVa pioneered in the late 1960s. As we saw in chapter one, such works involved a field of detritus—felt cloth, ball bearings, broken glass, and so on—spread in a low, seemingly arbitrarily arranged pile on a gallery floor. LeVa indicated his interest in the possibility of such "distributions" as a model for space itself, with a 1968 scatter piece entitled *North South East West*—a directional quatrain that became one of the central motifs of the next era's sculpture (Figure 4.9). LeVa

Figure 4.9   Barry LeVa, *North South East West*, 1967. Felt, ball bearings.

later recalled, "I became less and less interested in the ordering of parts and more concerned with horizontal scale, vastness."[89]

Returning to Leider's essay for a moment, we see that it ends with the following somewhat gnomic lines:

> Art is also art re-arranged, and *Spiral Jetty* does what it can. There was Andre's *Lever*, and Brancusi's *Endless Column* before that. You don't get a piece like *Lever* to turn in on itself by fooling around with a length of rubber hose, as Smithson has undoubtedly discovered by looking at New York art for the last few years.[90]

Leider here connects Carl Andre and Robert Smithson by referring to the formal property of potentially infinite lateral expansion. Unlike a length of hose, which can easily be made into a closed circle, neither *Lever* nor *Spiral Jetty* can be rendered a stable or definable object (Figures 4.10 and 4.11). Both literally and figuratively, they reach out into the landscape,

Figure 4.10   Carl Andre, *Lever*, 1966. 137 firebricks.
National Gallery of Canada.

defying (at least symbolically) our expectation that a sculpture should be a conclusive form. *Lever*, a simple row of firebricks installed along the floor of a gallery, could keep going, if more bricks were added. Smithson's famous spiral earthwork, similarly, could continue to "turn in on itself" to infinity. In both cases, the lack of fixity is also temporal. As Leider was among the first to notice, Smithson's earthwork changes with the elements, acquiring a crust of salt and yellow mineral deposits, while *Lever* is destroyed when it is de-installed, becoming once more a pile of construction material. As the artist Dan Graham wrote of Andre's work in 1967, "the constituents are *literally* transported from view when the exhibition is terminated (the parts having been recovered and perhaps put to an entirely nonrelated use as part of a different whole in a different future)."[91]

While these gestures might seem entirely abstract—pointing towards the realm of the conceptual rather than the physical, perhaps—Andre saw his sculpture as having a specifically crafted character. This was, for him, as much a matter of politics as of process. He had been instrumental in the founding of the Art Workers Coalition, a New York group that protested various conservative tendencies within the art bureaucracy with which they

Figure 4.11. Robert Smithson, *Spiral Jetty*, 1970. Great Salt Lake, Utah.
Black rock, salt crystals, earth, red water (algae).
Courtesy of the Estate of Robert Smithson/DACS, London/VAGA. Image
courtesy of James Cohan Gallery, New York. Collection: DIA Center for
the Arts, New York. Photo by Gianfranco Gorgoni.

worked. While the Museum of Modern Art and the Metropolitan Museum were the main targets of criticism (both having boards of trustees that were perceived as profiting from the Vietnam War), the AWC also printed anti-war propaganda and agitated for improved financial support for artists.[92] Leider's travelogue in *Artforum*, as it happens, was published in the same issue as a symposium on the subject of "the artist and politics," in which a number of artists registered varying opinions on the subject. First in the roster was Andre, who wrote, "Given: art is a branch of agriculture. Hence we must farm to sustain life… Life is the link between politics and art."[93] This populist pastoral metaphor was a consistent part of Andre's rhetoric throughout the late 1960s and early 1970s. "My social position," he declared, "in the classic Marxist analysis is, I'm an artisan … to exchange my goods that I exchange for other people for their goods is my economic function."[94] Andre insisted that his work was performed within a morally charged calculus of production, in which materials and procedures should be guided by the practical concerns of efficiency, availability and ecology. Even after he attained success as an artist, his credo was "make work as if you were poor."[95]

Andre came naturally by this craftsman's attitude, or so he would have had his public believe. As he has frequently remarked in interviews, his grandfather was a brick mason and his father a woodworker. He appealed to these roots in discussing his early "exercises" in wood sculpture (1959), which were made with a radial arm saw in the basement of his parents' home in Quincy. Andre remarked that he liked using the saw because it "embodied thousands of years of human experience in cutting."[96] He continued to create pieces of what he called "perverse carpentry" until about 1964, when he gradually abandoned woodworking procedures, finally erasing all but the distant memory of joinery from his work. A body of work composed of timbers or Styrofoam beams stacked in a relatively complex fashion was gradually succeeded by simpler serial arrangements such as *Lever* and related pieces in firebrick, the well-known series of floor sculptures composed of metal plates, and scatter works using little cubes of wood or metal.

Again, though these works seem rather abstract, they could be seen as announcing a much more direct approach to craft on Andre's part, unmediated even by tools. As in Morris's and LeVa's work, even the exact form taken by the work could be inconsequential; Andre declared that "the scatter pieces can move because how they are is not more interesting one time than another time."[97] This relaxation of the means of assembling the elements (or, as he put it, "particles") of the sculptures distanced Andre still further from literal craft procedures, but laid further emphasis on the process of arrangement itself. Certainly, Andre preserved his self-presentation as a workman.[98] In 1976, when asked to identify an artist's social responsibility, he replied, "I should prefer to say, to the values of a craft—a process of making and selecting—and to the task of making that craft intersect with contemporary life as it is felt and seen. This includes the responsibility of considering that the craft may have become atrophied or redundant."[99] Thus Andre did not abandon the artisanal, but rather sublimated its value structure and formal concerns. He himself described this sublimation as a shift from "sculpture as form" to "sculpture as structure" to "sculpture as place":

> I began with form—or woodcutting, essentially—chiseling into timbers after the manner of Brancusi ... coming to a kind of structural position which was probably new to the twentieth century but also was persistent or had existed in neolithic works... Then, passing through that into place which was also a neolithic property, I think, in the countryside of southern England, Indian mounds, and things like that.[100]

By this logic, the physical fact one encounters in an Andre is merely an incidental instantiation of the "work," which can be materialized or not according to a given set of conditions. David Bourdon noted this dichotomy in Andre's sculptures as early as 1966, writing that "when the artist sees sculpture as place, there is no room for actual sculptures to accumulate."[101] This argument seems closer to the mark than the comments of other critics who have seen Andre's sculptures as being an "ironclad wedding of object to environment."[102] In fact, the sculptures operate dialectically with regard to site-specificity: like any object, they mark the place in which they are located, but they also initiate an encounter with what Andre called "generic space."[103]

In 1966, Andre's fellow Minimalist Tony Smith had been taken by the limitless spaces outside of the gallery. In his account of driving on the New Jersey Turnpike, Smith wrote: "The experience on the road was mapped out but not socially recognized ... There is no way you can frame it, you just have to experience it."[104] Andre said much the same in a 1970 interview:

> My idea of a piece of sculpture is a road. That is, a road doesn't reveal itself at any particular point or from any particular point ... we don't have a single point of view for a road at all, except a moving one, moving along it. Most of my works—certainly the successful ones—have been ones that are in some way causeways—they cause you to make your way along them or around them or move to the spectator over them. They're like roads, but certainly not fixed point vistas. I think sculpture should have an infinite point of view. There should be no one place, nor even a group of places where you should be.[105]

Andre puts an interesting spin here on the standard account of Minimalist theatricality, as put forward by Michael Fried in his well-known essay "Art and Objecthood" three years earlier.[106] Fried criticized the lack of interest in temporal boundaries voiced by Tony Smith, which he saw as typical of one's experience in the presence of Minimal (or, as he called it, Literal) art. Because of a lack of interior definition, he argued, the onlooker has no way to guide his or her visual journey through the work. For Fried, this makes for dull sculpture. But for Andre, the meandering experience of the viewer who is presented with an anti-compositional object is a positive attribute. Such a work dislodges the viewer spatially, not only returning him or her to the "real," as Smith might have said, but also conjuring an "infinite point of view," a mental space more fantastic than actual.

A sculpture like *Lever*, then, might best be conceived as a kind of artisanal technology of place-making, rather than as a bounded artwork. It operates on the viewer's sense of location like a tool—hence the title—changing one's experience of the gallery space as one walks around it. When it was first shown, *Lever* extended through two separate rooms in the Jewish Museum, so that there was no possible side view of the whole piece. It could only be seen in its entirety by sighting down the length of the sculpture from one end. The point was not to articulate the Jewish Museum's particular room layout, but rather to use the device of dramatic foreshortening to destabilize space itself. *Lever* should be seen as a particularly abstruse form of pastoral. It is a simple path that leads to an infinite and unspecified region: "another" place; a place of escape; a place that is inaccessible; a place that exists only as a point on an ethical compass.

Andre's version of pastoral also had to do with the politics of material. He expressed his attachment to such basic substances as wood, lead and stone in the pop-eastern, mystical terms common to the era: "I think, as Lao-Tzu wrote, 'the uncarved block is wiser than the tablet incised by the duke.' I've always tried to reach that state of the uncarved block, which is the 'now' (if not the *tao*) of the block."[107] The physicality of Andre's art, which Robert Smithson called his "metaphorical materialism," may initially seem incommensurable with his interest in "generic" space.[108] Yet these were two sides of the same coin. *Lever* operates through both an assertion of extreme perspective within regular space, but it also makes an obvious connection to the materials and procedures of masonry. Similarly, Andre's floor pieces are "places" where one becomes intimate with material, as the viewer is brought into contact with the tactile elements of sculptural form that usually go unnoticed: "the sound of a piece of work and its sense of friction ... [its] sense of mass."[109] From Andre's perspective, this materialism was overtly political. It pointed not to the indolence of classical shepherd, but rather to the simple work of the craftsman—the type exemplified by the "woodbutcher" house builders that Leider had visited in Canyon.

Andre's gestures to that other, better place—the displacement central to the pastoral mode—inevitably led to an attempt to escape the gallery in literal terms. In 1968, he created two works, *Rock Pile* (a five-and-a-half foot high pile of schist) and *Log Piece* (twenty-one logs, stripped of their bark and laid end to end) in a forest near Aspen, Colorado. This venture into the landscape seems like a logical conclusion of the thought process set in motion by *Lever*, but Andre described the project as a failure. Echoing Leider's sentiments, he said shortly afterwards: "I have a definite feeling that Aspen needed very little of my art. I think to a great extent my work was inappropriate there."[110] By and large, his future explorations of the pastoral would be limited to gallery-bound installations. Thus, two 1975 collections of sculptures, entitled "The Way North," "The Way East," and so on through the cardinal directions and their various combinations ("The Way Northeast," "The Way Northwest," etc.), did suggest that the place signified by the work was anywhere but here. But Andre could only point to "The Way." When the place of escape became real rather than figurative, his work fell flat.

It was just this problem that Robert Smithson's *Spiral Jetty* attempted to unravel. When Smithson traveled to Utah, he did so partly to demonstrate that nature was not a site of solace. For him, every encounter with nature was inevitably a demonstration of the sublime forces of entropy, which swallowed artistic subjectivity into a vast downward spiral: "the finite present of the center annihilates itself in the presence of the infinite fringes."[111] It is as if Smithson called Andre's bluff—as if he had walked along the infinite line of *Lever*, and tried to face up to the consequences. This tendency had been present in Smithson's gallery works, particularly his site/non-site sculptures, which consisted of rocks or other material gathered somewhere in the landscape and brought to the gallery, with maps and typescript descriptions indicating the "site" where the material was found. As Gary Shapiro has written, each of these works is "a frame constructed around an empty space."[112] But unlike Andre, whose works gesture towards absent space with a hopeful idealism, Smithson offers only the red herring of a diligently documented not-here, captured as if in a trap. As the artist put it in 1972, "the non-site exists as a kind of deep three-dimensional abstract map that points to a specific site of the surface of the earth," but this information provides no real insight into the conditions of the site, which "is open and really unconfined and constantly being changed." The sites, then, "are not destinations; they're kind of backwaters or fringe areas."[113] The viewer is left caught somewhere between the non-site and the site, neither of which satisfies.

As Leo Marx has argued, the idea of nature as a sublime, hostile terrain has long been central to American art, beginning with the nineteenth-century landscape paintings of Thomas Cole, George Innes, and Frederic Church. And to some extent, Smithson can be seen as placing himself in relation to this tradition.[114] But as is often the case with Smithson, this set of references was conflated with another, older tradition. The art historian Erwin Panofsky has shown how the art and literature of the Renaissance vacillated between an acceptance of the temporal nature of the pastoral refuge, and a disavowal of that temporality—in effect, between a pastoral that resigns itself to its own ephemerality, and a pastoral that idealistically refuses to admit its own demise. The former model had its ultimate expression in Nicolas Poussin's canvas *Et in Arcadia Ego*, in which a group of shepherds are gathered around a tomb inscribed with that Latin phrase, which might be translated "I am also in Arcadia." As Panofsky writes, the picture functions as a *memento mori*—a scene of "contemplative absorption in the idea of mortality."[115] Death too is in Arcadia, and there is no escape from that finality.

Smithson adopted this pessimistic position wholeheartedly, writing in 1968: "the 'pastoral,' it seems, is outmoded. The gardens of history are being replaced by the gardens of time."[116] The nuances of language here are important: "history," for Smithson, is time perceived through a humanist lens, a self-centered point of view. "Time," by contrast, has no special connection to any one perspective. It stands in relation to no one center. Furthermore, while history is susceptible to notions of forward progress, time is undifferentiated. It is governed only by the law of entropy, in which all things tend towards an abyss. Thus, while

Andre idealistically pointed "The Way North" and "The Way West," Smithson provided only a litany of directions leading nowhere. In the essay that accompanied the *Spiral Jetty*, a senseless refrain of directions—North, North by East, Northeast by North, and so on around the compass—culminating in an sardonic twist on the classical pastoral: "The helicopter maneuvered the sun's reflection through the Spiral Jetty until it reached the center... *Et in Utah ego*."[117] Art historian Caroline Jones characterizes this heaping-up of vectors as an Oceanic dispersal, in which the traditional sublime of the infinite landscape is conflated with a "technological sublime." The tractor, two dump trucks, and front loader that made the *Spiral Jetty*, as documented in a film by Smithson that constitutes a part of the work, do not create; they digest, in what Jones calls "visceral scenes of massive, ravenous, shuddering machines that devour rock and slowly disgorge it into the water."[118]

Thus, just as Andre's idealism was wrapped up in the rhetoric of the artisanal, Smithson directly opposed himself to craft, and instead sought to operate at the scale of industry. As early as 1965, he had praised Donald Judd for his lack of "sentimental notions about 'labor'" and "subjective craftsmanship," and by 1968 he was ready to declare that "the private studio notions of 'craft' [have] collapsed."[119] *Spiral Jetty* was the logical continuation of a series of works that referred to industrial landscapes (as in his work *Non-site: Ruhr District*, which was composed of slag taken from the center of German mining and material fabrication).[120] Smithson did not see industry as an ordering force, but rather as an engine that drives the wheels of entropy ever more quickly. Furthermore, as Ron Graziani has pointed out, the location of *Spiral Jetty* was rich in industrial associations. Rozel Point, on the Great Salt Lake in Utah—was adjacent both to an abandoned oil well and to Promontory Point, where the Golden Spike was driven to symbolically connect the transcontinental railroad in 1869. He could not have chosen a sight more redolent of the victory of the machine over the garden.[121]

LANDSCAPES: GORD PETERAN AND RICHARD SLEE

For Smithson, craft and the pastoral were both dinosaurs, models of art that needed displacing. Given the force and cogency of his anti-idealism, it is tempting to allow him to have the last word. Certainly, after *Spiral Jetty*, it would be difficult for any artist to occupy a position of retreat into nature without conceding that, at the very least, they had been warned of the underlying naïveté of that gesture. However, given that Smithson's crushing cynicism has done little to quell the ongoing enthusiasm for pastoral craft, it is worth pointing to two recent artists who have engaged the subject with a lighter touch. A first example comes from the Toronto artist Gord Peteran, whose hybrid chair *Prosthetic* was described in chapter one. Peteran's *Workbench (Compass)* is just what its title advertises: a found workbench with a compass sunk into its top, an example of what Marcel Duchamp would have called an "assisted readymade" (Figure 4.12). The piece came about during an artistic residency in which Peteran visited the remote campus of Anderson Ranch Arts Center in Colorado (one of the summer craft schools with which this chapter began). Peteran's passage to this site

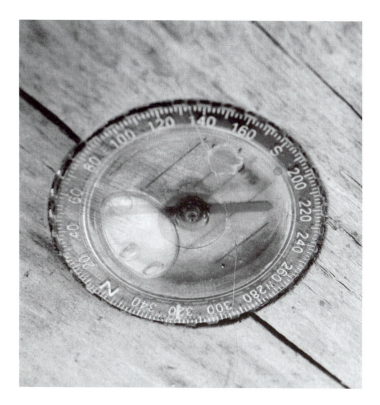

Figure 4.12   Gord Peteran, *Workbench (Compass)*, 2002.
Found beech workbench, found compass.
Courtesy of the artist. Photograph: Brian Porter.

was perhaps more similar to Phil Leider's than Art Carpenter's, inasmuch as he travelled from city to country. Though he mainly made landscape paintings while in the mountains, Peteran did find time for this one conceptual gesture. He drilled a hole in the surface of a fellow furniture maker's expensive new workbench and sunk a compass into it. We have seen the connection between craft and the cardinal directions too many times to miss the point being made here—that a maker's bench, and the studio surrounding it, is a still center with which to navigate the world. Yet there is something of the satirical, of the Shakespearean fool, in Peteran's act of vandalism. At Anderson Ranch, a banker or lawyer can adopt a posture of noble disengagement, apart from the fray, and pursue a higher calling of an honest day's work. Peteran seems to have regarded this idealistic setting with more than a little skepticism, but also considerable affection. His implanted compass nods sympathetically in the directions of pastoral—the quest for somewhere else. At the same time, it delivers the simple, unanswerable observation that Smithson posed to all pastoralists: "You are here."

Peteran played the fool, too, in maintaining a distance from the other artists at Anderson Ranch. This was typical of him; he presents himself not as the main character in the play of contemporary furniture, and perhaps not even a character that advances the plot, but rather as an observer who sits on the sidelines, making cracks that expose the true state of affairs. Much the same could be said for the unassuming figure of Richard Slee, who is almost universally hailed as Britain's leading ceramic artist, but whose exact significance has proved elusive even to his most dedicated admirers. The countervailing principles of "ambiguity and economy," in Nicholas Rena's words, are the only unifying tendencies (apart from the use of ceramics) that bind Slee's wildly diverse work together.[122] Three overscaled gilt hooks hanging on a wall; a plastic bucket filled with Easter eggs; a cartoon Volkswagen beetle; a silver platter and a frying pan, each sprouting mushrooms; a bit of gum stuck to the front door: all of these were included in a single showing of the artist's work at a gallery in 2006.[123] What does it all mean? Perhaps in this multiplicity, this embrace of the mutually irreconcilable, Slee has found a way to adopt all the doubt of the pastoral position, without any of the certainty that usually accompanies it. These are objects that could exist happily in a museum, a gift shop, a gallery, or a commune; they are equal parts art work, collectible, commodity, and Pet Rock. Like Peteran, Slee is an artist who expresses complex reservations about his own métier—even to the extent of doubting the value of his own reservations. "When a wise man gives thee better counsel, give me mine again," says Lear's fool. "I would have none but knaves follow it, since a fool gives it." (Act II, Scene iv.) Slee puts it more concisely: "It's a worrying thing, being part of something."[124]

The works that show Slee's pastoral credentials most clearly are a series of landscapes, made in the mid-1990s, which feature ceramic hillocks dotted with found plastic or glass knick-knacks (see Plate 12). His fellow potter Alison Britton described the works as "small and ironic pastorals, 'pieces of England,'" and noted that in them "the sort of cultured landscape conjured up by the park at Stourhead, perhaps, (grottoes, classical myths, and fake hills) is gently mocked."[125] Garth Clark also sees in Slee's works a degree of social satire, pitched intentionally low—a "working class cottage aesthetic" that digs away at the foundations of British national identity.[126] Clark perceptively contrasts him with the arch-ironist Jeff Koons, who is of the same generation and who also works frequently with ceramic. The difference, for Clark, is that the two operate "at different ends of the class structure."[127] It doesn't take much to figure out which end is which—Koons's life-size gilt porcelain figurines and Slee's abject little tchotchkes are a classic case of upstairs/downstairs.

Bringing these observations to bear on Slee's landscape works might result in a reading about class collision: tawdry kitsch figurines from the charity shop, gamboling scandalously on rolling hills of patrician green. There is something to this idea, and the notion of Slee as a sort of comic equivalent to the thundering Marxist anti-pastoral of Raymond Williams is an attractive one. What this reading misses, though, is the degree to which these landscape works seem to constitute a world of their own, a world as devoid of class struggle as Virgil's arcadia. All the observations that are routinely made about Slee—his use of a teasingly opaque "private language," his flirtation with the sewing-machine-meets-an-umbrella-on-an-operating-table aesthetics of Surrealism—still hold. But in their pastoral content, the landscapes reveal a more general truth about Slee's work that is usually harder to see: it always seems to lie between parentheses. Hesitation and uncertainty are its defining characteristics. Slee's works flinch from commitment, forever raising the specter of an uncomfortable truth, and then holding that truth in abeyance. Like a sheepfold, or summertime itself, they offer space and time in which to take a big step back, in the perhaps vain hope that things will appear more clearly when seen from a distance.

5   AMATEUR

One of the most cherished myths about craft is that it is inherently disruptive to modern art. As Justin Clemens recently put it, "craft—precisely because of its degraded status—remains an insistent problem and an affront to high aesthetics."[1] As we have seen, this is not always the case. Craft is more often conceived as a necessary "other," a useful disturbance that plays a necessarily unacknowledged role in modern art's critical apparatus. Yet in one important respect, Clemens is absolutely correct. Craft does act as an "affront," a spanner in the works, precisely when it is in its most "degraded" state. Commercially viable studio craft—expertly handblown glass, sculptural jewellery, and the like—poses no problems. On the contrary: like a Victorian servant aping his or her betters, studio craft inadvertently ratifies the hierarchical arrangement of the art world by aspiring so transparently to a status that it cannot claim.

When craft manifests itself as an expression of amateurism, however, it becomes genuinely troublesome. The problem begins with the word itself. "Amateur" means, roughly, "lover," from the Latin *amare* (to love), and one of the hallmarks of amateur activity is a lack of critical distance from the object of desire. If modern art, seen from a perspective like Adorno's, is grounded in searching self-awareness, then amateurism is a form of creativity that can never be integrated into this model. In the popular imagination, hobby crafts are on a par with such activities as stamp collecting and weekend sport—activities done in a spirit of self-gratification rather than critique. Such amateur pursuits constitute their own worlds of reference. One need only call to mind the dynamics of a model train weekend or a science fiction convention to grasp the interiority of amateur social structures. Such closed worlds are easily dismissed from the outside. Yet the disdain goes both ways. The amateur mindset implies a complete indifference to the self-critical values of the avant garde. The problematic concept of "outsider" art is only the most extreme version of this way of thinking. The term refers to the creative output of figures like Henry Darger and Adolf Wölfli, who are definitively cut off from the narrative of modern art, because they are "self taught," imprisoned, mentally ill, or otherwise disconnected from modernity *per se*. In fact, such "outsiders" are only amateur artists under another name, but the reception of their work involves an effacement of this identity through an insistence on their native genius. This act of projection involves not only a deeply conservative set of assumptions about art (universalist aesthetics, a paternalistic view of the artist, etc.), but also hostility to artistic discourse itself.

Yet, for all its potential to upset the apple cart, amateurism troubles the art world very little in practice. This is because hobbyists tend to be quite passive in social terms. Indeed, in its modern form, amateurism should be seen first and foremost as a result of the surplus economy. Sewing in the living room or woodworking in the garage are activities that reflect a culture of prosperous excess. In a sense, the hobbyist is the positive mirror image of the worker who has been made redundant at the factory. The unemployed are chillingly described by Zygmunt Bauman as "wasted lives," the leftover human products of modernity—those to whom society says, "The others do not need you. They can do as well, and better, without you."[2] The successful management of such purposeless populations has been key to modern politics; idle hands make for potentially revolutionary work. Similarly, the successful displacement of unused time into harmless leisure activities has been vital to the project of capitalist expansion. Furthermore, insofar as there are huge profits to be gained by selling commodities (in the form of materials and tools) to aspiring craftspeople, amateurs perform a valuable, if largely unconscious, service to the economy. From a strict Marxist perspective, then, hobby craft is the very embodiment of false consciousness: when fashioning a Christmas ornament or an end table by hand, amateurs believe themselves to be exercising creativity, or at least to be creating something more authentic than what can be bought at the local mall. But in fact, the effect of such activity is exactly the reverse. Precisely because they are made so lovingly, homemade crafts betray the degree to which their makers are integrated into the larger structure of capitalist ideology, in which commodity forms are the primary carriers of meaning.[3] The experience of amateurism may feel like autonomy, but in fact nothing could be more predetermined (a fact captured brilliantly by the name of a leading company in the field of how-to advice, "Martha Stewart Living"). In this sense too, hobbyism is the antithesis of an avant garde.

Of course, there is another way of looking at amateurism, which would take as its initial point of reference not the craft supply store or DIY shop, but the eighteenth-century parlor. Amateur craft today seems to be both a public and classless phenomenon, with products pedaled to every imaginable niche in the market. Even the young subcultural "crafters" who have emerged in the past few years, who maintain a fiercely independent stance on the basis of thick irony, Internet chat rooms, and open-source knitting patterns, have their anointed media celebrities. (One is Debbie Stoller, author of the widely distributed series of "Stitch'n'Bitch" how-to books, who advises "chicks with sticks" to "get their knit on." As ever, the future of craft is now.)[4] At one time, however, amateur craft was a mostly private affair—the exclusive domain of the wealthy, and more particularly, of aristocratic women, who spent their time in "accomplishments" such as quillwork, embroidery, and decorative painting. The attraction of these activities was their purposelessness. If a young lady had the time in which to master such conspicuously wasteful crafts, one could be sure that she was a member of the leisure class.[5] Yet even in the eighteenth century, there was skepticism about the worth of such pursuits. Mary Granville Delany, perhaps England's greatest exponent of cut-paper work and a woman who also excelled at gardening, drawing, writing, and embroidery, worried that her closet was "*too much filled* with amusements of no real estimation; and when people commend any of my performances I feel a consciousness that my time might have been better employed (Figure 5.1)."[6]

This sentiment was recorded at a time in which female creativity was constrained by a moral economy much more overt and oppressive than the mass media. But the imputation that amateur crafts are self-indulgent, even shameful, is by no means unfamiliar. So, while amateurism can be the very definition of unconscious cultural practice, it can also prompt anxieties of the most self-conscious kind. The tradition of pre-modern amateurism is a grand one, taking in not only masterpieces like Delany's, but also the art collecting of *virtuosi*, the founding of scientific disciplines, and the writing of great literature. Today, though, hardly anyone likes being seen as amateurish. Indeed, as the sociologist Robert Stebbins has demonstrated, amateur pursuits, once initiated, inevitably tend to follow an arc of increasing professionalization. "The durable benefits" of a hobby, Stebbins writes, "spring from the refusal to remain a player, a dabbler, or a novice in it. Rather, the activity is transformed into an avocation in which the participant is motivated by seriousness and commitment, as these are expressed both in regimentation (such as practice and rehearsals) and in systematization (such as schedules and organization)."[7] A corollary of this general rule is that there is corresponding pressure on the other side of the amateur-professional divide. In theory, hobbyists are beneath the notice of the expert. In practice, though, the line between the two is often a blurred one. The boundary must constantly be policed, both through the power of institutions and the maintenance of skill or conceptual difficulty among individual professionals. Some have even argued that the upward pressure of amateurs is a primary means of propelling creative fields forward. As the educator Jacques Barzun put it in the 1950s: "We may complain and cavil at the anarchy which is the amateur's natural element, but in soberness we must agree that if the amateur did not exist it would be necessary to invent him."[8]

Modern craft movements have been increasingly marked by such competitive pressures. At the turn of the century, it was desirable for men and (especially) women involved in the Arts and Crafts movement to be seen as enlightened amateurs; in fact, as Jennifer Harris has pointed out, "At a time when work, especially paid work, meant a serious loss in social status for middle-class women, it became essential for unmarried and destitute gentlewomen to find 'suitable' work. 'Art-work,' particularly those crafts granted social sanction by their growing popularity as hobbies among the upper- and upper-middle classes, seemed to provide the solution."[9] After 1945, however, amateurism was seen as a great problem for the crafts, and professionals sought to distance themselves from association with hobbyism whenever possible. In a prospectus written for the omnibus craft exhibition *Objects: USA* in 1968, curator Lee Nordness wrote: "the term crafts confusedly connotes in many people's minds something done as an avocation, something done as a therapy, something done by the aged. Actually, what is being created by the top artisans in the United States should be associated with such names as Benvenuto Cellini, [Peter

Figure 5.1   Mary Granville Delany, *Physalis, Winter Cherry*,
1772–88. Paper collage.
British Museum.

Carl] Fabergé, and Paul Revere."[10] In invoking these names from the past, Nordness was appealing to an era in which courts and guilds ratified the professional standing of individual craftspeople. With the subsiding of the historical methods of standardization imposed by these regulative bodies, craft in general has been plunged headlong into an ongoing crisis of image management. Just as modern art, as an autonomous and visual field of practice, must define itself against craft, professional craftspeople who wish to model themselves upon modern artists must distinguish themselves from the hobbyists that nip at their heels.

Modern art is immune to such pressure to some extent, because anything is permissible within its "exhibitionary complex."[11] There is no such thing as an amateur contemporary artist, only an unsuccessful one.[12] Just as craftspeople in the eighteenth century were sanctioned by the guild system, modern artists are authorized by museums, galleries, art schools, publications, and exhibitions. So far, so good. Yet, as we saw in Chapter 1, art is not only in the business of endorsing itself as a field of practice. It is also devoted to a corresponding assault on its own condition, and especially its own institutions. It constantly asks: who determines what is good art, anyway, and on what basis? And what are the losers to do about it? These are the big questions that form the backdrop for this fifth and final chapter, which describes three cases in which amateur craft has been employed by artists as a rebuke to the prevailing state of affairs in the art world. What binds these examples together is the theme of marginalization by art's institutional power structure. Rightly or wrongly, the ceramic artist Robert Arneson concluded that his chosen medium of clay consigned him to the outer limits of the art world. Judy Chicago and other Feminist artists, with much greater justification, railed against the sexism that beset their careers. In both of these cases, amateurism functioned as a rhetorical device—a reminder that the playing field was not equal—but also as a means of working through the particularity of a marginal subject position. The last case study takes up the more recent examples of Mike Kelley and Tracey Emin. These two artists, not among the losers by any stretch of the imagination, are lucky enough to be working in a post-disciplinary and post-Feminist art world. Their context is one in which the aggrieved stances of Arneson and Chicago should (at least in theory) be unnecessary. As we shall see, however, Kelley, Emin and their peers continue to exhibit a fascination with amateurism, perhaps in a desperate attempt to find something, anything, that might be unacceptable to the limitless field of art.

"THE WORLD'S MOST FASCINATING HOBBY": ROBERT ARNESON

Robert Arneson, the California potter, was almost unbearably aware of craft's association with amateurism. On the one hand, he complained bitterly about the situation. In art schools, he pointed out, clay departments were invariably stuck in the basement. He crafted his pedagogical intent in such a way as to counteract this prejudice: "to treat ceramics as an art and this meant we had to deal with ideas and content. I am not concerned with process in the craft tradition."[13] In this respect his goals resembled those of Peter Voulkos, who was an early and important influence. At the same time, though, Arneson mocked his own involvement in clay, dismissing it as "just a lot of work in white mud calling itself art."[14] He offered flip aphorisms that captured his conflicted sentiments, such as "ceramics is the world's most fascinating hobby," and described his working process in patronizingly domestic terms: "I take the clay and squeeze it, steps one, two, three, just like Betty Crocker. Then I cook it, and for how long. [sic] The problem with ceramics anyway, everything [looks] like a knick-knack. Nobody in their right mind would get involved with it . . . It's just a goddamn craft." Yet, in the next breath, he mused: "But it's important to make something . . . you know . . . majestic."[15]

Robert Arneson began his career in clay as a student of the Spanish potter Antonio Prieto at Mills College in Oakland. He finished the program there in 1958, and went on to teach as Prieto's assistant beginning in 1960. At Mills, Arneson could not avoid getting a thorough education in the finer points of ceramic technique. Prieto was a skilled potter by any standard, a conservative figure who believed that perfect execution was the soul of worthwhile pottery (Figure 5.2).[16] Arneson's decisive break with this philosophy occurred in September of 1961, when he and Prieto were demonstrating wheel throwing together at a craft fair. On a whim, Arneson made a beer bottle-shaped vessel on the wheel, capped it, and labeled it "No Deposit." The act incorporated Peter Voulkos's strategy of closing off the vessel as a way of refusing functionality, but the literalness of the gesture and the applied slogan, with its unstated conclusion of "no return," constituted a different means of attacking traditional pottery.[17] Soon after Arneson parted company with Prieto and began to develop a body of organic sculptures that were absolutely consistent with the Otis manner. But Arneson ran up against a wall at this point. Painfully aware that he was working in a borrowed style, he gave up working in clay for a year, returning to the medium only in 1963 when he found a permanent position teaching ceramics at the University of California at Davis.

It would be difficult to imagine a less promising situation from which to launch a revolution. While the Otis program had at least been connected to the burgeoning Los Angeles art community, Davis was a state agricultural college. It sported a surprisingly strong art faculty, but its ceramic facilities were non-existent when Arneson arrived. He was forced to set up shop in a wartime Quonset structure that already contained a forge and metalwork studio, as well as the campus police headquarters (complete with a jail cell) and a food experimentation lab.[18] However, the attitude of Arneson's own ceramic work was quite appropriate to this down-at-heel setting, later described by alumni as a "clubby masculine garage workshop."[19] The parochial milieu of Davis was the perfect place for him to pursue his increasing fascination with the marginality of the ceramic medium itself.

In considering Arneson's problematic relationship with amateurism, it is useful to think in terms of the concept of "taboo." I use the term here in its anthropological sense, to designate an object or substance that slips between what Emile Durkheim called positive and negative "cult value."[20] A taboo is alternately venerated or prohibited, depending on context: it fascinates and disgusts at the same time.[21] The idea of taboo also captured the imagination of Sigmund Freud, who configured it in psychoanalytic terms:

> The principle characteristic of the psychological constellation which becomes fixed in this way … is what might be described as the subject's *ambivalent* attitude towards a single object, or rather towards one act in connection with that object. He is constantly wishing to perform this act (the touching), and looks on it as his supreme enjoyment, but he must not perform it and he detests it as well.[22]

Arneson's engagement with ceramics suggests the mindset of taboo both in its overall tone and its literal iconography. He often analogized glaze and clay with substances that are coded as taboo in Western culture: blood and feces. In 1962, Arneson began a series of "eviscerated pots," brown stoneware vessels that were slashed and painted with

Figure 5.2   Antonio Prieto and Eunice Prieto working at the California College of Arts and Crafts, 1947.
Antonio Prieto papers, Archives of American Art, Smithsonian Institution.

a bright red glaze, and the following year he exhibited his notorious *Funk John*, a hand-built ceramic toilet with scatologically explicit contents. This latter piece was censored from the exhibition "California Sculpture" at the Kaiser Center in Oakland, and subsequently destroyed.[23] Numerous critics and historians have noticed a parallel between this incident and the curiously similar fate of Marcel Duchamp's own infamous *Fountain*, which was also expunged from public exhibition and then lost. It has even been suggested that Duchamp's toilet served as the model for Arneson's *Funk John*, and that the work could therefore be seen as an elaborate art historical joke: a handmade Readymade.[24] But according to his own testimony, Arneson chose the toilet not because of an iconic historical reference, but on the contrary, because it was "the ultimate ceramic," that is, "something that had no art heritage." *Funk John* was, then, a statement on the condition of clay itself.[25]

And what a statement it was. A collection of "ceramic emblems" (as Arneson later called them) floating in the toilet's bowl brought an uncomfortable iconography to hand-rolled coils, the fundamental building blocks of handbuilt pottery.[26] Even as these bits of clay were debased, they were also fetishized—even, to indulge in a bit of Arneson-style word-play, "enthroned." Here is the contradiction of the taboo substance, most prominent exactly when it is most reviled. It is tempting to read *Funk John* as a condensation of Arneson's own anxiety about shaping clay; after all, he himself later referred to his work as "a kind of self-analysis."[27] Certainly, others were quick to psychologize. Incensed by a feature article on Arneson in *Craft Horizons*, one irate letter writer commented: "Whether too rigorous toilet training, surprising his parents at having intercourse, or something entirely different stymied Robert Arneson's emotional growth is for a psychiatrist to evaluate—and Arneson ought to see one regularly."[28] As puerile as such attacks now seem, they were probably just the sort of reactions that Arneson hoped to elicit. By suggesting that there was something scandalously infantile about his own (and others') fascination with wet clay, he implied that making ceramics was a bodily function, like excretion, respiration or copulation—the opposite of the intellectual process that some of craft's champions would have liked it to be.[29]

An even more tendentious aspect of Arneson's *Funk John* was that it did not shy away from the kitsch associations of ceramics. Most of his works of the 1960s were based on some debased ceramic form: toilets, sinks, fake flowers, flowerpots, cookie jars, cheap trophies, and especially bricks, on which he made literally hundreds of variations (Figure 5.3). Arneson often emphasized the unpretentiousness of these forms by embellishing them with store-bought hobby glazes and paste-on decals. By 1965, he was working almost exclusively in white low-fire earthenware, a material that complemented his cheap decorative techniques.[30] Because it lacked the tensile strength and brute tactility of stoneware, this clay suggested a ceramics of form and concept rather than physical demonstration. For Arneson, though, it also appealed because it was symbolically marginalized. White earthenware is often the first clay that is given to beginners, and by using it Arneson was able to symbolically occupy his craft's lowest rung—a position knowingly satirized in a series of pieces that focused on clay education, including plates that bore introductory "how-to" instructions showing how a plate is thrown on a wheel, or a book of "secret glazes" made of ceramic.

Arneson's sense of marginality was also captured in the term "Funk" itself. The word was first applied to Arneson and his students when they were included in an exhibition of that name, curated by Peter Selz for the art gallery at the University of California at Berkeley in 1967.[31] This terminology might raise hackles today: the African-American concept of "Funk" had been co-opted for an all-white group of artists. Robert Farris Thompson has written that the word "funk" descends etymologically from the Ki-Kongo word *lu-fuki*, meaning "the smell of the body," whence the association with earthiness and physicality that the term carries.[32] Indeed, the connotation of blackness may have been a factor in this choice of terminology; 1967 was the height of the civil rights movement, and what more potent symbol of the oppressed could be found than African-American culture? Not coincidentally, the immediate antecedents of the sculpture that Selz identified as Funky (the work of Bruce Conner and Wally Hedrick particularly) had flourished in the Beat culture of the Bay Area, which was of course deeply influenced by African-American music and culture.[33] And of

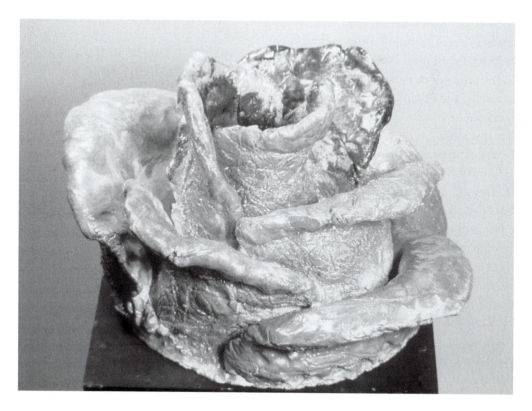

Figure 5.3   Robert Arneson, *Ceramic Rose*, ca. 1968–9. Glazed ceramic. Milwaukee Art Museum.

course, the term "funk" itself entered the American lexicon primarily through the efforts of such black musicians as James Brown and George Clinton, not the activities of a group of white artists in San Francisco. Arneson's self-construction as a disenfranchised figure may also have involved these racial overtones. He was entirely comfortable with the term and contributed to its popularity—he had after all created *Funk John* in 1963, four years before Selz's show. When Arneson was later called upon to explain the word, he used it to draw a three-way comparison between hobbyists, the jazz subculture, and his own activities: "We would say, 'let's do some dime store stuff with those funky glazes from the little old lady ceramic shops.' Lots of people threw the word around then. It comes from jazz. After the clubs closed, the jazz musicians would get together and blow. It was funky. It was for themselves."[34]

Whatever the complexities of Arneson's self-proclaimed marginalization may have been, it was certainly not just a pose. He found only limited reception for his work in the art world. In a 1965 review, for instance, the Minimalist sculptor Donald Judd panned him: "The main shapes of the pieces, which are askew and lumpy, resemble Oldenburg's plaster objects somewhat. The plentiful and literal details are like the more innocent detail of some folk art or long-orphaned art . . . Literal, somewhat naïve detail is not very interesting. At any rate, Arneson's scatology isn't complex enough."[35] It was only in the 1970s, when Arneson began executing works in the more recognizable art mode of portrait busts, that the mainstream art press took much notice of him—to the exclusion of his Funky confreres.[36] In the craft world, though, it was a different story. When Joseph Pugliese penned an article recapping the ceramics of the 1960s for *Craft Horizons*, he used Arneson's self-portrait *A Hollow Jesture* as the lead image (Figure 5.4). Arneson's tongue may have been sticking out, but it was too late to pretend that he was just a knowing crackpot in the peanut gallery— he found himself, ironically enough, the leader of a new ceramics movement. Pugliese's article reflected chagrin with the state of affairs that had resulted from the proliferation of Arneson's imitators: ". . . in the past several years, too many works in clay have become essentially decorative, increasingly obvious, and considerably less interesting than works in other media."[37] More recently, Mitchell Merback has pointed out, "[when] weaned from its underground roots, Funk was positioned as new and avant-garde at the very moment it had ceased to be either."[38] To the extent that Funk had been a subculture that flourished beneath the notice of the craft establishment, bringing it into the spotlight effectively destroyed it.

As the Funk movement proliferated, it lost in quality what it gained in followers, gradually petering out into a derivative confection of brightly colored glazes, finicky workmanship, and lame visual puns. In the process, the internal anxieties about amateurism in Arneson's work (and consequently, its critical edge) were lost. The hobby glaze became a common-place in American studio ceramics for several years, a development that established figures in the field like Paul Soldner, one of Voulkos's closest colleagues, dismissed with knee-jerk hostility. "Kids are getting more and more effeminate in their art work," Soldner complained

Figure 5.4 Robert Arneson, *A Hollow Jesture*, 1971. Glazed earthenware.
Fine Art Museums of San Francisco. Partial gift of Dorothy and George
Sace to the Fine Arts Museums Foundation, 2002.148.2.

in 1970. "It's part of the minimal kick and the highly lustered 'old lady' glazes and the use of sensual qualities as against the more masculine ones."[39] The later works of Arneson himself, which revolve mainly around the themes of portraiture, rarely have the conceptual acuity of his early Funk. Yet he remained obsessed with his own status as a potter and an artist. Whether lampooning himself outright, indicating his sense of art historical inferiority (most effectively through a series of works about Jackson Pollock), or depicting himself as a clay-like entity who was subject to violent stretching, pounding, and pressing, he implied that his anxieties had never been resolved. In this regard, despite (and as always with craft, because of) the limits of his work, Arneson stands as a convincing model for a craft-based practice, all the more expansive because of its self-referentiality.

FEMINISM AND THE POLITICS OF AMATEURISM

Just as Robert Arneson was drifting away from his confrontation with amateurism, Feminist artists were beginning to enter the fray. As it had been for Arneson, the trope of amateur craft was, for Feminists, a way of recognizing the enforced conditions of their own practice. But whereas Arneson's troubles had to do with the associations of his chosen medium, Feminist concerns were broader—grounded in the presumption that women's creativity itself was domestic and non-professional. As Kate Millet wrote in her popular and contentious book *Sexual Politics*, "although they achieved their first economic autonomy in the industrial revolution and now constitute a large and underpaid factory population, women do not participate directly in technology or in production. What they customarily produce (domestic and personal service) has no market value and is, as it were, pre-capital."[40] This was a theme reiterated by Feminists in all spheres of public life. But it had particular resonance among women artists, whose professional status was often frustratingly ambiguous (as in the cases of Eva Hesse and Miriam Schapiro, both of whose artistic careers were long considered to be addenda to those of their husbands). By calling attention to the tasks of social maintenance that had long remained invisible to a patriarchal culture, Feminists dramatized the singular difficulties of being a woman artist in the early 1970s, who was often a professional artist by choice but also something else (a mother, a housekeeper, a teacher) by necessity.[41]

Of course, Feminist artists did not simply inhabit the sphere of domestic amateurism uncritically.[42] They arrived at a formulation that was more subtle than Arneson's. Where he offered the completely debased category of "the world's most fascinating hobby," Feminists both recognized the marginality of certain media and processes and simultaneously insisted on a certain respect for such work. They called attention to the long history of domestic arts—textile arts such as spinning, quilting, embroidery, fancywork, and lace-making especially, but also work in paper, decorative painting on furniture and ceramics, and even the "craft" of homemaking itself—and argued that these amateur activities should be recuperated as a lost art history.[43] As far as the present day went, the logic of the Feminist movement demanded that a woman artist should create work that would attain broad cultural legitimacy, while also being somehow identifiable as "women's work." The upshot was a strategic quandary: should women artists try to capture art world attention from their own marginal base (such as the co-operative galleries that proliferated in the 1970s), or alternatively, as Amelia Jones has written, "[have] work exhibited and discussed within high art institutions and discourses while attempting to critique them at the same time"?[44]

Amateurism became a middle ground through which women artists could articulate the very difficulty of their position. In this respect, the writer Virginia Woolf provided a model. Despite her misgivings she valued her pseudo-professional status and her "room of one's own," because they distanced her from the overtly sexist literary institutions of her day.[45] In this spirit, Feminists conceived of amateurism as a strategy that held both the traditional home and the mainstream art world at arm's length. Craft was the most material expression of that strategy. It served double duty as a symbol of unjustly quashed creativity, and a token of the Feminist desire to break out of the stultification of domesticity. Thus the typical Feminist account of craft stresses its "[association] with trivialized and degraded categories of 'women's work' outside of the fine arts," even as it emphasizes craft's potential for liberating self-expression.[46] The British art historian Rozsika Parker summed up this ambivalent attitude towards craft in her 1984 text *The Subversive Stitch*. Embroidery, Parker wrote:

> has been the means of educating women into the feminine ideal, and of proving that they have attained it—witness the history of samplers, for instance—but it has also proved a weapon of resistance to the painful constraints of femininity… Limited to practising art with needle and thread, women have nevertheless sewn a subversive stitch, managing to make meaning of their own in the very medium intended to foster polite self-effacement.[47]

Parker aptly characterized both the advantages and the problems that Feminists knowingly assigned themselves in taking up amateur craft as an artistic vocabulary. On the positive side, they acquired a ready-made alternative art history, and gained a language of form that summoned up vast realms of women's experience. On the negative side, they found themselves confronted by the questionable notion that craft was inherently female, and by the negative aspects of that gendering. This issue lay at the heart of a 1987 exhibition, also entitled "The Subversive Stitch," inspired by Parker's book. Historic women's textiles and contemporary British art works were gathered into a pair of exhibitions in Manchester, followed by a tour to other venues in England. The curator of the project's contemporary section, Pennina Barnett, summed up the prevailing attitude of the participating artists as "an ambivalence towards sewing and textile work. On the one hand they respect the tradition of needlework… Yet there is also the feeling that by sewing they are practicing a painstaking feminine craft which has low status and strong domestic connotations."[48] Barnett reflected this sense of unease by adducing disturbing details from the history of women's textile art, such as this poignant verse from an 1830 girl's sampler:

Seek to be good but not to be great
A Woman's noblest station is retreat
Her fairest virtues fly from public sight,
Domestic worth still shuns too strong a light.[49]

Much of the contemporary work she gathered together was premised on Parker's attempt to "show the contradictory faces of embroidery, demonstrating how it has been both a source of pleasurable creativity and oppression."[50] Some artists took satirical aim at the problematic association of women with amateur craft by satirizing the history of domestic needlework itself. Lyn Malcolm, for example, fashioned a domestic vignette in which various needlework elements spelled out the phrase "Why Have We So Few Women Artists?" (an Anglicization of the famous essay title by Feminist art historian Linda Nochlin). Others resorted to the mediation of photography or film, which as Barnett put it "set the subject at one remove," situating textile imagery within a suitably critical framework.[51]

Also included in the exhibition were protest artworks made in textile media, emblazoned with slogans such as "Forward Ever Backward Never," which could scarcely be seen as expressing nostalgia for the days when embroidery connoted domestic virtue. Such craft objects had particular currency at the time, due to the ongoing occupation of Greenham Common, Berkshire, as a Women's Peace Camp (see Plate 13). From its beginnings in 1981, the stated goal of this permanent counter-cultural emplacement was to protest the presence of American nuclear missiles at an adjacent airbase; but it soon became a spiritual center for British Feminists. It also served, rather more incidentally, as a hub of amateur craft production. Homemade banners, clothing and makeshift shelters constituted a powerful collective aesthetic, which was powerfully influential on certain Feminist artists. One such figure was Janis Jefferies, who remains a key figure in the intersection between professional fiber art and Feminist textiles. Early in her career, Jefferies had studied with the Polish weavers Tadek Beutlich and Magdalena Abakanowicz. Her early work adapted the implicitly Feminist vaginal imagery and the thick, hand-knotted and woven structures that had made Abakanowicz an international phenomenon in the early 1970s.[52] After a stint at Greenham Common, Jefferies incorporated the demonstration culture there into her artwork, creating photocollages and domestic needlework objects featuring imagery from the camp. She also took a leading role in the creation of a tapestry commemorating the women there, whom she described as having "literally woven themselves into the site of their protest ... with an assortment of banners and quilts as in the manner of a textile dragon."[53] Her later work and writings have continued to explore the textiles as a political instrument. For Jefferies and other Feminist artists of her generation, the notion of a flexible, evenly dispersed weave has itself come to seem like a model for a more democratic and egalitarian social "fabric"— a metaphor that has become only more potent with the emergence of the World Wide Web.[54]

As Feminists in 1980s Britain came to see textile craft as intrinsically political, some weavers began to object to those who failed to live up to this critical standard. As Faith Gillespie put it in 1987, "Our turning to craftwork is a refusal. We may not all see ourselves this way, but we are working from a position of dissent. And that is a political position."[55] A reversal of the same logic led the Canadian Feminist artist Ann Newdigate to attack the Lausanne Biennial, a main venue for the exhibit of fiber art installations by Abakanowicz and others, for "creating a High Craft sphere which sought to distance itself from the Low Craft sphere. For the most part any submission which could be identified as pertaining to women's work, or figurative imagery evoking the vanquished French tradition, constituted the lower end of the Low Art sphere."[56] Such emphatically politicized positions perhaps overlooked the commonalities between Feminism and fiber art. After all, both were marginalized with respect to mainstream art institutions.[57] But most in the Feminist movement, both in Britain and in America, were skeptical that such exhibitions would ever constitute a real avenue of progress. Gillespie's "refusal" and Newdigate's rejection of "High Craft" were at least in part a denunciation of the fine art system itself. Some Feminists went so far as to characterize museums as obsolete institutions, much as early twentieth-century avant gardes had done. This position was extreme, but also justified by long experience with the intransigent sexism of museums and galleries. As late as 1995, the art historian and artist Johanna Drucker was only facing facts when she wrote, "Women still don't have the power base—individually or collectively—to make changes in the structures of the art world or the media world. Denial won't change that."[58]

Many women writing from this position identified quality itself—the conceptual foundation of museum collecting—as an ideological barrier, constructed for the express purpose of fencing out the art of women, minorities, and the working class. The African-American painter and quilt artist Faith Ringgold put it this way: "Quality is something that a white Anglo-Saxon protestant man does... Quality is expensive decoration for rich people who happen to be blind."[59] Nor was this an unusual viewpoint. The leading critic Lucy Lippard offered phrasing that softens but maintains Ringgold's core assertion:

> A populist definition of quality in art might be "that element that *moves* the viewer." A man probably can't decide what that is for a woman, nor a white for a person of color, nor an educated for an uneducated person, and so forth, which is where "taste" comes in. This in turn may explain why the "experts" have never been able to agree on which artists have this elusive "quality."[60]

This relativistic strain in Feminist thought was also reflected in the conduct of the movement's cooperative galleries, such as Womanspace in Los Angeles, which tried to "circumvent the 'star system'" by resisting the typical hierarchy, promotionalism, and commercialism of art galleries.[61] Already by the mid-1970s, Feminism had acquired the reputation, for good or ill, of encouraging women's art indiscriminately. Establishment critics such as Robert Pincus-Witten and Barbara Rose lambasted the movement for abandoning the notion of standards. Pincus-Witten commented that "pluralism means open-enrollment art," resulting in "bad art, primitive, illustrative art and narcissistic self-indulgence called art," while Rose simply stated that "If a woman paints while watching a soap opera, it's hobby art."[62] To these charges, Feminists returned equally angry accusations of snobbery. As Pennina Barnett wrote, "there are those who feel that this fine art business has gone far enough; isn't it all rather elite, and shouldn't the crafts get closer to industry and design, so that more than 'a few rich and idle men,' galleries and museums can enjoy them?"[63]

Yet not all Feminist artists shared this suspicion of objective qualitative standards. When Judy Chicago—perhaps the most influential of the first-generation Feminist artists in America—was asked about the problem of the commodification of art, she responded:

> I'm going to tell you something. I wouldn't mind if my art became a little more of a commodity. Actually it's the opposite problem for those of us who come from disenfranchised groups—it does not even represent a threat because not being able to enter the cultural commodity pool as a maker is one of the things that makes us disenfranchised.[64]

Chicago and her colleagues were on the horns of a dilemma: how to be accepted as major artists, while undercutting the standards on which artists were accepted as being important. Amateur craft was at the heart of two projects undertaken by Chicago during the 1970s, which mark a personal and to some extent an art historical transit in attitudes towards the questions of quality and professionalization: *Womanhouse* (1972) and *The Dinner Party* (executed between 1974 and 1979).

The first of these was a collaborative effort, staged by Chicago in partnership with Miriam Schapiro and their students in the Women's Art Program at the California Institute of the Arts (CalArts), which had recently moved to Valencia, beginning in 1971.[65] It was an auspicious setting for the world's first Feminist art program. Schapiro remembers the school as "a grand melée of radical procedures," including avant-garde dance and the craft-based, "nomadic" design ethic being taught by Victor Papanek.[66] *Womanhouse* was a transformation of a suburban house that was slated for demolition. Its interiors were completely reshaped into art installations that employed ornamental craft techniques, materials, and imagery traditionally associated with women, all aimed at a critique of women's infantilizing consignment to the home. Chicago later explained in her autobiography that the project was an explicit attempt to reframe domestic "women's work" into the substance of oppositional art:

> Women had been embedded in houses for centuries and had quilted, sewed, baked, cooked, decorated and nested their creative energies away. What would happen, we wondered, if women took those very same homemaking activities and carried them to fantasy proportions? Instead of making a pink-and-white, filmy, feminine but functional bedroom for one's daughter, the space might become pinker and whiter and filmier and filled with more and more ruffles until it was a complete environment. Could the same activities women had used in life be transformed into the means of making art?[67]

According to Chicago, then, the strategy at *Womanhouse* was to appropriate an amateur activity, and to intensify or multiply it until it transcended the normal boundaries of domesticity. This was also the understanding of the project voiced by outside observers. Lucy Lippard wrote that rather than "untying the apron strings," the artists involved in *Womanhouse* were "keeping the apron on, flaunting it, and turning it into art," while the artist Martha Rosler saw the project as consisting of "burlesquing and overstating the passive, dependent and depressive roles."[68]

Burlesque was indeed a common thread that ran through the *Womanhouse* environments. The space served as the setting for consciousness-raising sessions and performances by Faith Wilding and the other students in the CalArts program, which helped to create what Schapiro has called a "happening-environment."[69] This technique also guided many of the installations in the building. The act of applying cosmetics to the face, for example, was expanded to the drenching of one bathroom in lipstick-red paint, creating the effect of a horror movie interior. Chicago's own *Menstruation Bathroom* staged a graphic opposition between the "very, very sterile, all white" cleanliness of traditional domesticity and the organic physicality of blood-soaked tampons.[70] The installation in *Womanhouse* that made the most explicit use of craft technique was a similar exercise in exaggeration: Faith Wilding's *Crocheted Environment*, or *Womb Room* (Figure 5.5).[71] Wilding, who had been trained in weaving and other crafts during her upbringing at a utopian commune in Paraguay, also studied with fiber artist Walter Nottingham in River Falls, Wisconsin, prior to moving to the Los Angeles area in 1969. Under Nottingham's tutelage, Wilding came to know about the burgeoning fiber scene, and she credits her use of crocheting on a large-scale to the example of his work.[72] Upon moving to Los Angeles, her previous leftist affiliation (including activism with the organization Students for a Democratic Society) was channeled into energetic devotion to the Feminist program at Fresno, and later at CalArts.[73] Wilding's contribution to *Womanhouse* was a rare exception to the rule that, while fiber art proper and Feminism were closely linked in Britain, they tended to be separate worlds in the United States. Indeed, *Crocheted Environment* was strikingly similar to the fiber environments by the great Polish weaver Magdalena Abakanowicz that had been exhibited in museums around the Los Angeles area in 1971 and 1972. (Wilding lived in Pasadena at the time, and recalls visiting Abakanowicz's exhibit at the museum there several times: "it remains a fantastic memory of entering womblike red woven space.")[74] The space exemplified the ambition that Wilding ascribed to *Womanhouse* in general: to stage "a sharp critique of the confinement of female creativity to a limited sphere."[75]

Sadly, the fate of *Womanhouse* underscored the lack of institutional support for women artists in the early 1970s. Despite the enormous public success of the project, including television and national magazine coverage, the building was eventually destroyed as planned, and its artworks lost. To Wilding's dismay, *Crocheted Environment* was stolen; "someone just cut the whole thing off at the roots, so to speak."[76] Schapiro and Chicago parted company in 1973 and turned increasingly to their own artistic undertakings—Schapiro

Figure 5.5   Faith Wilding, *Womb Room (Crocheted Environment)*.
1971. As refabricated for the exhibition "Division of Labor" at the
Bronx Museum, 1995.
Courtesy of the artist. Photograph: Becket Logan.

to her fabric-and-paint "femmages," which brought a Feminist analysis to the decorative supplement (see Chapter 1), and Chicago to an ambitious, all-consuming installation project entitled *The Dinner Party* (Figure 5.6). If *Womanhouse* was the quintessential example of Feminist art staged at the margins, with normative standards of quality held in contempt, then Chicago's new endeavor was a bold reversal of that strategy, a bid for institutional authorization. With its equilateral triangular shape and interior territory of interlocking tiles painted with the names of 999 women, the installation has more the feeling of a fortification than a domestic dining room. The amateurism of the installations at *Womanhouse*—so appropriate and evocative in that domestic environment—is still present, but only in the sense that pinned butterflies are present in a collector's cabinet. Hobby craft was now overlaid with a heavy veneer of the professional. Chicago's design for

Figure 5.6 Judy Chicago, *The Dinner Party*, 1974–79. Painted porcelain, needlework.
Courtesy of Through the Flower.

the installation referred to her own past (before her overtly Feminist days) as a sculptor of the "Finish fetish" school, a Southern California style of the 1960s was premised on clean, perfect surfaces in which marks of the hand were effaced.[77] The style had proved successful in landing ceramists such as Ken Price in fine art museums, and it is telling that Chicago revived it here.

In adopting china painting techniques for her vaginal plates, Chicago was also alluding to the hobbyist associations of ceramics, like Arneson before her. In the catalogue for the project, she recalled a china painting class she took in 1972 in preparation for the execution of *The Dinner Party* as "a perfect metaphor for women's domesticated and trivialized circumstances. It was an excruciating experience to watch enormously gifted women squander their creative talents on teacups."[78] In vivid contrast to the lack of ambition that Chicago perceived in this amateur situation, she aimed to make a piece of power and authority. As she put it:

> I can discuss what my vision is. I wanted to make a piece that was beyond judgment. For example, if you go and you see the Sistine Chapel you don't say, "Oh, I don't like it." It's irrelevant whether you like it or not. Whether it's good or bad is irrelevant, it simply stands as a testament to human achievement. When I was in Europe traveling around I went to the Leger Museum and the Matisse Chapel and Picasso's house. And I so long to see that kind of achievement having been made by a woman.[79]

As one might expect from this level of aspiration, Chicago had little patience with the amateurism of the 200 volunteer women who executed *The Dinner Party*. She maintained a hierarchy patterned on a traditional guild, in which her own role as master artist was clearly demarcated from the subservient role played by her assistants. Thus, although the installation was achieved through amateur craft processes, Chicago herself no longer wanted to play the part of the amateur, even in the broadly satirical terms that she and the other women of *Womanhouse* had previously found so provocative. As Amelia Jones has noted, "rather than attempting to break down the distinctions between high and low, Chicago has openly acknowledged her continued investment in upholding such an opposition."[80]

ABJECT CRAFT: MIKE KELLEY AND TRACEY EMIN

In retrospect, it is hard to see *The Dinner Party* as anything but an enormous success. Chicago's installation visited fourteen museums and was wildly popular, attracting 100,000 visitors at one venue.[81] It is now considered the primary monument of Feminist art itself, and despite lingering ambivalence about the project, it is indeed taught in introductory art history surveys alongside Michelangelo's and Matisse's chapels, just as Chicago had wanted. While *Womanhouse* was destroyed shortly after its creation, *The Dinner Party* is now permanently installed at the Brooklyn Museum. In the late 1970s, though, this enfranchised status was hardly a foregone conclusion. Chicago's simultaneous mobilization and disavowal of amateur aesthetics invited (and received) critique from both sides. Left-wing critics lambasted her for hewing to an obsolete notion of the inspired artist, while conservatives denounced her as inordinately willing to sacrifice formal standards for the sake of content. Particularly vivid was the criticism from Feminists who saw the project as exploitative. Chicago was accused of mistreating the team of craftswomen who executed the embroidery and ceramics for *The Dinner Party*, who were scarcely recognized for their labor in print and gallery presentations of the work.[82]

Ethically speaking, Chicago's apparent disdain for the women working for her should not be excused—though it should also be noted that such a dynamic was hardly unique to her at the time, and arguably remains the norm today in large-scale contemporary art production. Yet, in a curious historical development, unspoken disdain is the very thing that seems most contemporary about *The Dinner Party*. Since the rise and wane of first-generation Feminism, contemporary artists have continued to employ the tropes of amateur craft, both as a means of production and as a recognizable sign of social content. Unlike Chicago, however, they have not sought to celebrate hobby craft by submerging it into subject matter and protecting it within a shield of professionalism. On the contrary, the most widespread strategy in the late 1980s and early 1990s was to exploit craft's "abject" position, its "lower than low" status in the cultural hierarchy.[83] Craft has captured the attention of artists because it is a site of cultural failure, a field of activity that is resigned to inferiority and debasement because of the complete supremacy and centrality of mass-manufactured commodities. The issues explored earlier in the book—craft's supplementarity and its brute materiality—return with a vengeance in abject art, as amateur craft is used alongside other tropes (the inside of the body, excrement, and obscenity) as a way of rupturing the placid surface of art production and display. This tendency is strikingly reminiscent of Robert Arneson's investigation of clay as a taboo substance, or the menstrual blood in Judy Chicago's bathroom installation at *Womanhouse*. But if Arneson's concerns were local to the condition of studio pottery, and Chicago's to the Feminist movement, recent work has used craft as a vehicle to arrive at more general theoretical positions. The artists Mike Kelley and Tracey Emin serve as two exemplary, but contrasting cases.

Though he hails from Detroit, Kelley has long been based in Los Angeles, and thus at the centerpoint of early Feminist practice in America. Over the course of an extraordinarily varied career (beginning with performance art and taking in a wide range of sound, installation and video work), he achieved perhaps his greatest notoriety in the late 1980s and early 1990s with a series of works employing hobbyist craft, including both found objects and hand techniques such as felt appliqué and knitting. Both in its title and its materials, *More Love Hours Than Can Ever Be Repaid*—a collection of found stuffed animals sewn on to a found handmade quilt—evokes the wretched excess and pathos of domestic craft activity (see Plate 14). In 1994, Kelley recalled the initial motivations for this body of work:

> Los Angeles was one of the main centers of feminism and also one of the last holdouts of a huge movement of essentialist feminists, especially in the performance art world. I was dealing with these people all the time. Basically I thought it was really wrong for these women to do pattern painting, because that was heroicizing the kind of feminine clichés that had been handed down to them... When I first [began to use knitting], it

was as a reaction to essentialist feminist art. Not to put it down, but to say, 'What if I do this, then what happens?' I have been accused of being just another man co-opting feminist art. Well, I refuse to say that knitting is only for women. That's sexist. It's just as much mine as theirs, because whether it's men or women that are supposed to knit is totally random.[84]

Kelley's argument typifies the attitude towards first-generation Feminist art held by recent artists, who tend to see the "essentialism" embodied by figures such as Chicago, their insistence on the absolute difference between men and women, as untenable. His main interest in craft is therefore not in its positive gender association, but its negative or marginal social character. He has described craft as culturally "invisible" and degraded: "here's a structure that's loaded with pathos… You want to kick it. That's what I wanted out of the thing—an artwork that you couldn't raise; there was no way you could make it better than it was."[85] For Kelley, craft is a species of kitsch, and the expenditures of effort and skill that are lavished on craft objects reap only pity.

It has been argued that Kelley's appropriation of craft intentionally effaces the history and intentions of Feminism even as it promotes a new kind of machismo.[86] But this is to simplify and caricature his position, as well as the context in which he was working. In the 1980s Kelley was only one artist of many who operated on the premise that craft, in the art world, could only be synonymous with inferiority. In certain quarters, this played out as a frustrated acknowledgment of the continuing disenfranchisement of women in the art world. The spotlight that Feminism had placed on the marginalized nature of amateur craft activities made them an appealing subject for artists who were looking for a language to express this general condition. Thus the parody of the amateur that appears in Kelley's work is also manifested in later Feminist art—from Cindy Sherman's "bad" color photography to the laboriously wrought sculptures of Janine Antoni to entire exhibitions such as the New Museum's 1994 "Bad Girls," which was devoted to the "carnivalesque" mode in second and third wave Feminist art.[87]

Seen against this background, while Kelley's work was conceived in terms that were oppositional to earlier Feminist art strategies, his use of craft might be seen as sympathetic with the broader Feminist project as it had developed in the 1980s. His general strategy has been to identify formal languages that appear to have fixed ideological content, and then to create contravening formal situations that destabilize that content. In his essay "The Mike Kelleys," John Welchman summarizes this deconstructive strategy as follows: "Whether it is noise repressed by music, craft by fine art, desire by conduct, or objects and ideas repressed by the codes of Minimalism and Conceptual Art, Kelley's impulse is to liberate, then free-associate with their traces, and mongrelize their syntactical relation."[88] Thus in *More Love Hours Than Can Ever Be Repaid*, Kelley employs brightly-colored, found stuffed animals as if they were the individual brushstrokes of a painting. The shift is similar to that enacted by Judy Chicago in the *Dinner Party*—low craft transported into the genre of high art—but the strident claims that Chicago made for such recontextualization are completely absent.

In their place is little more than an air of discomfort, a lack of fit between two competing worlds of form that creates problems for both. Despite the compositional reference to an abstract canvas, it is difficult to see the work in purely painterly terms—our associations with lovingly handmade objects, which may well combine sympathy with disdain, are simply too strong to overcome. Kelley is teasingly referring to the precedent of Feminism, but he is clearly more interested in ongoing popular usages of craft, and particularly in people's willingness to pour time and effort into objects that lie below the regard of most cultural institutions.

As the work's title implies, the plenitude of craft labor expended on these worthless objects, which Kelley found abandoned in thrift stores, makes sense only within an asymmetrical emotional economy of gift-giving. That system of value lies outside not only the art world but the standard flow of commodities in general.[89] They also are well out of reach of any artistic avant garde. Unlike Chicago, Kelley assumes that he can have little direct effect upon these cultural associations with craft and has no intention to do so in any case. He rather exploits a coded formal language in order to create works of internal dissonance. Another of Kelley's works, entitled *Craft Morphology Flow Chart*, offers a organizational system in which found sock monkeys and yarn octopi have been laid out on folding tables, classified arbitrarily into groups, photographed and measured. This send-up of the formal language of Conceptual art again exploits the fact (already implied by Duchamp's Readymades, but not central to the theoretical tradition that they initiated) that not all found objects are created equal. The pathos of the stuffed animals, the sad individuality that Kelley describes as "the uncanny aura of the craft item," inevitably escape the piece's systematic logic.[90] In the final analysis, Kelley needs craft for a work like this because it is indigestible. It cannot be made to sit still for a normative statistical exercise. In its very lowness, craft disrupts the normally all-encompassing language of art.

The British artist Tracey Emin has achieved even more fame than Kelley through the use of a similar idiom of debased craft. If Kelley's public persona is elusive and multiple, and his works stubbornly resistant to conclusive reading, then Emin is a diametrically opposite character on the landscape. Her art functions as a confirmation of her celebrity rather than vice versa. Ulrich Lehmann has described the cultural artifact that is Tracey Emin as "a (fictional) self-construction," a fabricated and consciously maintained cliché composed of intimate biographical details, explicit sexual confessions, and above all, the constant revelation of the artist's body.[91] Emin's careful management of this cultural material, ironically, always serves to create the impression that her true subjectivity is on offer. In short, Lehmann argues, "Tracey Emin" principally functions not as an artist, but as a trademark. Just as it would be a mistake to criticize Kelley for lampooning the tropes of Feminist art, it would equally be incorrect to see Emin as glibly indulgent. Her work is a mechanism that performs the double act of guaranteeing authenticity, but which in fact takes into account the replication of her self as a highly successful commodity. This trademarking is the end result of Emin's collapsing of traditionally distinct binaries such as public/private, artist/model (in a 1996 nude performance piece cum artist's residency entitled "Life Model Goes Mad"), curator/exhibitor (in the "Tracey Emin Museum" that she maintained in London, which was also her studio) and above all, professional/amateur.[92]

Craft occupies a key position in this process of continual unveiling, and is Emin's most effective way of occupying a *faux* amateur position. (She also draws "badly," misspells words, and makes frequent informal references to her circle of friends, but unlike craft, these tactics might easily be taken as classical avant garde gestures.) Again, Emin's use of craft, despite its formal similarities to Kelley's, is the opposite of his in both content and intent. Kelley has said, "with my doll works, the viewer isn't led to reflect on the psychology of the artist but on the psychology of the culture."[93] The opposite is clearly true of Emin's *appliqués*. Like her fellow Turner prizewinner, the potter Grayson Perry (who learned the skills necessary to make his confessional autobiographical ceramics in an adult education class), Emin's work maps tales of personal rejection through a marginalized craft language. So much is clear from her most famous work, *Everyone I Have Ever Slept With, 1963–1995* (1995), a tent with the names of Emin's sleeping partners (both sexual and Platonic) appliquéd to the interior, or the seemingly unending series of quilts, furniture and bags that she has embroidered with a welter of personal slogans and motifs (see Plate 15).

While Kelley's use of craft is generalized and anthropological, Emin's is specific and autobiographical—a form of self-portraiture.[94] This distinction in turn rests on a difference in process. Kelley mainly employs found objects as a way of introducing craft into his work, and when he does not, he invariably employs found imagery. Emin, by contrast, executed all her work herself by hand until recently (she now hires skilled assistants, with the result that the workmanship in her art has noticeably improved). Kelley exposes the arbitrariness with which certain formal practices are assigned to certain producers—knitting to women, for example. Emin by contrast relies on just this "essentialist" association as a means to assert her own (specifically female) subject position. Her employment of craft as an abject formal language exemplifies the tendency, furiously criticized by Rosalind Krauss, to employ the seemingly disruptive matter of the abject only as a way of renewing old certainties about identity. Whereas Krauss praises Kelley, whose work is involved in an endless operation of destabilization, she rejects any art that, like Emin's, is based upon "a 'truth' that is spoken again and again, the truth that is the master signified of a system of meaning for which the wound is feminine, the truth that the woman is wounded."[95]

Yet, if Emin's art is problematic in its replication of cultural "truths" that would better be deconstructed, it may in another sense be productive in a way that Kelley's art is not. There can be little doubt that Emin is narcissistic, and that the persona that she constantly presents to the world is a collage of cherished scars. If it is possible to write of "Mike Kelleys," in the plural, there is no sense that Tracey Emin views herself in multiple or internally contradictory terms. She is simply "the slag from Margate" redeemed through art. She is therefore celebrated by supportive critics as "an honest realist," a phrase that inadvertently but revealingly connects her to the most conservative strains within twentieth-century art.[96]

Yet Emin is also narcissistic in the approving sense in which Amelia Jones has used that term: "the self turns inside out, as it were, projecting its internal structures of identification and desire outward ... such formulations *make evident* what modernism has labored to conceal."[97] Emin's elaborate parade of the self, her seeming desperation to tell us everything, inevitably calls the motivations of her audience—we the viewers—into question. For if her embarrassing narratives suggest an exhaustion of artistic authority, then why are we still looking? In the end, Emin is no less effective than Kelley in her "thinking through craft," in the sense that I have tried to explore that phrase throughout this book. She demonstrates in no uncertain terms that, for all that craft is an embarrassment for the construct of modern art, it seems that the modern art world cannot do without it.

6 CONCLUSION

Work, *practice*, and *site*: three words that contemporary art would have a tough time getting along without. Anything made by an artist can be a work; anything an artist does can be a practice; and anywhere this happens can be a site. This lack of definition is indispensable in today's climate of polymorphic production. The traditional genres (landscape, portrait, still life, vessel) and media (painting, pottery, photography) that once imposed order on artistic production are now of purely historical interest. They still exert a hold on the imagination, certainly, and artists take them up for their own purposes, but they no longer act as the grounds of discipline. In the absence of such commonalities, a generic conception of artistic production has become the norm.

Thus, whether an artist makes something from paint and canvas, metal, or videotape, whether it is the size of a building, or so small as to be invisible to the naked eye and whether it is encountered in a gallery, a city park, or on a computer screen, that thing (even if it is not a "thing" at all) can still be called a "work." So handy is this open-ended word that it has displaced the term "object" itself, which was used just as frequently (and for similar reasons) in the 1960s. Robert Morris spoke of "object-type art," while Marcel Broodthaers found object useful as a "zero word."[1] The marquee craft exhibition of the postwar period, *Objects: USA*, exploited the term's imprecision to include teapots, avant-garde sculpture, and everything in between.[2] However, as Lucy Lippard's book title *Dematerialization of the Art Object* suggests, the term was already insufficient to cover the range of current artistic practices by 1972. Unable to cope with the emergence of installation, earth art, video, and performance, object gave way to work.

Equally useful is "practice," which, bolstered by its homology with "praxis" (a Marxist philosophical term meaning roughly "theoretical knowledge put to use"), has become the universal occupation of today's creative class. Practice, like work, is a relative newcomer, having displaced "action," which again suffered from too much definition. While action carries strong connotations of the freighted gestures of the Abstract Expressionists, a practice can reasonably include every aspect of an artist's life. Chris Burden's infamous performance, *Shoot*, in which he arranged to be shot through the arm by a rifleman, was an action. Rirkrit Tiravanija's daily serving of Thai curry to gallery visitors is a practice, along with other multifarious, non-productive, do-it-yourself art phenomena that have proliferated under the recently-fashionable heading of "relational aesthetics."[3]

"Site," meanwhile, is the word of choice not only for artists but even for institutions such as SITE: Santa Fe—an art museum in all but name. Site conflates the place of an artwork's production with that of its reception, and in this respect alone represents an improvement upon the now old-fashioned term "studio." The artist's studio, as in the case of Brancusi, is characterized by artisanal (rather than mass) production. A studio is inhabited by a limited number of workers, under the leadership of a single individual who is the author of anything made there. Like an object and an action, a studio is singular and confined, rather than multiple and open. In her book *The Machine in the Studio*, Caroline Jones has provided a rich account of the passing away of the studio as the normative concept applied to places of artistic production.[4] She locates the shift, again, in the 1960s, when American artists like Frank Stella, Andy Warhol, and Robert Smithson embraced serial and industrial production, adopted the personae of managers rather than makers, and ultimately left the enclosed environment of the studio behind entirely in order to produce site-specific work *in situ*. The power of the site can be witnessed in action in Smithson's works, which constituted a deconstructive assault on the studio and the gallery simultaneously.[5] This is not to say that contemporary artists no longer work in studios, obviously, or even that the old magic of these spaces cannot be put back into play. It is not the studio itself, but the secure authorial power that it once embodied that can never be fully recaptured.

The foregoing may seem a rather general way to begin the conclusion to this book. But it might go a long way toward understanding the identity crisis that faces a fourth problem word: "craft" itself. The much-discussed decision by the American Craft Museum in New York to change its name to the Museum of Arts and Design, or the dropping of the final two words from the name of the California College of Arts and Crafts, signify more than local concerns. The American Craft Council and its sister organization, the British Crafts Council, are consciously undertaking parallel processes of re-definition, the former revamping its journal *American Craft* and considering re-entry into the fray of contemporary art exhibitions, and the latter closing its London exhibition space (to much dismay amongst loyalists) and restructuring itself as a development and support organization. Each of these individual institutions has its own story, related more to questions of commercial viability than theoretical integrity, and it is too early to predict the outcome of any of these attempts at rebranding and redirection. But it would be well for all of these institutions to remember that, issues of nomenclature aside, studio craft has not managed to adapt itself well to the historical shifts in contemporary art described above. As a field of production, studio craft is still unswervingly devoted to the creation of "objects." It is defined by the mastery and enactment of a set of readily identified "actions" (throwing a pot, making a basket, etc.). And, as its very name suggests, it has not yet begun to grapple with the realities of the "post-studio" environment.

Ironically, as I hope this book has demonstrated, craft without the "studio" modifier has always been a crucial factor in the sphere of modern and contemporary art. Matters are no different today. In fact, craft seems positively fashionable in the present moment, as artists, architects, and designers evince a fascination with process and materials not seen since the heyday of the Counterculture in the late 1960s. (Amusingly, this fervor for craft is often discussed under the heading of "production values," as if what was being described were Hollywood film and not art.)[6] When the 2004 Whitney Biennial was positively received by critics for its "youth-heavy emphasis on gloss and craft," it caused considerable head-scratching amongst craftspeople accustomed to complaining about art world prejudice.[7] In Britain, meanwhile, three of the recent winners of Britain's prestigious Turner Prize are deeply involved with issues of craft: Tracey Emin, Grayson Perry, and Simon Starling. As we have seen, Emin's engagement with craft depends on an implicit presumption of its pathos, and the same could be said of Perry's work, which employs pottery as a vehicle for the exposure of a hair-raisingly frank interior monologue.[8]

Whatever one thinks of the cults of personality around Emin and Perry, though, no one could doubt the seriousness and complexity with which Simon Starling employs the concepts of craft. His prize-winning work *Shedboatshed* might possibly be a sign of things to come: a work in which all the thinking operates through process, but which makes no assumptions about the preconditions or results of that endeavor. Starling's work consists of a shed that the artist found along the banks of the Rhine river, transformed into a raft, paddled down the river, and re-erected at a museum in Basel (see Plate 16). The word "craft" has a double meaning here, as both an activity and a genre of object. Woodcraft turns into a watercraft, and back again. Starling's personal interaction with the universal concerns of shelter and transit could only occur through the medium of artisanal activity. *Shedboatshed* makes no claims about an intrinsically superior craft "ethic," and in its displacement of materials from one site to another (a combination of baroque excess and rigorous efficiency) seems even to lampoon the first law of ecologically responsible tourism—"take nothing but photographs, leave nothing but footprints." But Starling is nonetheless staging artisanal work through art in a way that Kenneth Frampton would doubtless approve of: a highly aware way of being-in-the-world. Serious thinking about our own personal place in the environment, Starling suggests, will inevitably involve thinking through craft.[9]

The conceptual depth of Starling's practice, and even the celebrity of artists like Perry and Emin, have gone some way towards rehabilitating craft in the eyes of the British art world; but their success has certainly not redounded to the benefit of poor old studio craft. In fact, the current fascination with means of production—not just on the part of these British artists, but many others across the globe—may be happening despite, and not because of, efforts to promote the crafts as a separate-but-equal branch of the visual arts. Grayson Perry himself has been notably forceful in his dismissal of the studio craft movement, writing:

> I see the craft world as a kind of lagoon and the art world in general as the ocean. Some artists shelter in this lagoon, because their imagination isn't robust enough to go out into the wider sea. Although there are some very good things being made, the craft world at the moment is set up to preserve something that can't look after itself.[10]

Perry's metaphor, which plays on the pastoral idea of a protected space of retreat, returns us to the fact that studio craft's dilemma may be better captured not in the word "craft" at all, but rather "studio." The romance of the work space, having been comprehensively dismantled (or at least critiqued) elsewhere in contemporary art, is still alive and well in the crafts. This is partly due to the fact that crafted objects are by their very nature evocative of the way in which they were made, a trait that is amplified by the organization of the craft movement into discrete institutions and groups along media lines. The sheer appeal of craft-in-action also doubtless plays a role: the hot and sweaty theatrics of the glass hot shop, the fountains of wood shavings produced by turners at the lathe, the magical transformations that occur on the pottery wheel, and even the slower, mesmerizing back-and-forth of a loom or the raising of a vessel from sheet metal. The problem with this seductive aspect of craft is that it props up a hidebound attitude towards the nature of artistic enterprise. Looking back at the advent of Conceptualism from the vantage point of 1986, the British artist Victor Burgin isolated the rejection of the action and the object as a particularly important breakthrough: "Art practice was no longer to be defined as an artisanal activity, a process of crafting fine objects in a given medium, it was rather to be seen as a set of operations performed in a *field* of signifying practices, perhaps centred on a medium but certainly not bounded by it."[11]

If people who care about craft above all else are to shake off the air of crabby conservatism that hangs about that word, they must not hold the notions of studio, action, and object as sacred. Fortunately, however, because of their longstanding attachment to these terms and all they imply, it could be argued that those who have invested deeply in craft now enjoy a unique vantage point from which to engage in critical practice—a chance, that is, to become newly relevant to the art world as a whole.

At several points in this book, I have tried to draw attention to historic and contemporary works that operate in just this way, by exploiting what seems to be a predicament. Robert Arneson, Judy Chicago, Gijs Bakker, Mike Kelley, Gord Peteran, Miriam Schapiro, Richard Slee, Emma Woffenden, and Yagi Kazuo, each in his or her own way, take their strength as artists from some aspect of craft's intrinsic weakness. Each occupies what seems on one level to be a traditional studio environment, operating within the tightly defined parameters of certain activities in order to make discrete objects. Yet they also undercut the stability of these fixed points in the artistic equation. For them craft is not only a way of thinking; it is also a foil. For Arneson, Bakker, Peteran, and Slee, the object is a self-regarding in-strument that calls the basis of its own value into question. Yagi and Woffenden distance themselves from normative ideas of craft as an action, so as to reveal the stakes of working material more clearly. For Chicago, Schapiro, and Kelley, the physical and social space in which craft objects are made becomes a means of displacing value structures. In each of these cases, the potential frameworks for artistic production were generic—work, practice, and site—but craft's specificity and limitedness offered a possibility for useful friction. In such sleights of hand, the challenge is always to see craft not as a subject for celebration or self-congratulation, nor as a disqualification for serious artistic enterprise, but rather as a problem to be thought through again and again.

I should add, in closing, that this book has been written partly in a spirit of instigation. I have mostly discussed the relation of craft to the avant garde, and have devoted comparatively little attention to "traditional" craftspeople who occupy a proudly conservative position. This is because, frankly, I do not think that all craft demands critical analysis. A modern object that ticks all the craft boxes—an object that simply *is* supplemental, material, skilled, pastoral, and amateur—may be fascinating from the perspective of a historian, but it does not necessarily present an interesting case for theoretical discourse. So, when a maker insists that the best way to understand their object is to use it, I am sometimes inclined to agree. My two most prized possessions are a Warren MacKenzie bowl and an Art Carpenter Wishbone chair. I wrote much of this book sitting in the latter, only a few feet from the former, and looking at both in the idle moments between sentences. I would hotly dispute any claim that either of these objects is culturally insignificant, aesthetically unsatisfying, or otherwise valueless. The histories of such objects, and the people that made them, are long overdue. They should be written with as much sensitivity and care as craft historians can summon. On the other hand, to write those histories accurately, we must concede that they occupy a safe position in the landscape of the visual arts—a lagoon, perhaps. We should all be glad for the availability of such an option, but that feeling should not necessarily make us feel compelled to "interpretation" per se. For the historian, theorist, or critic who is interested in the problem of craft, the challenge is not to subject every crafted object to an equivalent degree of analysis, but rather to identify and do justice to the reality of craft's position within modern culture. Above all, this means resisting the impulse unthinkingly to celebrate craft in all its manifestations. Thinking through craft is a useful exercise, and never more so than when it creates uncertainty.

NOTES

INTRODUCTION

1. Thomas Crow, "Modernism and Mass Culture in the Visual Arts," in Crow, *Modern Art and the Common Culture* (New Haven: Yale University Press, 1996), p. 33.
2. Johanna Drucker, *Sweet Dreams: Contemporary Art and Complicity* (Chicago: University of Chicago Press, 2005).
3. Theodor Adorno, *Aesthetic Theory*, trans. Robert Hullot-Kentor (London: Athlone Press, 1997), p. 3. A classic, if idiosyncratic, demolition of the craft-as-art project is Bruce Metcalf, "Replacing the Myth of Modernism," *American Craft* 53/1 (Feb./Mar. 1993), pp. 40–7. On questions of what gets named as art see also Thierry de Duve, *Kant After Duchamp* (Cambridge, MA: MIT Press, 1996).
4. Albers herself made this point in an interview with Martina Margetts; see "Thoroughly Modern Anni," *Crafts* 74 (May/June 1985), p. 16.
5. Robert Morris, "American Quartet," *Art in America* 69/10 (Dec. 1981), reprinted in Morris, *Continuous Project Altered Daily* (Cambridge, MA: MIT Press, 1993), p. 252. See also Thomas Kuhn, *The Structure of Scientific Revolutions* (Chicago: University of Chicago Press, 1962); Caroline Jones, "The Modernist Paradigm: The Artworld and Thomas Kuhn," *Critical Inquiry* 26 (Spring 2000).

CHAPTER I: SUPPLEMENTAL

1. Theodor Adorno, *Aesthetic Theory*, trans. Robert Hullot-Kentor (London: Athlone Press, 1997), pp. 1–2.
2. Lambert Zuidervaart, *Adorno's Aesthetic Theory: The Redemption of Illusion* (MIT, 1991), p. 88ff.
3. Pierre Bourdieu, "Outline of a Sociological Theory of Art Perception" (1968), in Bourdieu, *The Field of Cultural Production* (New York: Columbia University Press, 1993), p. 236. For Bourdieu's views on autonomy see his *The Rules of Art* (Cambridge: Polity Press, 1996; orig. pub. as *Les Regles d'Art*, 1992), p. 106ff.
4. Adorno, *Aesthetic Theory*, p. 2. Peter Bürger makes a parallel argument to Adorno's in his widely read *Theory of the Avant Garde* (Manchester: Manchester University Press, 1984).
5. Adorno, *Aesthetic Theory*, p. 6. For a transposition of this idea into the realm of art criticism, see Elizabeth Sussman and David Joselit (eds), *Endgame: Reference and Simulation in Recent Painting and Sculpture* (Cambridge, MA: MIT Press, 1986).
6. Adorno, *Aesthetic Theory*, p. 12. Johanna Drucker has recently argued that contemporary art has become just such a commodity, and must now abandon cherished fantasies of pure autonomy and engage with its own complicity. I hope that what follows is consistent with such a position, in that art's gestures to craft are a way of thinking through such complicity—an idea that Drucker herself has delineated in her writing on "production values." See Johanna Drucker, *Sweet Dreams: Contemporary Art and Complicity* (Chicago: University of Chicago Press, 2005); Johanna Drucker, "Affectivity and Entropy: Production Aesthetics in Contemporary Sculpture," in M. Anna Fariello and Paula Owen (eds), *Objects and Meaning: New Perspectives on Art and Craft* (Lanham, MD: Scarecrow Press, 2004).
7. Theodor Adorno, "Functionalismus Heute," delivered to the German Werkbund on 23 Oct. 1965. Originally published in *Neue Rundschau* 77/4 (1966); translated and reprinted as "Functionalism Today" in *Oppositions* 17 (Summer 1979), pp. 30–41: 36.

8. Adorno, *Aesthetic Theory*, p. 179.

9. Jacques Derrida, *Of Grammatology* (Baltimore: Johns Hopkins University Press, 1977), p. 144.

10. Robert Plant Armstrong, *The Powers of Presence: Consciousness, Myth, and Affecting Presence* (Philadelphia: University of Pennsylvania Press, 1981), p. 37.

11. Elissa Auther, "The Decorative, Abstraction, and the Hierarchy of Art and Craft in the Art Criticism of Clement Greenberg," *Oxford Art Journal* 27/3 (2004), pp. 339–64.

12. Immanuel Kant, *The Critique of Judgment*, trans. James C. Meredith (Oxford: Clarendon Press, 1952), p. 68. Unlike other *parerga* (such as the garments on statues or the colonnades on buildings), Kant criticizes the gold frame because of its status as ornamentation: "it is introduced [to] win approval for the picture by means of its charm [*Reiz*]—[it] does not itself enter into the composition of the beautiful form." Thus it is not an enhancement to the beauty of the art object, but rather "finery [*schmuck*, also the German for cosmetics] and takes away from genuine beauty" (p. 61).

13. Jacques Derrida, *The Truth in Painting*, trans. Geoff Bennington and Ian McLeod (Chicago: University of Chicago Press, 1987; orig. pub. 1978), p. 61.

14. Derrida, *The Truth in Painting*, p. 63.

15. For a comparison of Derrida's and Adorno's positions see Christoph Menke, *The Sovereignty of Art: Aesthetic Negativity in Adorno and Derrida*, trans. by Neil Solomon (Cambridge, MA: MIT Press, 1999), especially Ch. 5 *passim*.

16. Derrida, *The Truth in Painting*, p. 61.

17. Littleton made this remark at the National Sculpture Conference in Kansas in 1972. Interviewed subsequently, he commented: "All I meant by that is that technique is available to everybody, that you can read the technique, if you have any background. Technique in and of itself is nothing. But technique in the hands of a strong, creative person, like [Peter] Voulkos or Dante Marioni, takes on another dimension. And it's that other dimension that is the product of our educational system, of our uniquely American freedoms, and so on." Interview with Harvey K. Littleton conducted by Joan Falconer Byrd, March 15, 2001 (Smithsonian Institution: Nanette L. Laitman Documentation Project for Craft and Decorative Arts in America).

18. On Brancusi's influence on postwar British craft, see Tanya Harrod, *The Crafts in Britain in the Twentieth Century* (New Haven: Yale University Press, 1999), pp. 271, 274, 373.

19. On the general influence of Brancusi in postwar art, see Roxana Marcoci, "The Anti-Historicist Approach: Brancusi, 'Our Contemporary,'" *Art Journal* 59/2 (Summer, 2000), pp. 18–35.

20. John Perreault, *Artopia* (weblog, 28 June 2004), accessed 18 July 2006.

21. John Coplans, "Brancusi as Photographer" (1980), in Stuart Morgan (ed.), *Provocations by John Coplans* (London: London Projects, 1996).

22. Anna C. Chave, *Constantin Brancusi: Shifting the Bases of Art* (New Haven: Yale University Press, 1993), p. 13.

23. Chave, *Constantin Brancusi*, p. 10.

24. Quoted in Chave, *Constantin Brancusi*, p 28.

25. Chave, *Constantin Brancusi*, pp. 13, 208–9.

26. Ibid., p. 210.

27. Scott Burton, "My Brancusi," *Art in America* (March 1990), pp. 149–59.

28. Chave, *Constantin Brancusi*, pp. 193, 242ff.

29. See Leo Steinberg, "Jasper Johns: The First Seven Years of His Art," in Steinberg, *Other Criteria: Confrontations with Twentieth-Century Art* (New York: Oxford University Press, 1972).

30. Burton, "My Brancusi," p. 149.

31. See Toni Greenbaum, *Messengers of Modernism: American Studio Jewelry 1940–1960*, edited by Martin Eidelberg (Montreal: Montreal Museum of Fine Arts/Flammarion, 1996); Toni Greenbaum, "Bizarre

Bijoux: Surrealism in Jewelry," *The Journal of Decorative and Propaganda Arts*, vol. 20 (1994), pp. 196–207.

32. Toni Lesser Wolf, "Mid-Century Jewelry and Art Smith," in Camille Billops (ed.), *Art Smith: A Retrospective* (New York: Jamaica Arts Center, 1990), n.p.

33. Peter Lyon, *Design in Jewellery* (New York: The McBride Company, 1957), pp. 77–8, 79, 84.

34. Margaret DePatta, American Craft Council Research Service Craftsman's Questionnaire, 3 March 1961 (American Craft Council artist file). On Moholy-Nagy's teaching in Chicago, see Rainer W. Wick, *Teaching at the Bauhaus* (Ostfildern-Ruit: Hatje Cantz, 2000), p. 356ff.

35. DePatta quoted in Laurie Glass, "The Jewelry of Margaret DePatta," *Artweek* (6 March 1976), p. 9.

36. Yoshiko Uchida, "Margaret DePatta," in *The Jewelry of Margaret DePatta: A Retrospective Exhibition* (Oakland: The Oakland Museum, 1976), p. 15.

37. DePatta quoted in *Jewelry by Margaret DePatta: A Memorial Exhibition* (New York: Museum of Contemporary Crafts,1965), pamphlet, n.p. On DePatta and Moholy-Nagy see also Robert Cardinale and Hazel Bray, "Margaret DePatta: Structural Concepts and Design Sources," *Metalsmith* (Spring 1983), pp. 11–13.

38. Yoshiko Uchida, "Jewelry by Margaret DePatta," *Craft Horizons* (Mar./Apr. 1965), pp. 22–4: 23.

39. Uchida, "Jewelry by Margaret DePatta," p. 22.

40. Greenbaum, *Messengers of Modernism*.

41. Toni Lesser Wolf, "Mid-Century Jewelry and Art Smith," n.p.

42. Toni Lesser Wolf, "Goldsmith, Silversmith, Art Smith," *Metalsmith* 7/4 (Fall 1987), pp. 21–5: 21.

43. Herman Friedel and Dorothea Baumer, *Körperkultur: Otto Künzli und Gerd Rothmann* (Vienna: Galerie am Graben, 1982).

44. "Jewellery Redefined," *Crafts* 38 (Sept./Oct. 1982), pp. 42–6. See also Linda Sandino, "Studio Jewellery: Mapping the Absent Body," in Paul Greenhalgh (ed.), *The Persistence of Craft* (London: A&C Black, 2002); Judith Aston, "The Emergence of the 'New Jewellery' in Holland, Britain, and Germany in the 1970s," Master's thesis, V&A/RCA Course in the History of Design, 1991.

45. Rose Slivka, "Exhibitions," *Crafts* 64 (Sept./Oct. 1983), pp. 44–5: 45.

46. Susanna Heron, letter to the author, May 20, 2007.

47. Susanna Heron, *Bodywork* (London: Crafts Council, 1980), p. 11. See also Susanna Heron, "Jewellery Undefined," *Crafts* 61 (Mar./Apr. 1983), pp. 38–43; Ralph Turner, *The Jewellery Project* (London: Crafts Council, 1983).

48. For a discussion of this aspect of Heron's work, and an account of her work after she discontinued her jewelry practice, see Caroline Collier, "Elements," in *Susanna Heron: Elements* (Warwick: Mead Gallery, Warwick Arts Centre, 2003).

49. Harrod, *The Crafts in Britain in the Twentieth Century*, p. 428.

50. Christopher Reid, "Clowning Seriously," *Crafts* 59 (Nov./Dec. 1982), pp. 18–21: 18.

51. Greenbaum, *Messengers of Modernism*.

52. Goldin, who died in 1978, was the first critical advocate for the group. In a series of articles, she tied their work to an unacknowledged decorative tradition within modernism. Goldin had been a teacher of Kushner and MacConnel's at the University of California at San Diego around 1970, and according to Joyce Kozloff was the only critic who attended the meetings of the Pattern and Decoration group beginning in 1975 (Joyce Kozloff, correspondence, 6 March 2000). For an early statement by Goldin, see "The 'New' Whitney Biennial: Pattern Emerging?" *Art in America* 63/3 (May 1975), pp. 72–3. For an account of the commercial fortunes of Pattern and Decoration art, see Richard Armstrong, "A Short History of the Holly Solomon Gallery," Holly Solomon Gallery Inaugural Exhibition catalogue (New York: Holly Solomon Gallery, 1983); and Alexandra Anderson-Spivy, *Robert Kushner* (New York: Hudson Hills Press, 1997).

53. John Perreault, "Issues in Pattern Painting," *Artforum* 16/3 (Nov. 1977), pp. 32–6. The late appearance of this article is explained by the fact that Perreault was the art critic for the *Soho Weekly News* throughout

the decade, following his work at *Village Voice* ending in 1972. The *Artforum* article was preceded by supportive pieces written by Perreault in these local papers, but "Issues in Pattern Painting" was his first nationally published discussion of the movement. Intriguingly, the small constellation of New York writers sympathetic to Pattern and Decoration seems to have served as a proving ground of sorts for the American Craft Museum (formerly the Museum of Contemporary Crafts and presently the Museum of Art and Design) in New York. Perreault went on to be head curator at the museum and subsequently the director of Urban Glass workshop in Brooklyn. April Kingsley, whose critical interests also included the Pattern and Decoration movement, also became a curator at the museum, and Janet Kardon, who was museum's director from 1987 to 1996, curated both a 1979 exhibition on Robert Kushner and a show on Pattern and Decoration called "The Decorative Impulse" in 1979 (Philadelphia: University of Pennsylvania, Institute of Contemporary Art, 1979).

54. Carrie Rickey, untitled review, *Artforum* 17/5 (Jan. 1979), pp. 61–2. Critic Jeff Perrone also drew attention to the similarity between Stella's and Jaudon's paintings. See Perrone, "Approaching the Decorative," *Artforum* 15/4 (Dec. 1976), p. 27. For other comparisons of Minimal art and Pattern and Decoration, see Kay Larson, "For the First Time Women Artists are Leading Not Following," *Art News* 79/8 (Oct. 1980), p. 67; and John R. Clarke, "The Decorative Revisited: Five on Fabric," *Arts Magazine* 56/9 (May 1982), p. 143. Stella himself had by the 1970s turned to boldly colored patterning in his painting, and in fact Jaudon and Stella were both included in Amy Goldin's 1977 exhibition "Pattern and Decoration" held at the Museum of the American Foundation for the Arts in Miami.

55. Michael Fried, *Three American Painters: Kenneth Noland, Jules Olitski, and Frank Stella* (Cambridge: Fogg Art Museum, 1965). Chave, employing a line of Hélène Cixous's, writes of Jaudon's inversion of Stella: "The visual idiom she chose for her work … was the established modernist idiom of geometric abstraction, but she would use that idiom in a sense *against* itself, turning it around, 'taking it in her own mouth,' to use Cixous's words, or 'polluting' it, to use her own." Anna C. Chave, "Disorderly Order: The Art of Valerie Jaudon," in René Paul Barilleaux (ed.), *Valerie Jaudon* (Jackson: Mississippi Museum of Art, 1996), p. 16.

56. Jeff Perrone, untitled review, *Artforum* 26/1 (Sept. 1977), p. 75.

57. Rickey, untitled review, *Artforum* 17/5, p. 62.

58. Carrie Rickey, "Joyce Kozloff," *Arts Magazine* 52/5 (Jan. 1978), p. 2.

59. As the artist put it, "in Italy, in 1972, I saw the craft, the beauty, the care and love in Italian painting—not just the painting, but the frame, and the painting within the frame." Interview of Joyce Kozloff by Judy Siegel (1975), printed as "Talk About Decoration," *Women Artists News* 2/5 (Nov. 1976), and again in *Women Artists News* 16/17 (1991/2), pp. 6–7. For a discussion of Kozloff's use of tiling, see her interview with Jeff Perrone, "Two Ethnics Sitting Around Talking About WASP Culture," *Arts Magazine* 59/7 (Mar. 1985), p. 82.

60. Jaudon quoted in Carrie Rickey, "Four Tendencies in Search of a Movement," *Flash Art* 90–91 (June–July 1979), p. 23.

61. Johanna Drucker, *Theorizing Modernism: Visual Art and the Critical Tradition* (New York: Columbia University Press, 1994), p. 97.

62. Drucker, *Theorizing Modernism*, p. 98.

63. Ibid., p. 99.

64. Jeff Perrone, "Approaching the Decorative," p. 27.

65. In addition to at least two other "collaborations" with Cassatt, Schapiro appropriated works by Delacroix and Gauguin in 1975. She chose to partially obscure the images of these male artists with overlays of fabric, while leaving the Cassatt images intact. See Thalia Gouma-Peterson, *Miriam Schapiro: Shaping the Fragments of Art and Life* (New York: Harry N. Abrams, 1999), pp. 78–9.

66. Schapiro, "Notes From a Conversation on Art, Feminism, and Work," in Sara Ruddick and Pamela Daniels (eds), *Working It Out* (New York: Pantheon Books, 1977), p. 292.

67. Schapiro went on, "What I'm saying now is very subversive. It is not something that is accepted in any way at all. Because if it were accepted you would have to acknowledge that women have brains, they have moxie, they have ability, they can move forward in the world, they can be philosophers, and that they can influence other people. The world is not ready to say this yet." Joan Arbeiter, interview with Miriam Schapiro, in Arbeiter, et al., *Lives and Works: Talks With Women Artists, vol. 2* (Lanham, MD: Scarecrow Press, 1996), pp. 141, 147.

68. Chave, "Disorderly Order," p. 45.

69. Jeff Perrone, "Fore-, Four, For, Etc.," *Arts Magazine* 54/7 (March 1980), p. 85.

70. See Ida van Zijl and Yvynne Joris, *Gijs Bakker and Jewelry* (Stuttgart: Arnoldsche, 1997); Ida van Zijl, *Gijs Bakker: Objects to Use* (Rotterdam: 010 Publishers, 2000); Aston, "The Emergence of the 'New Jewellery.'" Van Leersum passed away in 1984. Somewhat unusually for the crafts, gallerists have served a primary role in promoting and disseminating the ideas of the continental avant garde in jewelry, particularly Paul Derrez of Galerie Ra in Amsterdam, Ralph Turner of Electrum Gallery in London, and Helen Drutt in Philadelphia; all have supported Bakker. See Susanna Heron, "Jewellery Undefined," *Crafts* 61 (Mar./Apr. 1983), pp. 38–43; Peter Dormer and Helen Drutt, *Jewelry of Our Time: Art, Ornament and Obsession* (New York: Rizzoli, 1995).

71. Paolo Antonelli, "Nothing Cooler Than Dry," in Gijs Bakker and Renny Ramakers (eds), *Droog Design: Spirit of the Nineties* (Rotterdam: 010 Publishers, 1998), p. 13.

72. Rody Graumars, quoted in Bakker and Ramakers (eds), *Droog Design*, p. 17.

73. Gijs Bakker interviewed by Masajiro Kamijyo, *Axis* 101 (2003), p. 57.

74. See Marcus Fairs, "Droog," *Icon* (March 2005), pp. 80–5.

75. Quoted in Michael Horsham, "What Is Droog?" *Blueprint* (Oct. 1996).

76. For more on Peteran, see Glenn Adamson, et al., *Gord Peteran: Furniture Meets Its Maker* (Milwaukee: Milwaukee Art Museum/Chipstone Foundation, 2006).

CHAPTER 2: MATERIAL

1. This line, possibly apocryphal, is most often attributed to Ad Reinhardt. Peter Selz however recalls that the line was Barnett Newman's. Selz, letter to the author, 1 May 2007.

2. Scott Burton, "My Brancusi," *Art in America* (March 1990), pp. 149–59; Edith Balas, "Object-Sculpture, Base and Assemblage in the Art of Constantin Brancusi," *Art Journal* 38/1 (Autumn, 1978), pp. 36–46; James Meyer, *Minimalism: Art and Polemics in the 1960s* (New Haven: Yale University Press, 2001); Donald Judd, "Specific Objects," *Arts Yearbook* 8 (1965), reprinted in *Donald Judd: Complete Writings* (Halifax/New York: Press of the Nova Scotia College of Art and Design/New York University Press, 1975); Rosalind Krauss, "Sculpture in the Expanded Field," *October* 8 (Spring 1979), reprinted in Krauss, *The Originality of the Avant-Garde and Other Modernist Myths* (Cambridge, MA: MIT Press, 1985).

3. The seminal account is Rosalind Krauss, *Passages in Modern Sculpture* (New York: Viking, 1977). See also Alex Potts's overview *The Sculptural Imagination: Figurative, Modernist, Minimalist* (New Haven: Yale University Press, 2001).

4. Michael Fried, "Art and Objecthood," *Artforum* 5 (June 1967), pp. 12–23; reprinted in Fried, *Art and Objecthood: Essays and Reviews* (Chicago: University of Chicago Press, 1998); Rosalind Krauss, "Impulse to See," in Hal Foster (ed.), *Vision and Visuality* (Seattle: Bay Press/Dia Art Foundation, 1988). For an early objection to the theory of opticality see Leo Steinberg, "The Eye is a Part of the Mind," *Partisan Review* 20/2 (Mar./Apr. 1953), pp. 194–212.

5. Caroline A. Jones, *Eyesight Alone: Clement Greenberg's Modernism and the Bureaucratization of the Senses* (Chicago: University of Chicago Press, 2005), p. 7.

6. Philip Leider, "Literalism and Abstraction: Frank Stella's Retrospective at the Modern," *Artforum* 8/8 (Apr. 1970), pp. 44–51; reprinted in Jason Geiger and Paul Wood (eds), *Art of the Twentieth Century: A Reader* (New Haven: Yale University Press, 2003), p. 169. Emphasis in original. See also Allan Kaprow, "The Legacy of Jackson Pollock," *Art News* 57 (Oct. 1958), reprinted in Kaprow, *Essays on The Blurring of Art and Life*, edited by Jeff Kelley (Berkeley: University of California Press, 1995); and Robert Morris, "Some Notes on the Phenomenology of Making: The Search for the Motivated," *Artforum* 8/8 (Apr. 1970), reprinted in Morris, *Continuous Project Altered Daily* (Cambridge, MA: MIT Press, 1994); Carter Radcliff, *the Fate of a Gesture: Jackson Pollock and Postwar American Art* (Boulder, CO: Westview Press, 1998).

7. F. David Martin, "The Autonomy of Sculpture," *The Journal of Aesthetics and Art Criticism* 34/3 (Spring 1976), pp. 273–86: 273.

8. Thomas Crow, *Rise of the Sixties: American and European Art in the Age of Dissent* (New York: Harry N. Abrams, 1996), p. 108. See also Michael Fried, "Caro's Abstractness," in Richard Whelan, et al., *Anthony Caro* (New York: E. P. Dutton, 1975).

9. Richard Shiff, "Constructing Physicality," *Art Journal* 50/1 (Spring, 1991), pp. 42–7: 42. Shiff argues that Greenberg's anti-illusionistic model of painting required it to be not only optical but also "opaque," raising the question of the painter's touch.

10. Hal Foster, "The Crux of Minimalism," in *Individuals – A Selected History of Contemporary Art* (Los Angeles: Museum of Contemporary Art, 1986).

11. Greenberg was characteristically perceptive of this breakthrough even as he dismissed it. In 1967, he acidly observed that the "newness" of Minimalism was limited to "the shrinking of the area in which things can now safely be non-art," and wondered idly "whether or not the Minimalists themselves have really escaped the pictorial context." Clement Greenberg, "Recentness of Sculpture," in Maurice Tuchman (ed.), *American Sculpture of the Sixties* (Los Angeles: Los Angeles County Museum of Art, 1967), reprinted in J. O'Brian (ed.), *Clement Greenberg: The Collected Essays and Criticism*, vol. 4, pp. 250–6: 252.

12. Quoted in Hal Foster, Rosalind Krauss, Yve-Alain Bois and Benjamin H. D. Buchloh, *Art Since 1900: Modernism, Antimodernism, Postmodernism* (New York: Thames & Hudson, 2004), p. 492.

13. On Voulkos and other potters at Black Mountain, see Mary Emma Harris, *The Arts at Black Mountain College* (Cambridge, MA: MIT Press, 1987). On the Archie Bray Foundation, see "The Bray at 50," *American Craft* 61/2 (Apr./May 2001), pp. 56–61.

14. Cheryl White has persuasively argued that to align Otis clay directly with Abstract Expressionism is not a way to legitimate it, but rather a codification of its marginalization as a "regional version of the mainstream." White, "Towards an Alternative History: Otis Clay Revisited," *American Craft* 53/4 (Aug./Sept. 1993), pp. 120, 125. Also pertinent here is Garth Clark's work on Voulkos's circle, in which he calls the phrase "Abstract Expressionist Ceramics" into question. Clark points out, for example, that Voulkos's close personal connections with the New York School did not develop until the Otis program was two years underway. Clark, "Otis and Berkeley," in Jo Lauria, *Color and Fire* (Los Angeles: Los Angeles County Museum of Art, 2000).

15. Rose Slivka, "The New Ceramic Presence," *Craft Horizons* 21/4 (July/Aug. 1961), pp. 31, 32, 36.

16. Ibid., p. 34. For related arguments see Bernard Pyron, "The Tao and Dada of Recent Ceramic Art," *Artforum* (Mar. 1964), reprinted in Garth Clark (ed.), *Ceramic Art: Comment and Review 1882–1977* (New York: E. P. Dutton, 1978), pp. 143–52.

17. Voulkos had images of Picasso's pots hanging on the walls of his studio. See Garth Clark and Margie Hughto, *A Century of Ceramics in the United States, 1878–1978* (New York: E. P. Dutton/Everson Museum of Art, 1979), p. 135. See also Georges Ramie, *Picasso's Ceramics* (New York: Viking Press, 1976). It should be noted that Peter Selz, the key early curatorial champion of Voulkos's work, disputes Slivka's viewpoint: "I do not think that Voulkos was really so much concerned with the optical aspects of his painted pots. Certainly, when I decided to give him a show at MOMA and when I sent his work to the Paris Biennial, it

was the tangible, sculptural aspects of his work which was at issue." Peter Selz, letter to the author, 1 May 2007.

18. Soldner and Voulkos described one such pot, entitled *Love Is A Many Splendored Thing*, as a breakthrough piece in Voulkos's oeuvre. See "Ceramics: West Coast," *Craft Horizons* 26/6 (July 1966), p. 26.

19. The *Craft Horizons* review of the "Abstract Expressionist Ceramics" show was typical in this regard: "The Los Angeles potters had no program… They respected no rules, not even utility; rather, they impressed their wills on the material and suited their methods to their individual expressive needs." Helen Giambruni, "Abstract Expressionist Ceramics," *Craft Horizons* 26/6 (Nov./Dec. 1966), pp. 17, 61: 17.

20. Leedy was another point of contact with Abstract Expressionist painters, having had a fistfight with Willem deKooning in the Cedar Bar—he later recalled, "the result was that he liked me and I had the privilege of experiencing first hand some of his concerns." Jim Leedy, "Thoughts About My Work," American Craft Council artist's file. See also Matthew Kangas, *Jim Leedy: Artist Across Boundaries* (Seattle: University of Washington Press, 2000).

21. John Coplans, untitled review of "Work in Clay by Six Artists," *Artforum* 1/8 (Feb. 1963), p. 46.

22. The two favorable reviews in mainstream art journals were each only one paragraph in length: Dore Ashton, untitled review, *Arts and Architecture* 77/4 (Apr. 1960), p. 7; Walter Dennison, untitled review, *Arts Magazine* 36/6 (Mar. 1960), p. 61. Ashton also contributed a favorable review to the *New York Times*: "New Talent Display at Museum," *New York Times* 2 Feb. 1960, p. 40. Coplans's comments appear in Scott Sterling's historical video "Revolutions of the Wheel, Part Four: Peter Voulkos and the Otis Group" (Queens Row Films, 1997). For Rose Slivka's account of the exhibition see Slivka, *Peter Voulkos*, p. 55; Rose Slivka and Karen Tsujimoto, *The Art of Peter Voulkos* (Oakland: The Oakland Museum/Kodansha, 1995), p. 52. Jim Melchert recalls in detail the circumstances of the exhibition and its effect on Voulkos's career: "…the other thing that I think was a real setback for him was that he was given a show by Peter Selz at the Museum of Modern Art in a room that was sort of members' gallery, where someone would be selected as an introduction. And Pete had these wonderful sculptures. I mean, nobody was making clay sculpture like that. Tall, potent images. What was the show in the main gallery just at that time, but the Twenty Americans—Dorothy Miller's show, in which she was showcasing for the first time Claes Oldenburg, Frank Stella, Bob Rauschenberg… But I don't think there was any response at all to Pete's work at the time. I don't know that there were reviews of it, whatever, but it got no attention. And there's all this talk about the other show. The timing was extremely unfortunate. And the bias against clay was still very strong in New York, whereas it hadn't entirely disappeared here on the west coast, but things were much better for an artist interested in clay here than back in New York. And I think Pete desperately wanted attention in New York. Since you're not going to get it with clay, I think that was one of the attractions of bronze." Jim Melchert interviewed by Maddy Jones, Apr. 4/5, 1991, Archives of American Art, Smithsonian Institution.

23. See Richard Marshall and Suzanne Foley, *Ceramic Sculpture: Six Artists* (New York: Whitney Museum of Art, 1981). For a perceptive account of the reception of the Whitney show see Beth Coffelt, "East is East and West is West: The Great Divide," *California Living Magazine* (4 Apr. 1982), pp. 22–30.

24. Rosalind Krauss, *John Mason: Installations from the Hudson River Series* (Yonkers: Hudson River Museum, 1978), pp. 12–13.

25. For an instructive comparison in the world of painting, see Yve-Alain Bois, Thomas Crow, Hal Foster, David Joselit, Elisabeth Sussman and Bob Riley, *Endgame: Reference and Simulation in Recent American Painting and Sculpture* (Boston: Institute of Contemporary Art/MIT Press, 1986).

26. Paris joined the art faculty at Berkeley in 1960, and helped Voulkos found his bronze foundry, the Garbanzo Works. See Thomas Albright, *Art in the San Francisco Bay Area, 1945–1980* (Berkeley: University of California Press, 1985), pp. 141–5; Joseph Pugliese, "Work in Progress," *Artforum* 2/7 (Jan. 1964), p. 34.

27. Quoted in Peter Selz (ed.), *Harold Paris: The California Years* (Berkeley: University Art Museum, 1972), p. 13. Also see Selz's descriptions of the walls, reprising the quote, in Selz, "Harold Persico Paris," in *Beyond the Mainstream* (Cambridge: Cambridge University Press, 1997), pp. 268–77.

28. Fidel Danielli, untitled review, *Artforum* 7/2 (Oct. 1968), p. 68.

29. Melchert, "Peter Voulkos: A Return to Pottery." *Craft Horizons* (Sept./Oct. 1968). Melchert worked with Voulkos from 1959–61, and taught at the San Francisco Art Institute from 1961–65.

30. Voulkos's first opportunity to fire at an *anagama*—that of his longterm collaborator Peter Callas—was in 1979. See Karen Tsujimoto, "Peter Voulkos: The Wood-fired Work," in Slivka and Tsujimoto, p. 112ff.

31. For a lengthy statement on Zen by De Staebler, see "The Inside of the Outside," *Ceramics Monthly* (Sept. 1986), pp. 36–8; on Zen and the New York School, see Helen Westgeest, *Zen and the Fifties* (Zwolle: Waanders Publishing/Cobra Museum, 1996).

32. Elaine Levin, "Stephen De Staebler," *Ceramics Monthly* (Apr. 1981), p. 58; and Dore Ashton, "Objects Worked by the Imagination for their Innerness: The Sculpture of Stephen De Staebler," *Art Magazine* (Nov. 1984).

33. Harvey Jones, *Stephen De Staebler: Sculpture* (Oakland: Oakland Museum, 1974), n.p. According to Elaine Levin, the encounter with the applied slab occurred in John Mason's studio in 1960, when Mason was teaching at Berkeley as a visiting instructor. In this account, the slab was placed atop one of the armatures that Mason had built for his large sculptures, armatures that De Staebler would soon reject in his own work. See Levin, "Stephen De Staebler," p. 56.

34. Quoted in Ashton, "Objects Worked by the Imagination for their Innerness"; and Sharon Edwards, "A Conversation with Stephen De Staebler," *Ceramics Monthly* (Apr. 1981), p. 62.

35. Ramsay Bell Breslin, "The Figure as Fragment," in *Stephen De Staebler: Recent Sculpture* (San Francisco: Campbell-Thiebaud Gallery, 1994).

36. See Stephen Prokopoff, *Marilyn Levine: A Decade of Ceramic Sculpture* (Boston: Institute of Contemporary Art, 1981); Marc Treib, "On Reading Marilyn Levine," *Ceramics: Art & Perception* 59 (March 2005), pp. 44–7.

37. John Coplans, "The Sculpture of Ken Price," *Art International* 8/2 (Mar. 1964), p. 33. Emphasis in original.

38. Maurice Tuchman, *Ken Price: Happy's Curios* (Los Angeles: Los Angeles County Museum of Art, 1978), pp. 8–9. For other period responses to the project, see Jo Lauria, "Mapping the History of a Collection: Defining Moments in Ceramics at LACMA," in Lauria, *Color and Fire*, pp. 28–31.

39. Jorge Luis Borges, "Pierre Menard, Author of the Quixote," in *Ficionnes* (New York: Grove Press, 1962).

40. On the precocious postmodernism of Price's other work of the time, see Mark DelVecchio, *Postmodern Ceramics* (New York: Thames & Hudson, 2001), p. 15.

41. John Coplans, "The Sculpture of Kenneth Price," *Art International* 8/2 (March 1964), p. 34.

42. Louise Cort and Bert Winther-Tamaki, *Isamu Noguchi and Japanese Ceramics: A Close Embrace of the Earth* (Washington, DC: Arthur M. Sackler Gallery/University of California Press, 2003).

43. Cort and Winther-Tamaki, *Isamu Noguchi and Japanese Ceramics*, p. 157–60.

44. Bert Winther-Tamaki, "Yagi Kazuo: The Admission of the Nonfunctional Object into the Japanese Pottery World," *Journal of Design History* 12/2 (1999), pp. 123–41: 137. See also Bert Winther-Tamaki, *Art in the Encounter of Nations: Japanese and American Artists in the Early Postwar Years* (Honolulu: University of Hawaii Press, 2001), p. 89ff; Moroyama Masanori, *Crafts in Everyday Life in the 1950s and 1960s* (Tokyo: National Museum of Modern Art, 1995), pp. 22–3.

45. Cort and Winther-Tamaki, *Isamu Noguchi and Japanese Ceramics*, pp. 174–5.

46. See Garth Clark, "Lucio Fontana's Ceramics," in John Pagliaro (ed.), *Shards: Garth Clark on Ceramic Art* (New York: Ceramic Arts Foundation/DAP, 2003); Yves Peyré, *Fautrier, ou les Outrages de L'Impossible*

(Paris: Editions du Regard, 1990), p. 397ff.; Katharina Schmidt, *Cy Twombly: The Sculpture* (Ostfildern: Hatje Cantz Verlag, 2000).

47. Jean Dubuffet, "A Pleines Mains" (1946), translated in Sarah Wilson, "Paris Post War: In Search of the Absolute," in Frances Morris (ed.), *Paris Post War: Art and Existentialism* (London: Tate Gallery, 1993), p. 33.

48. Alexandra Munroe alludes to this reading of Yagi's ceramics in "*Circle:* Modernism and Tradition," in Munroe (ed.), *Japanese Art After 1945: Scream Against the Sky* (New York: Harry N. Abrams, 1994), p. 128.

49. Yve-Alain Bois and Rosalind Krauss, *Formless: A User's Guide* (New York: Zone Books, 1997). Bois and Krauss attribute this quality to Fontana's work in clay, citing his *Ceramica Spaziale* as "the simple interjection of an obscenity into the aesthetic house of cards" (p. 56).

50. Osamu Suzuki, "Kazuo Yagi and the People," in *The Works of Kazuo Yagi and Mentally Handicapped People* (Shigaraki: The Museum of Contemporary Ceramic Art, The Shigaraki Ceramic Cultural Park, 1993), p. 11.

51. Taichi Yoshinaga, "Kazuo Yagi and the Clay Work of Mentally Handicapped People," in *The Works of Kazuo Yagi and Mentally Handicapped People*, p. 14.

52. Jean Dubuffet, "*L'Art Brut* Preferred to Cultural Art" (1948), reprinted in Charles Harrison and Paul Wood, *Art in Theory, 1900–1990: An Anthology of Changing Ideas* (Oxford: Blackwell, 1992), pp. 593–5: 595.

53. On Bataille see Yve-Alain Bois and Rosalind Krauss, *Formless*; and Dawn Ades and Simon Baker, *Undercover Surrealism: Georges Bataille and Documents* (London: Hayward Gallery/MIT Press, 2006).

54. Bert Winther-Tamaki, *Art in the Encounter of Nations*, pp. 92–3.

55. Yagi Kazuo, "Rosanjin no toki ni tsuite (Concerning Rosanjin's Pottery)," in Yagi Kazuo, *Kokkoku no Hono (Steady Flame)* (Kyoto: Shinshindo Shuppan, 1981), p. 172. Translated in Louise Allison Cort, "Crawling Through Mud: Avant-Garde Ceramics in Postwar Japan," Sixth Annual Dorothy Wilson Perkins Lecture, Schein-Joseph International Museum of Ceramic Art at Alfred University, 14 Oct. 2003.

56. Quoted in Yoshiyuki Fuji, "Kazuo Yagi and the People in the Institutions," in *The Works of Kazuo Yagi and Mentally Handicapped People*, p. 17.

57. Lippard, "Eccentric Abstraction" (1966); reprinted in *Changing: Essays in Art Criticism* (New York: E. P. Dutton, 1971).

58. Lippard herself noted in a preface to the 1971 reprinting of her 1966 catalogue essay "Eccentric Abstraction" that she had "overestimated the Surrealist connection," and that the true defining feature of the movement was its concern for "materials and physical phenomena." Lippard, *Changing*, p. 98 ftnt. See also Briony Fer, "Objects beyond Objecthood," *Oxford Art Journal* 22/2 (1999), pp. 27–36.

59. Morris's exhibition at Castelli's warehouse space included Giovanni Anselmo, William Bollinger, Eva Hesse, Steve Kaltenbach, Bruce Nauman, Alan Saret, Richard Serra, Keith Sonnier and Gilberto Zorio. Marcia Tucker and James Monte, *Anti-Illusion: Procedures/Materials* (New York: Whitney Museum of American Art, 1969).

60. Marcia Tucker in *Anti-Illusion*, p. 27.

61. Quoted in Christopher Phillips, *Photography in the Modern Era: European Documents and Critical Writings, 1913–1940* (New York: Metropolitan Museum of Art, 1989), p. 101. See also Rainer Wick, *Teaching at the Bauhaus* (Ostfildern-Ruit: Hatje Cantz, 2000).

62. James Meyer, "The Genealogy of Minimalism: Carl Andre, Dan Flavin, Donald Judd and Robert Morris" (PhD dissertation, Johns Hopkins University, 1995), p. 134.

63. Robert Morris, "Some Notes on the Phenomenology of Making: The Search for the Motivated," *Artforum* 8/8 (Apr. 1970).

64. Rosalind Krauss, "The Mind/Body Problem: Robert Morris in Series," in Kimberly Paice, et al., *Robert Morris: The Mind/Body Problem* (New York: Solomon R. Guggenheim Museum, 1994), p. 4.

65. Robert Morris interviewed by Paul Cummings, 10 March 1968; Archives of American Art, Smithsonian Institution. In the interview Morris also mentions the *Box with the Sound of its Own Making* as a precursor: "The first object I made when I came to New York was a box with sound, which is a cube about eight inches on a side. I recorded the sound of making this box and put a speaker in it so that it plays for three hours the sounds of its being constructed ... I mean this completely split the process and the object. And yet put them both back together again. So in some way I think this was a work that allowed me then to go ahead."

66. Morris, "Anti Form," *Artforum* 6/8 (Apr. 1968), pp. 33–5.

67. Robert Morris, "Some Notes on the Phenomenology of Making," in *Continuous Process Altered Daily*, p. 77. Morris's attitude towards process had its roots in the Fluxus movement and the related New York performance art scene of the 1950s, of which Morris and Kaprow were a part. For more on these connections, see Anna Chave, "Minimalism and Biography," *Art Bulletin* 82/1 (Mar. 2000), pp. 155–7.

68. Robert Pincus-Witten interpreted this repeated, almost inevitable failure in very broad terms: "the film points up the ultimate inability of the hand to function as a tool, for, were it able to have successfully carried out such an *a priori* task, one would have witnessed a theatrical performance. Instead, the film concerns itself with the breakdown of a positivist assumption because the hand after a moment is physically unable to negotiate the predetermined command. Thus, the value of the film lies in its clear indication that all assumed or received systems—linguistic, esthetic, experiential, formal—are in themselves subject to breakdown." "Richard Serra: Slow Information," *Artforum* 8/1 (Sept. 1969), p. 38; reprinted in Pincus-Witten, *Postminimalism into Maximalism: American Art, 1966–1986* (Ann Arbor: UMI Research Press, 1987).

69. For more on Serra's films, see Benjamin H. D. Buchloh, "Process Sculpture and Film in the Work of Richard Serra," in *Richard Serra: Works '66–'77* (Tübingen: Kunsthalle, 1978); reprinted in Hal Foster and Gordon Hughes (eds), *Richard Serra* (Cambridge, MA: MIT Press, 2000).

70. Rosalind Krauss et al., *Richard Serra: Props* (Dusseldorf: Richter Verlag, 1994), p. 32. See also Rosalind Krauss, *Passages in Modern Sculpture* (Cambridge, MA: MIT Press, 1977), p. 276.

71. Inspired by a 1970 trip to Japan, Serra switched from lead to steel and began constructing much larger works that lacked the internal tension of the *Props*. Sculptures such as the 1972 *Skullcracker* were so huge that they exerted implied force not on themselves, but on the viewer's body, which was placed under threat. As Rosalind Krauss puts it, "the lead props were to the stacked slabs of *Skullcracker* as cottage industry is to a steel mill." Krauss, *Richard Serra: Props*, p. 56. See also Krauss, "Richard Serra, A Translation," in Krauss, *Originality of the Avant-Garde and Other Modernist Myths* (Cambridge, MA: MIT Press, 1985); Yve-Alain Bois, "A Picturesque Stroll Around *Clara-Clara*," *October* 29 (Summer 1984), pp. 32–62; and Anna Chave, "Minimalism and the Rhetoric of Power," *Arts Magazine* 64/5 (Jan. 1990), pp. 44–63.

72. Tucker in *Anti-Illusion*, p. 35. Rosalind Serra's prop work *House of Cards* "is a shape in the process of forming against the resistance, but also with the help of the ongoing conditions of gravity." Krauss, "The Cultural Logic of the Late Capitalist Museum," *October* 54 (Autumn, 1990), pp. 3–17: 8.

73. Emily Wasserman, untitled review, *Artforum* 8/1 (Sept. 1969), p. 58. Another critic commented, "Serra may actually court this bizarre danger, taking a certain pleasure in eventual mishaps; for a collapse is the ultimate moral proof of the uncompromising nature of his premise, and enhances his aims from a theoretical point of view." Elizabeth Baker, "Critic's Choice: Serra," *Art News* 68/10 (Feb. 1970), p. 26.

74. Robert Morris, untitled statement for the exhibition "Conceptual Art and Conceptual Aspects" at the New York Cultural Center, 1970. Quoted in Ursula Meyer, *Conceptual Art* (New York: E. P. Dutton, 1972), p. 184.

75. Anne M. Wagner, *Three Artists (Three Women): Modernism and the Art of Hesse, Krasner and O'Keeffe* (Berkeley: University of California Press, 1991).

76. Eva Hesse, "Statement for Art in Series exhibition," Finch College Museum of Art, 1967; reprinted in Rosalind Krauss et al., *Eva Hesse: Sculpture 1936–1970* (London: Whitechapel Art Gallery, 1979).

77. Briony Fer, "The Work of Art, the Work of Psychoanalysis," in Gill Perry (ed.), *Gender in Art* (New Haven: Yale University Press/The Open University, 1999); Anna Chave, "A 'Girl Being a Sculpture,'" in Helen Cooper, *Eva Hesse: A Retrospective* (New Haven: Yale University Art Gallery/Yale University Press, 1992).

78. "Chronology," in Cooper, *Eva Hesse: A Retrospective* , p. 31.

79. Melissa Feldman, *Signs of Life: Process and Materials 1960–1990* (Philadelphia: University of Pennsylvania/Institute of Contemporary Art, 1990), p. 10.

80. Barry Le Va interviewed by Liza Bear, "…A Continuous Flow of Fairly Aimless Movement," *Avalanche* 3 (Fall 1971). Ralph Rugoff has compared Le Va's scatter works to Bruce Nauman's *Composite Photo of Two Messes on the Studio Floor* (1967), an image of "the 'non-art' debris left over from making a sculpture." Rugoff, *Scene of the Crime* (Cambridge, MA: MIT Press, 1997), p. 60.

81. Kimberly Paice et al., *Robert Morris: The Mind/Body Problem* (New York: Solomon R. Guggenheim Museum, 1994), p. 226. Herb Aach, writing (with considerable befuddlement) on Process Art in the pages of *Craft Horizons*, explained that threadwaste is "a remainder from knitting or spinning mills normally passed along on industrial lines for use as oil or cleaning rags or similar purposes." Aach, "The Materials of Art Versus the Art of Materials," *Craft Horizons* 29/4 (July/Aug. 1969), p. 38.

82. Ursula Meyer, "De-Objectification of the Object," *Arts Magazine* 43/5 (Summer 1969), pp. 20–2: 20.

83. See Mary Kelly, "Re-viewing Modernist Criticism," *Screen* 22/3 (Autumn 1981), pp. 41–62; reprinted in Brian Wallis (ed.), *Art After Modernism* (Boston: David R. Godine, 1984).

84. Susan Orlean, "Art for Everybody: How Thomas Kinkade Turned Painting into Big Business," *New Yorker* (15 Oct. 2001).

CHAPTER 3: SKILLED

1. Jackson Pollock interviewed by William Wright, 1950, reprinted in Ellen H. Johnson (ed.), *American Artists on Art from 1940 to 1980* (New York: Harper & Row, 1982).

2. Helen Chadwick interviewed by Chris Blackford, 1986, orig. pub. in *Rubberneck* 3, transcribed online at http://www.users.globalnet.co.uk/~rneckmag/chadwick.html, accessed 21 Jan. 2007.

3. Warren MacKenzie interviewed by Robert Silberman, 29 Oct. 2002, Archives of American Art, Smithsonian Institution, Nanette L. Laitman Documentation Project For Craft and Decorative Arts in America, n. p.

4. Giorgio Vasari, *The Lives of the Artists*, trans. Julia Conaway Bondanella and Peter Bondanella (Oxford: Oxford University Press, 1991), pp. 22–3.

5. For typical accounts of the Renaissance's supposed separation between idea-based art and skill-based craft, see Larry Shiner, *The Invention of Art: A Cultural History* (Chicago: University of Chicago Press, 2001); Roger Coleman, *The Art of Work: An Epitaph to Skill* (London: Pluto Press, 1988); John Houston, "Ghiberti and the Great Schism," *Crafts* 12 (Jan./Feb. 1975), pp. 30–3.

6. For more on Vasari's use of the story see Paul Barolfsky, *Michelangelo's Nose: A Myth and Its Maker* (University Park, PA: Pennsylvania State University Press, 1990).

7. Warren MacKenzie interviewed by Robert Silberman, n. p.

8. David Pye, "Right 'First Off,'" *Crafts* 58 (Sept./Oct. 1982), p. 13.

9. David Pye, *The Nature and Art of Workmanship* (Cambridge: Cambridge University Press, 1968), p. 9.

10. I am indebted to Sir Christopher Frayling, Rector of the Royal College of Art, for his remembrances about Lenthall.

11. Pye, *The Nature and Art of Workmanship*, pp. 23–4.

12. Christopher Frayling and Helen Snowdon, "Skill – A Word To Start an Argument," *Crafts* 56 (May/June 1982), pp. 19–21: 19. See also Helen Snowdon, "British Craftsmanship in the Machine Environment," unpublished thesis, Department of General Studies, Royal College of Art, 1979; and David Pye, *The Nature and Aesthetics of Design* (Bethel, CT: Cambium Press, 1978; orig. pub. As *The Nature of Design*, 1964). Pye writes that "skill is the exercising of constraint on movement … know-how, in making, is design" (p. 52).

13. Pye, *The Nature and Art of Workmanship*, p. 7.

14. Ibid., p. 4.

15. Pye, *The Nature and Aesthetics of Design*, p. 50.

16. Tanya Harrod, "Thinking Out Loud," *Crafts* 203 (Nov./Dec. 2006).

17. Pye, *The Nature and Art of Workmanship*, p. 13.

18. Peter Dormer, *The Art of the Maker: Skill and Its Meaning in Art, Craft and Design* (London: Thames & Hudson, 1994), p. 42; see also pp. 60ff.

19. Pye, *The Nature and Art of Workmanship*, pp. 72, 20. See also Polly Ulrich, "The Workmanship of Risk: The Re-Emergence of Handcraft in Postmodern Art," *New Art Examiner* 25/7 (Apr. 1998), p. 24–9: 27.

20. Michael Baxandall, *Painting and Experience in Fifteenth-Century Italy* (Oxford: Clarendon Press, 1972), p. 3. See also Michael Baxandall, *Patterns of Intention: On the Historical Explanation of Pictures* (New Haven: Yale University Press, 1985); Creighton Gilbert, "What Did the Renaissance Patron Buy?" *Renaissance Quarterly* 51 (1998), 392–450; and Michelle O'Malley, *The Business of Art: Contracts and the Commissioning Process in Renaissance Italy* (New Haven: Yale University Press, 2005).

21. Thomas Crow, *The Intelligence of Art* (Chapel Hill: University of North Carolina Press, 1999).

22. Michael Baxandall, *The Limewood Sculptors of Renaissance Germany* (New Haven: Yale University Press, 1980), p. 32.

23. Baxandall, *The Limewood Sculptors of Renaissance Germany*, p. 34.

24. Ibid., p. 36.

25. Towards the end of his long life as a wood turner and carver, Pye wrote charmingly, "wood is a most unpredictable material altogether. I learn something new about it almost every week." David Pye, "Notes on Technique," in *David Pye: Wood Carver and Turner* (London/Bath: Crafts Council/Crafts Study Centre, 1986), p. 31.

26. Crow, *The Intelligence of Art*, p. 77.

27. For a discussion of craft and teaching in the postwar context see "The Neglected Lesson," *Crafts* 46 (Sept./Oct. 1980), p. 36–9; Peter P. Grimmett and Allan M. MacKinnon, "Craft Knowledge and the Education of Teachers," *Review of Research in Education* 18 (1992), p. 385–456.

28. On Sloyd see Otto Salomon, *The Teachers Handbook of Sloyd* (Boston: Silver Burdett & Co., 1904); B. B. Hoffman, *The Sloyd System of Woodworking* (New York: American Book Company, 1892).

29. Robert H. Beck, "Progressive Education and American Progressivism," *Teachers College Record* 60/2 (Nov. 1958), p. 79.

30. Herbert M. Kliebard, *The Struggle for the American Curriculum, 1893–1958* (Boston: Routledge & Kegan Paul, 1986), pp. 70–2.

31. John Dewey, *Art as Experience* (New York: Minton, Balch & Co., 1934), p. 40. On Adler's and Dewey's early influence see T. J. Jackson Lears, *No Place of Grace* (Chicago: University of Chicago Press, 1983), p. 78–83.

32. John Dewey, *Experience and Education* (New York: Collier Books, 1938), p. 25.

33. Lawrence A. Cremin, *The Transformation of the School: Progressivism in American Education, 1876–1957* (New York: Vintage Books, 1961), pp. 56–7.

34. Quoted in Kliebard, *The Struggle for the American Curriculum*, p. 148.

35. H.E. Miles, "An Engineer's Report on Vocational Education." *School and Society* 14/351 (12 Sept. 1921), p. 190; and "Vocational Education," *Journal of Education* 101/7 (Feb. 12, 1925), p. 179.

36. Charles Judd, "Industry and the Liberal Arts," *School and Society* 8/209 (Nov. 29, 1918), p. 159. Judd was a professor of education at the University of Chicago, and was George Counts's mentor there.

37. Judith Rosenberg Raftery, *Land of Fair Promise: Politics and Reform in Los Angeles Schools, 1885–1941* (Stanford: Stanford University Press, 1992), pp. 50–1.

38. David A. Ward, "Vocational Courses and the Junior High School," *School and Society* 25/651 (18 June 1927), pp. 711, 712.

39. Robert J. Leonard, "Changing Conceptions of Vocational Education," *School and Society* 23/580 (6 Feb. 1926), p. 154. For another criticism of the inefficiency of traditional craft courses, see William Hunter, "Manual Arts in the Junior High School." *Industrial Education Magazine* 31/1 (July 1929), p. 14.

40. Quoted in Kliebard, *The Struggle for the American Curriculum*, p.148.

41. Daniel Tanner, *Crusade for Democracy: Progressive Education at the Crossroads* (Albany: SUNY Press/John Dewey Society, 1991), pp. 5–7.

42. For examples of the politicization of "experience," see Bruce Raup, *Education and Organized Interests in America* (New York: G. P. Putnam's Sons, 1936); Lawrence K. Frank, "General Education Today," *Social Frontier* 3/25 (Apr. 1937), pp. 209–10.

43. George S. Counts, "Dare the School Build a New Social Order?" reprinted in Norman Benson and Richard Lyons, *Controversies over the Purposes of Schooling and the Meaning of Work* (Lanham, MD: University Press of America, 1986), p. 58.

44. George S. Counts, *The American Road to Culture* (New York: John Day Co., 1930), p. 71. See also Counts, "The Spirit of American Education," *Teachers College Record* 59/8 (May 1958).

45. Franklin Bobbitt, cited in Kliebard, *The Struggle for the American Curriculum*, p. 197.

46. Earl Browder, "Education: An Ally in the Workers' Struggle," *Social Frontier* 1/4 (Jan. 1935), p. 23. Italics in original.

47. John Dewey, *Experience and Education*, p. 83.

48. Ordway Tead, "New Challenge for Industrial Education," *Social Frontier* 2/1 (Oct. 1935), p. 18.

49. Tead, "New Challenge for Industrial Education," p. 18.

50. Patricia A. Graham, *Progressive Education: From Arcady to Academe* (New York: Teachers College Press, 1967).

51. Peter F. Carbone, Jr. and Virginia S. Wilson, "Harold Rugg's Social Reconstructionism," p. 60.

52. Harold Rugg, *American Life and the School Curriculum: Next Steps towards Schools of Living* (Boston: Ginn & Co., 1936), pp. 412–13.

53. Cited in Carbone and Wilson, p. 75.

54. Harold Rugg, *Culture and Education in America* (New York: Harcourt, Brace & Co., 1931), p. 362.

55. Rugg, *American Life*, p. 440.

56. The following analysis is indebted to two overview studies: Rainer K. Wick, *Teaching at the Bauhaus* (Ostfildern-Ruit: Hatje Cantz, 2000); and Frank Horowitz and Brenda Danilowitz, *Josef Albers: To Open Eyes: At the Bauhaus, Black Mountain, and Yale* (New York: Phaidon, 2006).

57. Wick, *Teaching at the Bauhaus*, p. 117.

58. Walter Gropius, "The Theory and Organization of the Bauhaus" (1923), excerpt reprinted in Charles Harrison and Paul Wood (eds.), *Art in Theory* (Oxford: Blackwell, 1992), p. 340.

59. Gropius, *The New Architecture and the Bauhaus* (Cambridge, MA: MIT Press, 1965), p. 78.

60. Ibid., p. 53.

61. Larry Hickman, *John Dewey's Pragmatic Technology*, p. 62.

62. John Dewey, *Art as Experience*, p. 145.

63. See Frederick Schwartz, "Utopia for Sale: The Bauhaus and Weimar Germany's Consumer Culture," in Kathleen James-Chakraborty, *Bauhaus Culture: From Weimar to the Cold War* (Minneapolis: University of Minnesota Press, 2006).

64. Josef Albers, "Creative Education," address delivered at the Sixth International Congress for Drawing, Art Education, and Applied Art, Prague, 1928; reprinted in Hans Wingler, *Bauhaus*, trans. Wolfgang Jabs and Basil Gilbert (Cambridge, MA: MIT Press, 1969), pp. 142–3: 142.

65. Frank Whitford, *Bauhaus* (London: Thames & Hudson, 1984), p. 133. On Albers's distinction between professional and unprofessional techniques and his focus on the "immanent features" of material, see Wick, *Teaching at the Bauhaus*, pp. 167, 179–81.

66. Quoted in Mervin Lane (ed.), *Black Mountain College: Sprouted Seeds: An Anthology of Personal Accounts* (Knoxville: University of Tennessee Press, 1990), p. 37. Rainer Wick concludes that Dewey's ideas "seem to have had a an especially lasting influence on Albers." See Wick, *Teaching at the Bauhaus*, p. 174–5, 354.

67. "The Compulsory Basic Design Courses of Albers, Kandinsky, Klee, Schlemmer, and Schmidt," 1928, reprinted in Hans Wingler, *Bauhaus*, p. 144. Gropius also taught at Black Mountain, as did the potter Marguerite Wildenhain and the painter Lyonel Feininger, but Josef and Anni Albers were the only Bauhaus people who spent extensive time in North Carolina.

68. Quoted in Lane (ed.), *Black Mountain College*, p. 35.

69. This is so despite Albers's initial idea that the workshops at BMC might become self-supporting, and the continued interest taken by his wife Anni, who created weaving patterns for mass-production with some success into the 1960s. See Harris, *The Arts at Black Mountain College*, pp. 20–4. To deal appropriately with Anni Albers's commitment to industrial design would take a separate essay. On the one hand, her teaching activities at the college, centered around workshop production and the understanding of weaving technologies, show that she was developing an alternative, if not contradictory, use of craft alongside Josef's. On the other hand, she pursued a similar pedagogical technique in attempting to "put my students at the point of zero," as she expressed it. "I tried to have them imagine, let's say, that they are in a desert in Peru, no clothing, no nothing, no pottery even at that time (it has been now proved that archaeologically textiles have come before pottery), and to imagine themselves at the beach with nothing. And what do you do?" Anni Albers interviewed by Sevim Fesci, 5 July 1968, Archives of American Art, Smithsonian Institution, n.p.

70. Quoted in Martin Duberman, *Black Mountain College: An Experiment in Community* (New York: E. P Dutton, 1972).

71. Wingler, *Bauhaus*, p. 293.

72. Quoted in Paul Zucker, *New Architecture and City Planning: A Symposium* (New York: Philosophical Library, 1944).

73. John Dewey, "The Educational Function of a Museum of Decorative Arts," *Chronicle of the Museum for the Arts of Decoration of Cooper Union* 1/3 (Apr. 1937), pp. 93–9: 97.

74. Albert Laneir, in Interview with Ruth Asawa and Albert Laneir, conducted by Paul Karlstrom, San Francisco, California, 21 June and 5 July 2002, Archives of American Art, Smithsonian Institution, n.p.

75. Wick, *Teaching at the Bauhaus*, p. 185.

76. Ibid., p. 184.

77. Folke Nyberg, "From *Baukunst* to Bauhaus," *Journal of Architectural Education* 45/3 (May 1992), pp. 130–7: 130. Nyberg's call for a revival of craft-based architectural education is closely allied to Frampton's writings.

78. Charles Jencks and George Baird (eds), *Meaning in Architecture* (London: Barrie & Rockliff/The Cresset Press, 1969). Frampton's use of Arendt's terminology of "labor" and "work" in this text might be seen as an application of Existentialism to more familiar Marxist thinking about alienated labor. For Arendt, labor (*arbeiten* in German) is an organic process in which life is sustained and corresponds to the biological processes of the body, while work (*werken*) is oriented to the production of the built environment, technology, and other seemingly non-essential things. Frampton follows Arendt in arguing that modern consumer society, in which the processes of gratifying the body have become paramount, has not attended (as earlier cultures did) to the "work" of building the public realm. Hannah Arendt, *The Human Condition* (Chicago: University of Chicago Press, 1958).

79. Charles Jencks, "The Post-Modern Agenda," in Jencks, *The Post-Modern Reader* (London: Academy Editions, 1992), p. 12.

80. Alfred Barr, Jr., *Cubism and Abstract Art* (New York: Museum of Modern Art, 1936); see Susan Noyes Platt, "Modernism, Formalism, and Politics," *Art Journal* 47 (1988), p. 284–95.

81. J. B. Jackson, "Goodbye to Evolution," *Landscape* 13/2 (Winter 1963–64). "Instead of evolving, working towards a climax," Jackson wrote, "the human landscape is changing by a series of violent and unpredictable mutations" (p. 1).

82. Charles Jencks, in Jencks and Nathan Silver, *Adhocism* (London: Secker & Warburg, 1972), p. 15.

83. Terry Anderson, *The Movement and the Sixties* (New York: Oxford University Press, 1995), p. 265. Most of Drop City was composed of domes made from the tops of abandoned cars. See Ron E. Roberts, *The New Communes: Coming Together in America* (Englewood Cliffs, NJ: Prentice Hall, 1971), p. 47.

84. Art Boericke and Barry Shapiro, *Handmade Houses: A Guide to the Woodbutcher's Art* (San Francisco: Scrimshaw Press, 1973; *Shelter I* and *Shelter II* (Bolinas: Shelter Publications, 1973 and 1978); Richard Schmidt; *Handbuilt Homes: Funk, Fun and Fantasy* (Vance Bibliographies, 1986).

85. See Keith Melville, *Communes in the Counterculture* (New York: William Morrow, 1972); Paul Kagan, *New World Utopias* (New York: Penguin Books, 1975). On adobe building, see Richard Masterson, "Building with Adobe Bricks," *Studio Potter* 4/2 (Winter 1075–6), pp. 54–8. Masterson noted encouragingly: "While [adobe] requires large amounts of labor, it doesn't require highly skilled labor." (p. 54).

86. Charles Jencks, *Heterotopia: Los Angeles, The Riots & Hetero-Architecture* (London: Ernst & Son, 1993), p. 32.

87. Jencks, *Adhocism*, p. 81.

88. Ibid., pp. 15–16.

89. Ibid., p. 16. See Claude Lévi-Strauss, *The Savage Mind* (Chicago: University of Chicago Press, 1968; orig. pub. As *La Pensée Sauvage*, 1962).

90. Jencks, *Adhocism*, p. 56.

91. Robert Venturi, *Complexity and Contradiction in Architecture* (New York: The Museum of Modern Art, 1966), p. 103.

92. Jencks, *The Language of Post-Modern Architecture* (London: Academy Editions, 1977; 1984 edn), p. 160–1.

93. Ibid., p. 154. Venturi's quote appeared originally in "Diversity, Relevance, and Representation in Historicism, or *plus ça change*," *Architectural Record* (June 1982), p. 116.

94. Charles Jencks, "Preface" (1984), in *The Language of Post-Modern Architecture*, p. 6.

95. Charles Jencks, "Late-Modern Architecture" (1978), reprinted in Jencks, *Late-Modern Architecture and Other Essays* (London: Academy Editions, 1980), p. 13. In the late Modernist camp Jencks placed such figures as Arata Isozaki, Norman Foster, Kevin Roche, and Richard Rogers.

96. Charles Jencks, untitled book review of Juan Pablo Bonta, *An Anatomy of Architectural Interpretations: A Semiotic Review of the Criticism of Mies van der Rohe's Barcelona Pavilion*, in *The Journal of the Society of Architectural Historians* 35/3 (Oct. 1976), pp. 226–7.

97. The idea of sublation (*aufhebung*, literally "a raising to a higher level") originates in Hegel's dialectical theory of historical change. It refers to the way in which a principle that is contrary to the existing state of affairs is not simply negated, but rather preserved through containment within a new principle, thus creating a "higher" unity and overcoming conflict. A classic application of this theory to the moment in British cultural history under discussion is Dick Hebdige, *Subculture: The Meaning of Style* (New York: Methuen, 1979).

98. Harrod, *The Crafts in Britain in the 20th Century*, p. 440.

99. Ibid., p. 437.

100. Charles Jencks, *Towards a Symbolic Architecture: The Thematic House* (London: Academy Editions, 1985).

101. Jencks, "Preface," in *The Language of Post-Modern Architecture*, p. 7.

102. Wick, *Teaching at the Bauhaus*, pp. 322–4.

103. Kenneth Frampton, "Apropos Ulm," *Oppositions* 3 (1974), pp. 17–36; reprinted in Frampton, *Labour, Work and Architecture: Collected Essays on Architecture and Design* (London: Phaidon Press, 2002), pp. 51–2.

104. Frampton, "Apropos Ulm," p. 53.

105. Ibid., p. 53. For other accounts of the transformations in pedagogy at Ulm see Paul Betts, "Science, Semiotics, and Society: The Ulm Hochschule für Gestaltung in Retrospect," *Design Issues* 14/2 (Summer 1998), pp. 67–82; Greg Castillo, "The Bauhaus in Cold War Germany," in James-Chakraborty, *Bauhaus Culture*, pp. 182–8.

106. Frampton, "Apropos Ulm," p. 63.

107. For an overview see Tom Rockmore, *On Heidegger's Nazism and Philosophy* (Berkeley: University of California Press, 1991).

108. For Jacques Derrida's deconstructions of Heidegger see *The Truth in Painting*, trans. Geoff Bennington and Ian McLeod (Chicago: University of Chicago Press, 1987; orig. pub. 1978) and *Of Spirit: Heidegger and the Question* (Chicago: University of Chicago Press, 1991; orig. pub. 1987); see also David Wood, *Of Derrida, Heidegger and Spirit* (Chicago: Northwestern University Press, 1993).

109. Mark Wigley, *The Architecture of Deconstruction: Derrida's Haunt* (Cambridge, MA: MIT Press, 1993), pp. 18–19.

110. Martin Heidegger, "Building Dwelling Thinking" (1951) in Neil Leach, *Rethinking Architecture: A Reader in Cultural Theory* (London: Routledge, 1997), p. 104.

111. Heidegger, "Building Dwelling Thinking," p. 100.

112. Martin Heidegger, "The Origin of the Work of Art" (1935), reprinted in Heidegger, *Basic Writings* (New York: Harper Collins, 1993).

113. Martin Heidegger, "The Question Concerning Technology" (1954), reprinted in Heidegger, *Basic Writings*.

114. Heidegger, "The Question Concerning Technology."

115. For Frampton's views on Heidegger's "eco-philosophy," see Kenneth Frampton, *Studies in Tectonic Culture* (Cambridge, MA: MIT Press, 1995), p. 23–4.

116. Kenneth Frampton, "Towards a Critical Regionalism: Six Points for an Architecture of Resistance," in Hal Foster (ed.), *Postmodern Culture* (London: Pluto Press, 1983), pp. 16–30: 17, 21.

117. Frampton, "Towards a Critical Regionalism," p. 19, 28, 26. See also Kenneth Frampton, "America 1960–1970: Notes on Urban Images and Theory," *Casabella* 35 (Dec. 1971), pp. 25–37; and Denise Scott Brown, "Pop Off: Reply to Kenneth Frampton," in Denise Scott Brown and Robert Venturi, *A View from the Campidoglio: Selected Essays 1953–1984* (New York: Harper & Row, 1984).

118. Kenneth Frampton, "Prospects for a Critical Regionalism," *Perspecta* 20 (1983), pp. 147–62: 149.

119. Jencks, "Preface," in *The Language of Post-Modern Architecture*, p. 6. Jencks reserved special antipathy for Botta, along with other architects such as Leon Krier, whose investment in craft seemed to be the sign of a cult mentality. He described them as "Rational Architects, equivalent to the Society of Jesus. And these New Jesuits from Spain, Italy, Belgium and France have even insisted on building with ancient techniques of craftsmanship and stone." Charles Jencks, *What is Post-Modernism?* (New York/London: St Martin's Press/Academy Editions, 1986), p. 56.

120. Jencks, *The Language of Post-Modern Architecture*, p. 152.

121. See Debra Schafter, *The Order of Ornament, the Structure of Style: Theoretical Foundations of Modern Art and Architecture* (Cambridge: Cambridge University Press, 2003), p. 37ff.

122. Eduard Sekler, "Structure, Construction, and Tectonics," in Georgy Kepes (ed.), *Structure in Art and in Science* (New York: Braziller, 1965), p. 89, 92. On Sekler see Alexander von Hoffman (ed.), *Form, Modernism, and History: Essays in Honor of Eduard F. Sekler* (Cambridge: Harvard University Press, 1996). For an alternative historiographical tradition of the term see Conor Joyce, *Carl Einstein in* Documents *and His Collaboration with Georges Bataille* (Philadelphia: Xlibris, 2003), p. 279ff.

123. Frampton, *Studies in Tectonic Culture*, p. 23. See also Robert Meagher, "Techné," *Perspecta* 24 (1988), pp. 158–64.

124. Kenneth Frampton, "The Legacy of Alvar Aalto" (1998), in Kenneth Frampton, *Labour, Work and Architecture: Collected Essays on Architecture and Design* (London: Phaidon Press, 2002), p. 315; Frampton, *Studies in Tectonic Culture*, p. 311.

125. Frampton, *Studies in Tectonic Culture*, p. 307. For a parallel reading of Aalto's drawings see Mark A. Hewitt, "The Imaginary Mountain: The Significance of Contour in Alvar Aalto's Sketches," *Perspecta* 25 (1989), pp. 162–77.

126. Frampton, "Prospects for a Critical Regionalism," p. 159.

127. Kenneth Frampton, "The Work of Tadao Ando," orig. pub. 1991, in Frampton, *Labour, Work and Architecture*, p. 315.

128. Frederic Jameson, "The Constraints of Modernism," orig. pub. in *The Seeds of Time* (New York: Columbia University Press, 1994); rep. in Neil Leach, *Rethinking Architecture: A Reader in Cultural Theory* (London: Routledge, 1997), p. 253.

129. Jencks, *The Language of Post-Modern Architecture*, p. 15.

130. Frampton, *Studies in Tectonic Culture*, pp. 179–80.

131. Jencks, "Late-Modern Architecture," p. 14.

132. Kenneth Frampton, "The Return of the Repressed: Tectonic Structure and Symbolic Form, 1972–83," in *GA Architect: Arata Isozaki Vol. 1 1959–1978* (Tokyo: ADA Edition, 1991), p. 152.

133. This reading of Isozaki is borne out by writings of the architect himself. In 1972, for example, he wrote of his emerging style: "The ancillary structure is basically tactile and relates to human action and behavior. It responds to the distinctive quality of each place with a distinctive solution. In contrast to the basic structure governing the whole, which tends to be abstract and universal, the ancillary structure is thoroughly individualized and determines the character of reach place. Since their *raison d'être* is to dig in and respond to the character of each place, ancillary structures are mutually discontinuous, fragmentary and non-repeating." Arata Isozaki, "Anti-Architectural Notes III," 1972, quoted in *GA Architect: Arata Isozaki Vol. 1*, p. 183.

134. Kenneth Frampton, letter to the editor, *Journal of Architectural Education* 46/3 (Feb. 1993), pp. 199–200: 200.

135. "Spot Check: A Conversation between Rem Koolhaas and Sarah Whiting," *Assemblage* 40 (Dec. 1999), pp. 36–55: 43.

136. Margali Sarfatti Larson, *Behind the Postmodern Façade: Architectural Change in Late Twentieth-Century America* (Berkeley: University of California Press, 1993), p. 174. For a nuanced discussion of the "unseasonable" aspects of Frampton's theories see Jameson, "The Constraints of Modernism," p. 247–8.

137. Jencks, "The Post-Modern Agenda," p. 24.

138. Kenneth Frampton, "Topaz Medallion Address at the ACSA Annual Meeting," *Journal of Architectural Education* 45/4 (July 1992), pp. 195–6: 196. Frampton notes in this address: "I am well aware of the reactionary tendency of my argument, but nonetheless we would be foolhardy to overlook the ideological prejudices that have accompanied the introduction of computer-aided design into the general system of architectural production..." (p. 196)

CHAPTER 4: PASTORAL

1. Thomas G. Rosenmeyer, *The Green Cabinet: Theocritus and the European Pastoral Lyric* (Berkeley: University of California Press, 1969); Luba Freedman, *The Classical Pastoral in the Visual Arts* (New York: Peter Lang, 1989), p. 2.
2. Laurence Lerner, *The Uses of Nostalgia: Studies in Pastoral Poetry* (London: Chatto & Windus, 1972), p. 41 ff.
3. William Empson, *Some Versions of the Pastoral* (New York: New Directions, 1974; orig. pub. 1935), p. 22.
4. Thomas Crow, "The Simple Life: Pastoralism and the Persistence of Genre in Recent Art," in Thomas Crow, *Modern Art and the Common Culture* (New Haven: Yale University Press, 1996), p. 177.
5. Steven Walker, *A Cure For Love: A Generic Study of the Pastoral Idyll* (New York: Garland Publishing, 1987), p. 79. On the pastoral as a form of escapism, see Renato Poggioli, "The Oaten Flute," in Renato Poggioli, *The Oaten Flute: Essays on Pastoral Poetry and the Pastoral Ideal* (Cambridge: Harvard University Press, 1975; orig. pub. in the *Harvard Literary Bulletin*, 1957); Marshall Berman, *All That Is Solid Melts Into Air: The Experience of Modernity* (New York: Penguin Books, 1988 [orig. pub. 1982]), p. 134ff.
6. Edward S. Cooke, "The Long Shadow of William Morris: Paradigmatic Problems of Twentieth-Century American Furniture," in Luke Beckerdite (ed.), *American Furniture 2003* (Milwaukee: Chipstone Foundation/University Press of New England, 2003). For nineteenth-century precedents see Robert S. Fogarty, *All Things New: American Communes and Utopian Movements, 1860–1914* (Chicago: University of Chicago Press, 1990).
7. Raymond Williams, *The Country and the City* (New York: Oxford University Press, 1973), p. 54. Tanya Harrod identifies this sort of simplifying pastoral in the waning days of the British Arts and Crafts movement in *The Crafts in Britain in the Twentieth Century* (New Haven: Yale University Press, 1999), pp. 23–8.
8. Ed Rossbach, "Objects: USA Revisited," *Craft Horizons* 32/4 (Aug. 1972).
9. Fiona MacCarthy, *The Simple Life: C. R. Ashbee in the Cotswolds* (London: Lund Humphries, 1981), p. 9.
10. Raymond Williams, *The Country and the City* (New York: Oxford University Press, 1973), p. 54.
11. Williams later was interviewed about Empson's book and emphasized the importance of acknowledging one's own critical position as way of touching this reality: "...a second-hand formalism is in real danger of taking over what begins as a necessary theoretical acknowledgement that literature is a process of production. Any Marxism which fails to remember those means of production, which involve not just techniques but whole social relationships, is bound to be lost when it confronts a poem by Jonson or a novel by Jeffries. I would rather have risked the danger of which I was very aware in the book of simply saying this rural literature is not like the rural history—the naïve realism for which several people attacked me—than the opposite course of merely writing *Some Versions of Pastoral*." Raymond Williams, *Politics and Letters: Interviews with New Left Review* (London: NLB, 1979), pp. 304–5.
12. Williams, *The Country and the City*, p. 36.
13. Ibid., p. 41. On pastoral in the eighteenth century see also Ann Bermingham, *Landscape and Ideology: The English Rustic Tradition, 1740–1860* (Berkeley: University of California Press, 1986), Ch. 2; Michael McKeon, *The Secret History of Domesticity: Public, Private and the Division of Knowledge* (Baltimore: Johns Hopkins University Press, 2005), p. 414–22.
14. Williams, *The Country and the City*, pp. 3ff., and 298ff.
15. Leo Marx, "Pastoral and Its Guises," *Sewanee Review* 82/2 (Spring 1974), p. 351. Marx's seminal book *The Machine in the Garden: Technology and the Pastoral Ideal in America* (New York: Oxford University Press, 1964) inaugurated thinking about the pastoral in American studies.
16. For an overview of Romantic Nationalism in the Arts and Crafts movement, see Wendy Kaplan, *The Arts and Crafts Movement in Europe and America* (Los Angeles: Los Angeles County Museum of Art/Thames & Hudson, 2004). For the Italian Fascist appeal to a pre-industrial purity see Mark Antliff, "Fascism,

Modernism, and Modernity," *Art Bulletin* 84/1 (Mar. 2002), pp. 148–69. On the broader issue of imaginary pasts and modern nationalism, see Benedict Anderson, *Imagined Communities: Reflections on the Origins and Spread of Nationalism* (London: Verso, 1983); Eric Hobsbawm and Terence Ranger (eds), *The Invention of Tradition* (Cambridge: Cambridge University Press, 1983).

17. Quoted in Deyan Sudjic, "Veneer of Optimism," *Crafts* 61 (Mar./Apr. 1983), pp. 24–7.

18. For an elegant introduction to this large subject, see T. J. Jackson Lears, *No Place of Grace* (Chicago: University of Chicago Press, 1983), p. 60ff.

19. Tanya Harrod, *The Crafts in Britain in the Twentieth Century*, p. 55.

20. Stefan Muthesius, review of Alan Crawford, *C. R. Ashbee: Architect, Designer and Romantic Socialist*, *Oxford Art Journal* 9/2 (1986), pp. 82–4: 82.

21. Annette Carruthers, "The Guild of Handicraft at Chipping Campden," in Mary Greensted (ed.), *The Arts and Crafts Movement in the Cotswolds* (Phoenix Mill: Alan Sutton, 1993), p. 46; MacCarthy, *The Simple Life*, pp. 44, 87.

22. Alan Crawford, *C. R. Ashbee: Architect, Designer and Romantic Socialist* (New Haven: Yale University Press, 1985), p. 145.

23. Carruthers, "The Guild of Handicraft at Chipping Campden," p. 55.

24. Harrod, *The Crafts in Britain in the Twentieth Century*, pp. 58–60; 170–2.

25. Richard LaTrobe-Bateman, "The Pursuit of Style," *Crafts* 66 (Jan./Feb. 1984), p. 14–15. On LaTrobe-Bateman see Harrod, *The Crafts in Britain in the Twentieth Century*, p. 398.

26. For the League of New Hampshire Arts and Crafts, see Allen H. Eaton, *Handicrafts of New England* (New York: Harper & Bros., 1949), p. 295 ff; *Hands That Built New Hampshire* (Brattleboro, VT: Stephen Daye Press, 1940), p. 250 ff; and *Contemporary New England Handicrafts* (Worcester: Worcester Art Museum, 1943). For more on interwar regionalism in the crafts, see Janet Kardon (ed.), *Revivals! Diverse Traditions: The History of American Craft 1920–1945* (New York: American Craft Museum/Harry N. Abrams, 1994).

27. Bruce E. Johnson, "Eleanor Vance, Charlotte Yale, and the Origins of the Biltmore Estate Industries," in Robert Brunk (ed.), *May We All Remember Well*, vol. 2 (Asheville, NC: Robert S. Brunk Auction Services, 2001), pp. 241–66.

28. Andrew Glasgow, "The Southern Appalachian Craft Revival: A Historical Perspective of the Southern Highland Handicraft Guild Organization," in *Southern Arts and Crafts 1890–1940* (Charlotte: Mint Museum of Art, 1996), p. 80. See also Jane Kessler, "From Mission to Market: Craft in the Southern Appalachians," in Janet Kardon (ed.), *Revivals! Diverse Traditions*, p. 124.

29. Glasgow, "The Southern Appalachian Craft Revival," p. 86.

30. William Goodell Frost, "Our Contemporary Ancestors in the Southern Mountains," *Atlantic Monthly* 83/497 (March 1899), pp. 311–19.

31. Empson, *Some Versions of Pastoral*, p. 14.

32. Dean Herrin, "Poor, Proud, and Primitive: Images of Appalachian Domestic Interiors," in Gerald W. R. Ward, *Perspectives on American Furniture* (New York: W. W. Norton/Winterthur, 1988), p. 109. See also John Jacob Niles, *The Appalachian Photographs of Doris Ullman* (Penland, NC: The Jargon Society, 1971).

33. Allen H. Eaton, *Handicrafts of New England* (New York: Harper & Bros., 1949), p. 45.

34. Julia S. Ardery, *The Temptation: Edgar Tolson and the Genesis of Twentieth-Century Folk Art* (Chapel Hill: University of North Carolina Press, 1998), pp. 237–8.

35. Jane S. Becker, *Selling Tradition: Appalachia and the Construction of an American Folk, 1930–1940* (Chapel Hill: University of North Carolina Press, 1998), p. 205–7; Andrew Wallace, "The National Folk Festival: The Sarah Gertrude Knott Years," *Folklife Center News* 24/1 (Winter 2002).

36. Richard Bauman and Patricia Sawin, "The Politics of Participation in Folklife Festivals," in Ivan Karp and Steven Lavine (eds), *Exhibiting Cultures* (Washington: Smithsonian Institution Press, 1991). On exhibitions

of Appalachian folk art, see Becker, *Selling Tradition*, p. 209ff; John Michael Vlach, "Holger Cahill as Folklorist," *Journal of American Folklore* 98/388 (Apr. 1985), pp. 148–62.

37. For English language studies of the main participants, see Sidney Cardozo and Masaaki Hirano, *Uncommon Clay: The Life and Pottery of Rosanjin* (Tokyo: Kodansha, 1987); Timothy Wilcox, Yuko Kikuchi, et al., *Shōji Hamada: Master Potter* (Ditchling: Ditchling Museum/Lund Humphries, 1998); Sōetsu Yanagi and Kanjirō Kawai, *Shikō Munakata: The Woodblock Prints* (Tokyo, 1958); Tony Birks, et al., *Bernard Leach, Hamada, and Their Circle* (Marston House, 1992); Carol Hogben, *The Art of Bernard Leach* (London: Faber & Faber, 1978); Edmund deWaal, *Bernard Leach: St. Ives Artists* (London: Tate Gallery, 1997); and Emmanuel Cooper, *Bernard Leach: Life and Work* (New Haven: Yale University Press, 2003). For pictorial overviews of *mingei* objects see Martha Longenecker, *Kindred Spirits: The Eloquence of Function in American Shaker and Japanese Arts of Daily Life* (San Diego: Mingei International, 1995); Japan Folk Crafts Museum, *Mingei: Two Centuries of Japanese Folk Art* (Tokyo: Japan Folk Crafts Museum, 1995); and Amaury Saint-Gilles, *Mingei: Japan's Enduring Folk Crafts* (Rutland, VT: Charles E. Tuttle, 1989).

38. Sōetsu Yanagi, "The Kizaemon Tea Bowl," in *The Unknown Craftsman: A Japanese Insight Into Beauty* (Tokyo: Kodansha, 1972), p. 192. It should be noted that this essay, like the other selections in *the Unknown Craftsman*, was freely translated by Leach with assistance, and so represents a synthetic document intermingling aspects of both men's thinking.

39. Yuko Kikuchi, *Japanese Modernisation and Mingei Theory: Cultural Nationalism and Oriental Orientalism* (London: Routledge, 2004), p. 124ff.

40. Predictably, writers inclined to celebrate *mingei* as an apolitical aesthetics tend to emphasize Yanagi's critiques of colonialism. See for example Teiko Utsumi, "*Mingei* and the Life of Sōetsu Yanagi," in Japan Folk Crafts Museum, *Mingei*, pp. 15–16.

41. Yanagi first traveled to Korea in 1916 and went regularly thereafter. Hamada visited in 1919, 1936–7, and 1941–3, and Leach in 1918 and 1935. See Yuko Kikuchi, *Japanese Modernisation and Mingei Theory*; Susan Peterson, *Shōji Hamada: A Potter's Way and Work* (New York: Weatherhill, 1974); Bernard Leach, *Beyond East and West: Memoirs, Portraits and Essays* (London: Faber & Faber, 1978).

42. Tanya Harrod, *The Crafts in Britain in the Twentieth Century*, p. 184; Stefan Tanaka, *Japan's Orient: Rendering Pasts into History* (Berkeley: University of California Press, 1993), p. 248.

43. Kikuchi, *Japanese Modernisation and Mingei Theory*, p. 134.

44. Bernard Leach, "China, Corea, Japan," 1920, in Sōetsu Yanagi, Bernard Leach, et al., *An English Artist in Japan* (self-published manuscript, 1920; 1969 copy in Ceramics Department library, Victoria & Albert Museum), p. 45.

45. Edmund de Waal, "Not In Ideas But In Things," in Garth Clark (ed.), *Ceramic Millenium* (Halifax: Press of the Nova Scotia College of Art and Design, 2006), p. 353.

46. Peterson, *Shōji Hamada*, p. 81.

47. Peterson, *Shōji Hamada*, p. 191.

48. Harrod, *The Crafts in Britain in the Twentieth Century*, pp. 143, 257.

49. Michael Casson, *Pottery in Britain Today* (London: Tiranti, 1967), n.p.

50. See Bert Winther-Tamaki, *Art in the Encounter of Nations: Japanese and American Artists in the Early Postwar Years* (Honolulu: University of Hawaii Press, 2001); and Alicia Volk, *Made in Japan: The Postwar Creative Print Movement* (Milwaukee: Milwaukee Art Museum/University of Washington Press, 2005).

51. See Emmanuel Cooper, "Bernard Leach in America," in Robert Hunter (ed.), *Ceramics in America 2004* (Milwaukee; Chipstone Foundation/University Press of New England, 2004); Garth Clark and Margie Hughto, *A Century of Ceramics in the United States 1878–1978* (New York: E. P. Dutton, 1979), pp. 130–3; Susan Peterson, ""The Explosion of the Fifties," in Jo Lauria (ed.), *Color and Fire: Defining Moments in Studio Ceramics 1950–2000* (Los Angeles: Los Angeles County Museum of Art/Rizzoli, 2000); and Nicole

Coolidge Rousmaniere, "Yanagi's America," in Japan Folk Crafts Museum, *Mingei*. An abridged version of Rousmaniere's essay is in *Mingei Revisited: In Search of the Ethical Pot*, published as *Studio Potter* 25/1 (Dec. 1996), pp. 10–12.

52. Glenn Adamson, "California Spirit: Rediscovering the Furniture of J. B. Blunk," *Woodwork* 59 (Oct. 1999): 22–31; Daniel Rhodes, "The Potter and his Kiln," *Craft Horizons* 24/2 (Mar./Apr. 1969), p. 36–8; Daniel Rhodes, *Tamba: The Timeless Art of a Japanese Village* (Tokyo: Kodansha, 1970); Daniel Rhodes, "Legends of Ahimsa," *Studio Potter* 3/2 (Winter 1974–75), pp. 3–6; "The Search for Form," *Studio Potter* 13/1 (Dec. 1984), pp. 6–20; George Nakashima, *The Soul of a Tree: A Woodworker's Reflections* (Tokyo: Kodansha, 1981); Michael Stone, *Contemporary American Woodworkers* (Salt Lake City: Gibbs M. Smith, 1986); Louise Cort (ed.), *Isamu Noguchi and Japanese Ceramics: A Close Embrace of the Earth* (Berkeley: University of California Press, 2003).

53. See for example Langdon Warner, *The Enduring Art of Japan* (New York: Grove Press, 1952); Hugo Munsterberg, *The Folk Arts of Japan* (Rutland, VT: Charles E. Tuttle, 1958); Seiichi Okuda, *Japanese Ceramics*, translated and adapted by Roy Andrew Miller (Rutland, VT: Charles E. Tuttle, 1960); Fujio Koyama, *Japanese Ceramics from Ancient to Modern Times* (Oakland: Oakland Art Museum, 1961).

54. Warren MacKenzie, "Bernard Leach Remembered," in *Mingei Legacy* (San Diego: Mingei International Museum/NCECA, 2003).

55. Warren MacKenzie, letter to the author, 20 Apr. 2007.

56. For an overview of these and other similar potters, see *Mingei Legacy*; Nancy Means Wright, "The Studio Potter," *American Craft* 44/4 (Aug./Sept. 1984), pp. 17–20, 96; and "Eight Independent Production Potters," *Craft Horizons* 37/1 (Feb. 1977), p. 48.

57. Jody Clowes, "John Glick," *American Craft* 51/3 (June/July 1991), pp. 36–43.

58. Gerry Williams, "Editorial," *Studio Potter* 2/1 (Summer 1973), p. 4.

59. Gerry Williams quoted in Currier Gallery of Art, *Gerry Williams: Ceramics* (Manchester, NH: Currier Gallery of Art, 1970), p. 31; Gerry Williams, "Editorial: Reading the Entrails," *Studio Potter* 3/2 (Winter 1974–75), p. 4.

60. Harriet Cohen in "What is the Role of the Potter?" *Studio Potter* 5/2 (1977), p. 21.

61. Garth Clark and Margie Hughto, *A Century of Ceramics in the United States: 1878–1978* (New York: E. P. Dutton, 1979), p. 133.

62. Warren MacKenzie, "Criticism in Ceramic Art," *Studio Potter* 9/1 (1980), reprinted in Ronald Larsen (ed.), *A Potter's Companion: Imagination, Originality, and Craft* (Rochester, VT: Park Street Press, 1993), p. 29.

63. Warren MacKenzie, letter to the author, 20 Apr. 2007.

64. Warren MacKenzie, "The Aesthetics of Function: Traces of Memory," *Studio Potter* 13/2 (June 1985), p. 13.

65. John Reeve, "Warren MacKenzie and the Straight Pot," *Craft Horizons* (June 1976), p. 20.

66. Warren MacKenzie, *Kiln Firing: February 26, 1976* (Rochester, NY: Rochester Art Center, 1976), n.p. Similarly, MacKenzie commented early in his career, "each piece, in a sense, becomes a variation of an idea which may develop over hours, days, or months and require ten to several hundred pieces in order to come to full development. One pot suggests another." Quoted in "Alix and Warren MacKenzie," *Design Quarterly* 42 (1958), p. 58. See also Robert Silberman, "Down to Earth Idealist," *American Craft* (June/July 1989), pp. 32–9: 37.

67. Quoted in Susan Brown, "Warren MacKenzie: A Potter's Life," *Ceramic Review* no. 119 (Sept./Oct. 1989). MacKenzie has said, "There is something about living in Minnesota, or living in the Midwest, I think I'd say. My pots are really most at home in the Midwest, and I think there's a number of potters who have gravitated to this area because they find it sympathetic to hand pottery. And it doesn't have to be fancy hand pottery, such as you're likely to find in the big galleries in New York or San Francisco and so on, the latest

thing. They want pots they can use in their home." Warren MacKenzie, interview with Robert Silberman, 29 Oct. 2002. Smithsonian Archives of American Art, Nanette L. Laitman Documentation Project for Craft and Decorative Art in America, n.p.

68. Rose Slivka, untitled editorial, *Craft Horizons* (June 1976), p. 15.

69. Garth Clark, letter to the editor, *Studio Potter* (Dec. 1992).

70. Erik Gronborg, "The New Generation of Ceramic Artists," *Craft Horizons* 29/1 (Jan./Feb. 1969), p. 27. The critique went both ways. Many pastoral-minded potters objected strenuously to the extensive favorable coverage accorded to Funk during Rose Slivka's editorial stint at *Craft Horizons*. To take one of many examples, one Lotte Streisinger wrote, "the function of the craftsman is to provide an *antidote* and *corrective* to mechanization... If the craftsman does not uphold the enduring values of humanity and the works of the human hand, who will? And if nobody does, we are lost, lost, lost. Now I think you have a responsibility there, editors of *Craft Horizons*, and I seriously urge you to have an editorial policy meeting on this subject: which side are you on, the side of pop-groovy-bullshit, or the side of humanity?" Untitled letter, *Craft Horizons* 29/3 (May/June 1969).

71. For Leider's recollections on his departure from *Artforum*, see his interview with Amy Newman, "An Art World Figure Re-emerges, Unrepentant," *New York Times*, 3 Sept. 2000, pp. 31–2; and Newman, *Challenging Art: Artforum 1962–1974* (New York: Soho Press, 2000).

72. Philip Leider, "How I Spent My Summer Vacation or, Art and Politics in Nevada, Berkeley, San Francisco and Utah." *Artforum* 11/1 (Sept. 1970), pp. 40–6. Reprinted in Amy Baker Sandback (ed.), *Looking Critically: 21 Years of Artforum Magazine* (Ann Arbor: UMI Research Press, 1984), p. 43.

73. Leider, "How I Spent My Summer Vacation," p. 45. See also "Canyon," *Los Angeles Times Magazine* (7 Dec. 1971), n. p.

74. Leider, "How I Spent My Summer Vacation," p. 45.

75. For an extensive account of the sparring between Canyon inhabitants and the local authorities, see James Van Der Zee, *Canyon: The Story of the Last Rustic Community in Metropolitan America* (New York: Harcourt Brace Jovanovich, 1972). I am indebted to Canyon Steinzig for my own chance to visit Canyon in 1998. It hasn't changed much.

76. Leider, "How I Spent My Summer Vacation," p. 45.

77. Ibid., p. 41.

78. Ibid., p. 45.

79. Ibid., p. 45.

80. Arthur Espenet Carpenter, "The Rise of Artiture," *Fine Woodworking* 38 (Jan./Feb. 1983), pp. 98–103.

81. Author's interview with Carpenter, 18 June 1998.

82. For Carpenter's biography, see Michael Stone, *Contemporary American Woodworkers* (Salt Lake City: Gibbs M. Smith, 1986), p. 82ff.

83. By 1975, the Guild included twenty-one "masters" who taught weaving, furnituremaking, pottery, house building, enamel, metalwork, batik, film, and photography.

84. See Glenn Adamson, "California Dreaming," *Furniture Studio One* (Free Union, VA: The Furniture Society, 1999), pp. 32–42; and Rick Mastelli, "Art Carpenter: The Independent Spirit of the Baulines Craftsmans' Guild," *Fine Woodworking* 37 (Nov./Dec. 1982), pp. 62–8.

85. Alan Marks, "California Woodworking," *Fine Woodworking* 1/6 (Spring 1977), pp. 32–4. This was the first article printed in the magazine to focus on a regional style of woodworking, attesting to the distinctiveness of the aesthetic developed in California during the period.

86. John Kelsey, the founding editor of *Fine Woodworking*, was responsible for the christening, having used the term in several public lectures in the early 1970s.

87. Carpenter, "The Rise of Artiture," p. 98.

88. Robert Morris, "American Quartet," *Art in America* 69/10 (Dec. 1981), reprinted in Morris, *Continuous Project Altered Daily*, (Cambridge, MA: MIT Press, 1994), p. 243.

89. Barry Le Va interviewed by Liza Bear, "...A Continuous Flow of Fairly Aimless Movement," *Avalanche* 3 (Fall 1971).

90. Leider, "How I Spent My Summer Vacation..." p. 46.

91. Dan Graham, "Carl Andre," *ARTS Magazine* 42/3 (Dec. 1967/Jan. 1968), p. 34. For a consideration of this temporal contingency see Martha Buskirk, *The Contingent Object of Contemporary Art* (Cambridge, MA: MIT Press, 2003).

92. For accounts of AWC activities, see Lucy Lippard, "The Art Workers' Coalition: Not A History," *Studio International* 180/927 (Nov. 1970), pp. 171–4; Lucy Lippard, "The Dilemma," *ARTS Magazine* 45/2 (Nov. 1970), p. 27–9; Lil Picard, "Protest and Rebellion: The Function of the Art Workers Coalition," *ARTS Magazine* 44/7 (May 1970), pp. 18, 20.

93. "The Artist and Politics: A Symposium," *Artforum* 9/1 (Sept. 1970), p. 35.

94. Jeanne Siegel, "Carl Andre: Artworker," *Studio International* 180/927 (Nov. 1970), pp. 175–6.

95. Siegel, "Carl Andre: Artworker," p. 178.

96. Quoted in Hollis Frampton, "Letter to Enno Develing," 1969; first published in *Carl Andre* (Den Haag: Haags Gemeentemuseum, 1969), pp. 7–12; reprinted in Eva Meyer-Hermann, et al., *Carl Andre: Sculptor 1996* (Wolfsburg, Germany: Kunstmuseum Wolfsburg/Oktagon, 1996), pp. 60–2.

97. Lucy Lippard (ed.), "Time: A Panel Discussion," *Art International* 13/9 (Nov. 1969), p. 39.

98. Andre also presents himself as an artisan, appearing at public lectures in overalls and sporting an old-fashioned Mennonite beard. See Anna C. Chave, "Minimalism and Biography," *Art Bulletin* 82/1 (Mar. 2000), pp. 149, 157–8. Chave describes Andre's self-presentation as "a mix of innocently pastoral and industrial images" (p. 157). In this context, it may be significant that Andre was the only major sculptor of the 1960s to exhibit a work at the Museum of Contemporary Crafts. The piece, entitled "Monuments, Tombstones and Trophies," was a mound of sand meant to be placed atop a grave site; perhaps Andre intended it as an elegy to "disappearing" craft. See Dan Graham, "Carl Andre," p. 35.

99. Carl Andre and Jeremy Gilbert-Rolfe, "Commodity and Contradiction, or, Contradiction as Commodity," *October* 2 (Summer, 1976), pp. 100–4: 102.

100. Phyllis Tuchman, "An Interview with Carl Andre," *Artforum* 8/6 (Jan. 1970), p. 55.

101. David Bourdon, "The Razed Sites of Carl Andre," *Artforum* 5/2 (Oct. 1966), p. 17.

102. Diane Waldman, *Carl Andre* (New York: Solomon R. Guggenheim Museum, 1970), p. 6. Jack Burnham also insisted that "the context of [Andre's] pieces dominates his arrangement of them." Jack Burnham, *The Structure of Art* (New York: George Braziller, 1971), p. 135.

103. Tuchman, "An Interview with Carl Andre," p. 55.

104. Samuel Wagstaff, Jr., "Talking with Tony Smith," *Artforum* 5/4 (Dec. 1966), p. 19.

105. Tuchman, "An Interview with Carl Andre," p. 57.

106. Michael Fried, "Art and Objecthood," *Artforum* 5 (June 1967), pp. 12–23.

107. Lucy Lippard (ed.), "Time: A Panel Discussion," p. 23.

108. Robert Smithson, "A Museum of Language in the Vicinity of Art," *Art International* 12/3 (Mar. 1968), p. 21.

109. Tuchman, "An Interview with Carl Andre," p. 57.

110. Willoughby Sharp, 1968 interview with Carl Andre, *Avalanche* 1 (Fall 1970), p. 18.

111. Smithson, "A Museum of Language in the Vicinity of Art," p. 24.

112. Gary Shapiro, *Earthwards: Robert Smithson and Art After Babel* (Berkeley: University of California Press, 1995), p. 56.

113. Robert Smithson interviewed by Paul Cummings, 14/19 July 1972, Archives of American Art, Smithsonian Institution, n.p.

114. Leo Marx, *The Machine in the Garden*; see also Jennifer Roberts, *Mirror-Travels: Robert Smithson and History* (New Haven: Yale University Press, 2004).

115. Erwin Panofsky, "Et In Arcadia Ego: Poussin and the Elegiac Tradition," in Panofsky, *Meaning and the Visual Arts* (New York: Doubleday, 1955), p. 359.

116. Smithson, "A Sedimentation of the Mind," in Jack Flam (ed.), *Robert Smithson: The Collected Writings* (Berkeley: University of California Press, 1996), p. 105. This line follows a withering characterization of the natural surroundings of a work by Anthony Caro as "a leftover Arcadia with flowery overtones [that] gives the sculpture the look of some industrial ruin." (p. 104)

117. Smithson, "The Spiral Jetty," reprinted in Flam (ed.), *Robert Smithson: The Collected Writings*, p. 149.

118. Jones, *The Machine in the Studio: Constructing the Postwar American Artist* (Chicago: University of Chicago Press, 1996), p. 342.

119. Robert Smithson, "Donald Judd," in *Seven Sculptors* (Philadelphia: Philadelphia Institute of Contemporary Art, 1965), reprinted in Flam (ed.), *Robert Smithson: The Collected Writings*, p. 4; Robert Smithson, "A Sedimentation of the Mind: Earth Projects," *Artforum*, Sept. 1968; reprinted in Flam (ed.), *Robert Smithson: The Collected Writings*, p. 105. As early as 1966, critics responded to Smithson's particularly forceful rejection of "hand manipulation." See Toby Mussman, "Literalness and the Infinite," in Gregory Battcock (ed.), *Minimal Art: A Critical Anthology* (New York: E. P. Dutton, 1968), p. 248. See also Jones, *The Machine in the Studio*.

120. Ann Reynolds, "Reproducing Nature: the Museum of Natural History as Nonsite," *October* 45 (Summer 1988), pp. 109–27.

121. Ron Graziani, "Robert Smithson: An Esthetic Foreman in the Mining Industry (Part Two)," *Art Criticism* 13/1 (1998), pp. 8–9.

122. Nicholas Rena, untitled gallery statement, Barrett Marsden Gallery, 2006.

123. The exhibition in question was held at Barrett Marsden Gallery, London, from 17 Mar. to 22 Apr., 2006.

124. Quoted in John Houston, *Richard Slee: Ceramics in Studio* (London: Bellew, 1990), p. 16.

125. Alison Britton, review of 'Glazed Ceramics,' *Crafts* 149 (Nov./Dec.1997), p. 55.

126. Garth Clark, "Resident Alien From the Land of Pop: Richard Slee in Context," in *Richard Slee* (Stoke-on Trent: Potteries Museum/Lund Humphries, 2003); reprinted in John Pagliaro, ed. *Shards: Garth Clark on Ceramic Art* (New York: Ceramic Arts Foundation/DAP, 2003), p. 196.

127. Garth Clark, "Resident Alien From the Land of Pop: Richard Slee in Context", in *Richard Slee* (Stoke-on Trent: Potteries Museum/Lund Humphries, 2003), p. 61.

CHAPTER 5: AMATEUR

1. Justin Clemens, "Postmodernity or 'The Breaking of the Vessels,'" in Garth Clark (ed.), *Ceramic Millenium* (Halifax: Press of the Nova Scotia College of Art and Design, 2006), p. 137.

2. Zygmunt Bauman, *Wasted Lives: Modernity and Its Outcasts* (London: Blackwell, 2003), p. 12.

3. For an extension of this argument see Chris Rojek, *Capitalism and Leisure Theory* (New York: Tavistock/Methuen, 1985).

4. Debbie Stoller, *Stitch'n'Bitch: The Knitter's Handbook* (New York: Workman Publishing Company, 2004).

5. The reference is of course to Thorstein Veblen, *The Theory of the Leisure Class* (1899).

6. Quoted in Kim Sloan, *A Noble Art: Amateur Artists and Drawing Masters, c. 1600–1800* (London: British Museum Publications, 2000), p. 46. See also Ruth Hayden, *Mrs Delany: Her Life and Flowers* (London: British Museum Publications, 1980).

7. Robert A. Stebbins, "'Amateur' and 'Hobbyist' as Concepts for the Study of Leisure Problems," *Social Problems* 27/4 (Apr. 1980), pp. 413–17: 414. See also Robert A. Stebbins, "The Amateur: Two Sociological Definitions," *Pacific Sociological Review* 20/4 (Oct. 1977), pp. 582–606; Robert A. Stebbins, "Serious Leisure: A Conceptual Statement," *Pacific Sociological Review* 25/2 (Apr. 1982), pp. 251–72; Robert A. Stebbins, *Between Work and Leisure: A Study of the Common Ground of Two Separate Worlds* (Piscataway, NJ: Transaction Publishers, 2004).

8. Jacques Barzun, "The Indispensable Amateur," *Juilliard Review* 1 (1954), pp. 19–25: 25, reprinted in Barzun, *Critical Questions: On Music and Letters, Culture and Biography, 1940–1980* (Chicago: University of Chicago Press, 1982).

9. Jennifer Harris, "The Role of the Amateur," in *William Morris: Questioning the Legacy* (London: Crafts Council, 1996), p. 56.

10. Lee Nordness, "Prospectus for Objects: USA," 13 Feb. 1968. Lee Nordness business records and papers, Archives of American Art.

11. Tony Bennett, "The Exhibitionary Complex," *New Formations* 4 (Spring 1988), pp. 73–102. See also Arthur Danto, *After the End of Art: Contemporary Art and the Pale of History* (Princeton: Princeton University Press, 1997); and Thierry de Duve, *Kant After Duchamp* (Cambridge, MA: MIT Press, 1996).

12. For a development of this point see George Bailey, "Amateurs Imitate, Professionals Steal," *The Journal of Aesthetics and Art Criticism* 47/3 (Summer 1989), pp. 221–7.

13. Quoted in Neil Benezra, *Robert Arneson: A Retrospective* (Des Moines: Des Moines Art Center, 1986), p. 28.

14. Quoted in Paul Smith, *Clayworks: Twenty Americans* (New York; Museum of Contemporary Crafts, 1971), n.p.

15. Quoted in Beth Coffelt, "Delta Bob and Captain Ace," *San Francisco Sunday Examiner and Chronicle*, 8 Apr. 1974, p. 42.

16. Prieto worked with the rigorous, Bauhaus-trained émigré potter Marguerite Wildenhain at her California studio, Pond Farm. See Charles Talley, "School for Life," *American Craft* 51/2 (Apr./May 1991), pp. 36–9, 72–3.

17. As one unusually hyperbolic evaluation has it, "that capped beer bottle took Robert Arneson across the Rubicon. It transformed ceramics from craft into art. It proclaimed a doctrine that Arneson has taught and exemplified ever since: work from idea, not from form." Alfred Frankenstein, "The Ceramic Sculpture of Robert Arneson: Transforming Craft Into Art," *Art News,* 75/1 (Jan. 1976), p. 48.

18. Despite the milieu, Arneson built up a strong body of students in a short period of time who were to be the heart of the Funk ceramics movement: David Gilhooly, Margaret Dodd, Richard Shaw, Steven Kaltenbach, Peter Vandenberge, and Chris Unterseher. Bruce Nauman was also briefly a student of Arneson's. See John Natsoulas and Bruce Nixon, *Thirty Years of TB-9: A Tribute to Robert Arneson* (Davis: John Natsoulas Gallery, 1991); Hilarie Faberman, *Fired at Davis* (Stanford: Iris and B. Gerald Cantor Center for Visual Arts at Stanford University, 2005); Constance M. Lewallen, *A Rose Has No Teeth: Bruce Nauman in the 1960s* (Berkeley: Berkeley University Art Museum/University of California Press, 2007).

19. Natsoulas and Nixon, *Thirty Years of TB-9*, p. 17.

20. Emile Durkheim, *The Elementary Forms of the Religious Life* (New York: The Free Press/Macmillan, 1965 [orig. pub. 1915]), pp. 344–5 and ff.

21. As the art historian Yve-Alain Bois has observed: "the sacred is only another name for what one rejects as excremental." Bois and Rosalind Krauss, *Formless: A User's Guide* (New York: Zone Books, 1997), p. 51; see also p. 52ff. Also see A. R. Radcliffe-Brown, *Taboo* (Cambridge: Cambridge University Press, 1939), pp. 17–18; and Franz Steiner, *Taboo* (New York: Philosophical Library, 1956), p. 35.

22. Sigmund Freud, *Totem and Taboo* (London: Routledge & Kegan Paul, 1950), p. 30.

23. "California Sculpture" was curated by John Coplans, with Pasadena Art Museum curator Walter Hopps and Oakland Museum director Paul Mills.

24. Garth Clark and Margie Hughto make a comparison between Arneson and Duchamp in *A Century of Ceramics in the United States, 1878–1978* (New York: E. P. Dutton, 1979), pp. 160, 271, as does Alfred Frankenstein in "Of Bricks, Pop Bottles and a Better Mousetrap," *This World* (6 Oct. 1974), p. 37.

25. "Robert Arneson in Conversation with Gwen Stone," *Visual Dialog* 2/1, p. 7.

26. Benezra, *Robert Arneson*, p. 23.

27. Coffelt, "Delta Bob and Captain Ace," p. 42.

28. Ulrica Rudd, letter, *Craft Horizons* 30/2 (Mar./Apr. 1970), p. 10.

29. Leo G. Mazow points to a tendency in Arneson's work of the 1960s to use the imagery of things that are "look[ed] down upon," from abject toilets and feces to seemingly innocuous bathroom scales and shoes. Mazow, *Arneson and the Object* (University Park, PA: Palmer Museum of Art/George Adams Gallery, 2004), p. 20.

30. In 1962 Ron Nagle and Jim Melchert had introduced white earthenware in their teaching at the San Francisco Art Institute in an attempt to get away from the technical orientation of higher fire stoneware. Their use of white earthenware freed them from the masculine showmanship and materialist dramatics that drove the work of Voulkos and his circle at Otis. Melchert, a former acolyte of Voulkos's in Berkeley, played out an Oedipal struggle against the influence of his mentor that was similar to Arneson's own struggles, but at much greater proximity. Melchert's formal break with Voulkos, the 1962 work *Leg Pot*, was an intentional renouncement of the Otis aesthetic—horizontal instead of vertical, eccentrically asymmetrical instead of hieratically frontal, and recumbent instead of priapic. (Author's conversation with Jim Melchert, 29 May 2003.)

31. Peter Selz, *Funk* (Berkeley: University Art Museum, University of California, 1967). See also Peter Selz, *Beyond the Mainstream: Essays on Modern and Contemporary Art* (Cambridge: Cambridge University Press, 1997).

32. Robert Farris Thompson, *Flash of the Spirit* (New York: Vintage Books, 1983), pp. 104–5.

33. Rebecca Solnit, *Secret Exhibition: Six California Artists of the Cold War Era* (San Francisco: City Lights Books, 1990).

34. Quoted in Audrey Strohl, "Life and Leisure," *Memphis Press-Scimitar* 29 Mar. 1979, p. 10. (George Adams Gallery artist file.)

35. Donald Judd, untitled review, *Arts Magazine* 39/4 (Jan. 1965), p. 69.

36. See for instance Dennis Adrian, "Robert Arneson's Feats of Clay," *Art In America* 62/5 (Sept./Oct. 1974, pp. 80–3).

37. Joseph Pugliese, "The Decade: Ceramics," *Craft Horizons* 33/1 (Feb. 1973), p. 48.

38. Mitchell Merback, "Beat Funk, Ceramic Funk, Defunct Funk: A Critical Flashback," *American Ceramics* 10/4 (1993), p. 33.

39. "Pottery Workers Very Feminine In Styles Today," *Ponca City, Oklahoma News* (May 3, 1970). American Craft Council archives, Objects: USA file.

40. Kate Millet, *Sexual Politics* (Garden City, NY: Doubleday & Co., 1969), p. 41.

41. See Helen Molesworth, "Housework and Artwork" *October* 92 (Winter 2000), pp. 71–97; Sue Rowley: "Going Public: Getting Personal," in Catriona Moore (ed.), *Dissonance: Feminism and the Arts 1970–1990* (Woolloomooloo, Australia: Artspace, 1994); Arlene Raven, *At Home* (Long Beach: Long Beach Museum of Art, 1983); Rozsika Parker, "Portrait of the Artist as a Housewife," *Spare Rib* 60 (1977), pp. 5–8.

42. See Phyllis Rosser, "No Place Like Home," in Joanna Frueh, Cassandra Langer, and Arlene Raven (eds), *New Feminist Criticism: Art Identity Action* (New York: HarperCollins, 1994).

43. For example, Patricia Mainardi, "Quilts: The Great American Art," *Feminist Art Journal* 2 (Winter 1973); Rachel Maines, "Fancywork: The Archaeology of Lives," *Feminist Art Journal* 3/4 (Winter 1974–5); Toni

Flores Fratto, "Samplers: One of the Lesser American Arts," *Feminist Art Journal* 5/4 (Winter 1976–77), pp. 11–15; Elaine Hedges and Ingrid Wendt, *In Her Own Image: Women Working in the Arts* (Old Westbury: Feminist Press/McGraw-Hill, 1980); and *Women's Traditional Arts: The Politics of Aesthetics*, *Heresies* 4 (1978). For a parallel discussion of women's amateur photography see Carol Armstrong, "From Clementina to Käsebier: The Photographic Attainment of the 'Lady Amateur'," *October* 91 (Winter, 2000), pp. 101–39.

44. Amelia Jones, "The 'Sexual Politics' of *The Dinner Party*: A Critical Context," in Amelia Jones (ed.), *Sexual Politics: Judy Chicago's* Dinner Party *in Feminist Art History* (Berkeley: University of California Press/Armand Hammer Museum of Art and Cultural Center, 1996), p. 88.

45. Bridgett Elliott and Jo-Ann Wallace, *Women Artists and Writers: Modernist (Im)positionings* (London: Routledge, 1994), Ch. 3 passim.

46. Arlene Raven, "Blood Sisters: Feminist Art and Criticism," in Lydia Yee, et al., *Division of Labor: "Women's Work" in Contemporary Art* (New York: Bronx Museum of Art, 1995), p. 47. See also Rozsika Parker and Griselda Pollock, *Old Mistresses: Women, Art and Ideology* (New York; Pantheon Books, 1981), pp. 50–81. These authors write: "what distinguishes art from craft in the hierarchy is not so much different methods, practices and objects but also where things are made, often in the home, and for whom they are made, often for the family, The fine arts are a public, professional activity. What women make, which is defined as 'craft,' could in fact be defined as 'domestic art.' The conditions of production and audience for this kind of art are different from those of art made in a studio and art school, for the market and the gallery. It is out of these different conditions that the hierarchical division between art and craft has been constructed; it has nothing to do with the inherent qualities of the object nor the gender of the maker" (p. 70).

47. Rozsika Parker, foreword, in Jennifer Harris, *The Subversive Stitch* (Manchester: Whitworth Art Gallery and Cornerhouse, 1988), p. 5. See also Parker, *The Subversive Stitch: Embroidery and the Making of the Feminine Ideal* (London: The Women's Press, 1984).

48. Pennina Barnett, "Women and Textiles Today," in Harris, *The Subversive Stitch*, p. 37. See also Pennina Barnett, "Afterthoughts on Curating 'The Subversive Stitch," in Katy Deepwell (ed.), *New Feminist Art Criticism* (Manchester: Manchester University Press, 1995).

49. Barnett, "Women and Textiles Today," in Harris, *The Subversive Stitch*, p. 38.

50. Rozsika Parker in Harris, *The Subversive Stitch*, p. 5.

51. Barnett, "Women and Textiles Today," in Harris, *The Subversive Stitch*, p. 48.

52. It is worth noting that Abakanowicz dismissed direct associations with femininity, insisting that her forms were about penetration and the body in a metaphorical, rather than sexual sense: "When I feel that I would like to construct a form, that you can go into, then of course the form is cut, to let you in. The most direct reaction is to connect it with erotic things, but a shell is also erotic, yes?" Jeff Makin, "Magdalena Abakanowicz," *Quadrant* 20/6 (June 1976), p. 53.

53. Victoria Mitchell (ed.), *Selvedges: Janis Jefferies: Writings and Artworks Since 1980* (Norwich: Norwich Gallery, 2000), p. 39.

54. See Mitchell (ed.), *Selvedges*; and Janis Jeffries, "Textiles," in Fiona Carson and Claire Pajaczkowksa, *Feminist Visual Culture* (London: Routledge, 2001).

55. Faith Gillespie, "The Masterless Way: Weaving an Active Resistance," in Gillian Elinor, Su Richardson, Sue Scott, et al. (eds), *Women and Craft* (London: Virago Press, 1987), p. 178.

56. Ann Newdigate, "Kinda Art, Sorta Tapestry," in Deepwell (ed.), *New Feminist Art Criticism*, p. 177.

57. For a consideration of these issues see Elissa Auther, "Classification and Its Consequences: The Case of 'Fiber Art,'" *American Art* 16/3 (Autumn, 2002), pp. 2–9; and my own "The Fiber Game," in *String*, a special issue of the journal *Textile* (Oxford: Berg Publishers, 2007).

58. Johanna Drucker, "New/Nude Difference," *October* 71 (Winter 1995), p. 20.

59. Quoted in Pat Mainardi, "Open Hearing at Brooklyn Museum," *Feminist Art Journal* 1 (Spring 1972), p. 6.

60. Lucy Lippard, "Sweeping Exchanges: The Contribution of Feminism to the Art of the 1970s," *Art Journal* (Fall-Winter 1980), reprinted in Lippard, *Get The Message? A Decade of Art for Social Change* (New York: E. P. Dutton, 1983), p. 153. One analyst of Lippard's writings sees the critic's move to Feminism in the early 1970s as a refusal of the "critic's right to set *him*self up as a judge because it is the artist who decides what is art. Thus, the role of the critic should be to describe the work and not make a prescription for what the art should be or do." Stephanie Cash, "The Art Criticism and Politics of Lucy Lippard," *Art Criticism* 9/1 (1994), p. 34.

61. Nancy Marmer, "Womanspace, a Creative Battle for Equality in the Art World," *Art News* 72/6 (Summer 1973), p. 39.

62. Judy Siegel, "Perils of Pluralism," *Women Artists News* 3/9 (Mar. 1978), reprinted in *Women Artists News* 16–17 (1991–2), pp. 88–9; and Sophie Rivera, "What is Feminist Art?" *Women Artists News* 1/6 (Nov. 1975).

63. Pennina Barnett, "Art or Craft… Who Decides?" in *Craft Matters: 3 Attitudes to Contemporary Craft* (Southampton: John Hansard Gallery, 1985), n.p.

64. Judy Chicago interviewed by Dinah Dossor, in Hilary Robinson (ed.), *Visibly Female: Feminism and Art, An Anthology* (London: Camden Press, 1987), p. 43.

65. Chicago founded the Feminist Arts Program in 1970 at Fresno State College, and moved it to Cal Arts the following year in partnership with Schapiro. At both venues the program was limited to female students and focused on consciousness-raising, cooperative art work, and the exploration of women's iconography. See Judy Chicago and Miriam Schapiro, "A Feminist Art Program." *Art Journal* 31/1 (Fall 1971), pp. 48–9. According to Faith Wilding, the *Womanhouse* project was first mooted by the art historian Paula Harper, but it was Chicago and Schapiro that steered the project to realization. Wilding, *By Our Own Hands: The Women Artist's Movement in Southern California 1970–1976* (Santa Monica: Double X, 1977), p. 25.

66. Miriam Schapiro interviewed by Ruth Bowman, Sept. 10, 1989. Archives of American Art, Smithsonian Institution, n.p.; Victor Papanek and Jim Hennesey, *Nomadic Furniture* (New York: Pantheon Books, 1973).

67. Judy Chicago, *Through the Flower: My Struggle as a Woman Artist* (Garden City, NY: Doubleday and Co., 1975), p. 104.

68. Lucy Lippard, "Household Images in Art," *Ms.* 1/9 (Mar. 1973), reprinted in Lippard, *From the Center: Feminist Essays on Women's Art* (New York: E. P. Dutton, 1976), p. 57; Martha Rosler, "The Private and The Public: Feminist Art in California," *Artforum* 16/1 (Sept. 1977), p. 69. See also Temma Balducci, "Revisiting *Womanhouse*: Welcome to the (Deconstructed) Dollhouse," *Women's Art Journal* 27/2 (Fall/Winter 2006), pp. 17–23.

69. Miriam Schapiro interviewed by Ruth Bowman, n.p.

70. Chicago, *Through the Flower*, following p. 106.

71. On a 1995 reconstruction of this installation, see Lydia Yee et al., *Division of Labor*; Miwon Kwon, "One Place After Another: Notes on Site Specificity," *October* 80 (Spring 1997), pp. 98–110: 99–100; and Faith Wilding, "Monstrous Domesticity," *M/E/A/N/I/N/G* #18 (Nov. 1995). The use of fiber in *Crocheted Interior* was echoed in other parts of the installation: a much simpler hanging of knotted cord by Judy Heddleston that graced the entrance way to the house; and a set of quilts that were hung on the walls of an upstairs hallway. See Chicago, *Through the Flower*, following p. 106 and pp. 113–14.

72. Correspondence with the author, 13 March 2000.

73. For Wilding's biography see her interview in Joan Arbeiter, Beryl Smith, and Sally Swenson, *Lives and Works: Talks With Women Artists, vol. 2* (Lanham, MD: Scarecrow Press, 1996).

74. Correspondence with the author, 13 March, 2000.

75. Faith Wilding, *By Our Own Hands*, pp. 27–8.

76. Correspondence with the author, 7 February, 2007.

77. Laura Meyer, "From Fetish Finish to Feminism: Judy Chicago's *Dinner Party* in California Art History," in Amelia Jones (ed.), *Sexual Politics*. Meyer does not mention the interesting fact that one of the ceramists to whom Chicago turned for technical assistance in firing the plates was Richard Shaw, who had recently developed a newly polished trompe l'oeil "finish fetish" style (see Chapter 2). This is noted in Elaine Levin, "Judy Chicago's Dinner Party," *Craft Horizons* 39/2 (Apr. 1979), p. 54. For an illustration of a vaginal-form "finish fetish" ceramic sculpture by Chicago (then Judy Gerowitz), see Douglas McClellan, "Sculpture," *Artforum* 2/12 (Summer 1964), p. 73.

78. Judy Chicago, *The Dinner Party: A Symbol of Our Heritage* (Garden City, NY: Doubleday/Anchor Press, 1979), p. 11.

79. Susan Rennie and Arlene Raven, "The Dinner Party: An Interview with Judy Chicago," *Chrysalis* 4 (1977), p. 96.

80. Jones, "The 'Sexual Politics' of the *Dinner Party*: A Critical Context," in Jones (ed.), *Sexual Politics*, p. 88. Tamar Garb has been more critical, writing: "That Chicago's piece aims to beat the 'modernist grande machine' at its own game is clear. Its scale is almost unparalleled, [and] its ostensible significance in terms of conjuring a spurious cumulative progress which culminates in the achievements of the Great Western Woman (at the pinnacle of which is Chicago herself) is painfully obvious…" Garb, "Engaging Embroidery," *Art History* 9 (March 1986), p. 132.

81. Amelia Jones, "The 'Sexual Politics' of the *Dinner* Party: A Critical Context," p. 89.

82. Audrey Farrell, "Judy Chicago: Art or Exploitation?" *Art Criticism* 10/2 (1995), pp. 94–106; Cassandra Langer, "Against the Grain: A Working Gynergenic Art Criticism," in Arlene Raven, Cassandra Langer, and Joanna Frueh, *Feminist Art Criticism: An Anthology* (New York: HarperCollins, 1988); Amelia Jones, "The 'Sexual Politics' of the *Dinner* Party: A Critical Context," in Jones (ed.), *Sexual Politics*.

83. This terminology is borrowed from Yve-Alain Bois and Rosalind Krauss, *Formless: A User's Guide* (Cambridge, MA: MIT Press, 1997).

84. Robert Storr, "An Interview with Mike Kelley," *Art in America* 82/6 (June 1994), pp. 90–3: 90.

85. Mike Kelley interviewed in Lucinda Barnes et al., *Between Artists: Twelve Contemporary American Artists Interview Twelve Contemporary American Artists* (Los Angeles: A.R.T. Press, 1996), pp. 108–9.

86. Terry R. Meyers, "The Mike Kelley Problem," *New Art Examiner* 21/10 (1994), pp. 24–9.

87. Marcia Tucker, *Bad Girls* (New York: New Museum of Contemporary Art, 1994), p. 22.

88. John C. Welchman, "The Mike Kelleys," in John C. Welchman, Isabelle Graw, and Anthony Vidler, *Mike Kelley* (New York: Phaidon, 1999), p. 57. Kelley himself puts it this way: "People project moral conclusions onto artworks by virtue of the social codes associated with various abstract motifs – clean lines next to fuzzy broken lines will be read as forms in conflict. I treat those moral interpretations as an intrinsic aspect of composition. There are conventions within modernist art history that have come to signify the abject, the confrontational, the pure. These conventions are now so naturalized that they seem almost random. I play games with them and invert them." "Isabelle Graw in Conversation with Mike Kelley," in Welchman, Graw, and Vidler, *Mike Kelley*, p. 32.

89. Mike Kelley, "In the Image of Man," *Carnegie International 1991* (Pittsburgh: Carnegie Museum of Art, 1991), p. 129; reprinted in Welchman, Graw, and Vidler, *Mike Kelley*, p. 128.

90. Kelley, "In the Image of Man," p. 128.

91. Ulrich Lehmann, "The Trademark Tracey Emin," in Mandy Merck and Chris Townshend (eds), *The Art of Tracey Emin* (London: Thames and Hudson, 2002), p. 66.

92. See Sarah Kent, "Tracey Emin: Flying High," in *Tracey Emin* (London: White Cube, 1998).

93. Mike Kelley, "Dirty Toys: Mike Kelley Interviewed," in Charles Harrison and Paul Wood, *Art in Theory: 1900–2000* (Oxford: Blackwell, 2003), p. 1100.

94. For Emin appliqué is, among other things, an autobiographically specific reference to her grandmother. See Rosemary Betterton, "Why Is My Art Not As Good As Me? Femininity, Feminism, and 'Life-Drawing' in Tracey Emin's Art," in *The Art of Tracey Emin*, p. 35 and *passim*. Kelley too employs autobiography in his art, but in ways that problematize the reconstruction of his own past from memory; see Anthony Vidler, "Mike Kelley's Educational Complex," in Welchman, Graw, and Vidler, *Mike Kelley*.

95. Rosalind Krauss, "The Destiny of the *Informe*," in Bois and Krauss, *Formless: A User's Guide*, p. 244.

96. Rudi Fuchs, "Tracey Emin: A Particular Honesty," in *Tracey Emin: When I Think About Sex… I Make Art* (London: White Cube, 2005), p. 18. For a dissenting view see Janis Jeffries, "Autobiographical Patterns," *Surface Design Journal* 21/4 (Summer 1997). Jeffries argues that Emin's 'bad girl' performance is so disruptive to stereotypical norms of femininity that it breaks "the repetition of unified pattern of experience pieced and patched into a coherent, overall whole" and thus "produce[s] an autographic of hybridity."

97. Amelia Jones, *Body Art: Performing the Subject* (Minneapolis: University of Minnesota Press, 1998), pp. 46, 52. Emphasis in original.

CONCLUSION

1. Robert Morris, "Anti Form," *Artforum* 6/8 (Apr. 1968), pp. 33–5; Marcel Broodthaers, "Ten Thousand Francs Reward" (1974), reprinted in *October* 42 (Fall 1987), pp. 37-41: 37.

2. Lee Nordness, *Objects: USA* (New York: Viking Press, 1970).

3. Nicolas Bourriaud, *Relational Aesthetics* (Dijon: Les Presse du Reel, 2002); Claire Bishop, "Antagonism and Relational Aesthetics," *October* 110 (Fall 2004), p. 51–79.

4. Caroline Jones, *The Machine in the Studio: Constructing the Postwar American Artist* (Chicago: University of Chicago Press, 1996).

5. See Jones, *The Machine in the Studio*; and Jennifer Roberts, *Mirror Travels: Robert Smithson and History* (New Haven: Yale University Press, 2004). See also Rosalind Krauss, "Sculpture in the Expanded Field," in Krauss, *The Originality of the Avant-Garde and Other Modernist Myths* (Cambridge, MA: MIT Press, 1985); originally published in *October* 8 (Spring 1979).

6. See Johanna Drucker, *Sweet Dreams: Contemporary Art and Complicity* (Chicago: University of Chicago Press, 2005). For a younger generation of craftsy artists, see Shu Hung and Joseph Magliaro (eds), *By Hand: The Use of Craft in Contemporary Art* (New York; Princeton Architectural Press, 2007).

7. Michael Kimmelman, "Touching All Bases at the Biennial," *New York Times* (12 Mar. 2004).

8. For sensitive readings of the issue of marginality in Perry's work see Garth Clark, "The Queen of Découpage: Grayson Perry's Guerilla Ceramics," in John Pagliaro, ed., *Shards: Garth Clark on Ceramic Art* (New York: DAP, 2003); and Jeffrey Jones, "Grayson Perry: The Pot is the Man," in Julian Stair (ed.), *The Body Politic: the Role of the Body and Contemporary Craft* (London: Crafts Council, 2000).

9. See Tag Gronberg, "Crafting the Modern: Simon Starling," *Journal of Modern Craft* 1/1 (March 2008).

10. Grayson Perry, "A Refuge For Artists Who Play It Safe," *Guardian* (Saturday 5 Mar. 2005). Perry has extended his argument as follows: "Craft, I feel, to people outside the exquisitely constructed ring fence of the Craft Council has become a hobby. It is a leisure activity practised by exhibitors at craft fairs who fashion novelty covers for vacuum cleaners and children who are bought bead jewellery kits by well-meaning aunts who think they watch too much television… Craft is becoming a zoo-bred animal that could not survive in the wild of the market place." Grayson Perry, "Let the Artisans Craft Our Future," *The Times* (5 Apr. 2006).

11. Victor Burgin, "The Absence of Presence," in *The End of Art Theory* (London, 1986); reprinted in Charles Harrison and Paul Wood, *Art in Theory, 1900-1990: An Anthology of Changing Ideas* (Oxford: Blackwell,

1992), p. 1097ff. A less concise but even more explicit defense of modern art's autonomous, contemplative character was offered to the studio craft readership by critic John Mays in 1986: "Hands cannot contemplate; and the creation of works for disinterested, hands-off contemplation has traditionally been a central concern of all Modern art production... Modern art itself, in all its variety, is proof that the historically anti-hand, anti-craft strategy continues to be radical and greatly rewarding. All this is a matter of passionate conviction among many art critics and curators alike, even if it is not usually put as bluntly as I've done here. The well-lit, empty, free and austere space in which painting and sculpture conventionally exist is cherished because it is there (and not in the familiar clutter of life) that Modern art yields up its complex, ironic truth about the world—not in being handled and known intimately, but in being contemplated by the educated eye." Mays, "Comment," *American Craft* 45/6 (Dec. 1985/Jan. 1986), p. 38-9.

INDEX